Building MCP Servers with C#

Connect AI Agents to Your .NET Applications with the Model Context Protocol

Gerald Versluis

Apress®

Building MCP Servers with C#: Connect AI Agents to Your .NET Applications with the Model Context Protocol

Gerald Versluis
Hulsberg, Limburg, The Netherlands

ISBN-13 (pbk): 979-8-8688-3009-9 ISBN-13 (electronic): 979-8-8688-3010-5
https://doi.org/10.1007/979-8-8688-3010-5

Managing Director, Apress Media LLC: Welmoed Spahr
Acquisitions Editor: Ryan Byrnes
Editorial Assistant: Gryffin Winkler

Cover designed by eStudioCalamar

Distributed to the book trade worldwide by Springer Science+Business Media New York, 1 New York Plaza, New York, NY 10004. Phone 1-800-SPRINGER, fax (201) 348-4505, e-mail orders-ny@springer-sbm.com, or visit www.springeronline.com. Apress Media, LLC is a Delaware LLC and the sole member (owner) is Springer Science + Business Media Finance Inc (SSBM Finance Inc). SSBM Finance Inc is a **Delaware** corporation.

For information on translations, please e-mail booktranslations@springernature.com; for reprint, paperback, or audio rights, please e-mail bookpermissions@springernature.com.

Apress titles may be purchased in bulk for academic, corporate, or promotional use. eBook versions and licenses are also available for most titles. For more information, reference our Print and eBook Bulk Sales web page at http://www.apress.com/bulk-sales.

Any source code or other supplementary material referenced by the author in this book is available to readers on GitHub. For more detailed information, please visit https://www.apress.com/gp/services/source-code.

If disposing of this product, please recycle the paper

For Oliver and Victor, the two most unpredictable agents I've ever deployed to production with zero testing. And for my wife, who somehow keeps them (and me) within acceptable parameters.

Table of Contents

About the Author

Gerald Versluis is a software engineer at Microsoft on the .NET team, building a cross-platform framework that lets developers target iOS, Android, macOS, and Windows with C# and .NET. He is deeply invested in AI-powered developer tooling and how it is changing the way we build software.

Beyond his day job, Gerald is an active voice in the .NET community—through his YouTube channel, his blog, and public speaking at events internationally.

When he's not writing code, he's apparently writing books.

About the Technical Reviewer

Codrina Merigo is a Microsoft MVP Alumni and SAFe PO/PM certified professional with a strong passion for building impactful mobile applications and exploring the evolving landscape of AI. With over seven years of experience in the Xamarin ecosystem and now deeply engaged in .NET MAUI, she has consistently focused on delivering high-quality, cross-platform solutions that balance performance, usability, and scalability.

Author of *AI-Enabled Apps with .NET MAUI: How to Build Cross-Platform .NET MAUI Apps with the Latest AI Capabilities*, she brings together hands-on development experience and a forward-looking perspective on integrating AI into modern applications.

She is particularly passionate about UX and UI design, with a keen eye for creating intuitive, user-centered experiences across platforms. In recent years, she has specialized in UI testing, best practices, continuous integration, and performance optimization within .NET MAUI projects, helping teams build more robust and maintainable applications.

Acknowledgments

A book about connecting things turns out to be a fitting thing to have written, because so many people connected to make it real.

Ryan and Humera at Apress took a chance on a topic that barely existed when we started and shaped it with steady hands and good judgment. Codrina went through the manuscript chapter by chapter as technical editor, pressing on every claim until it either held up or got rewritten, and the book is sharper for her feedback. Thank you!

I want to acknowledge the engineers and maintainers shaping the Model Context Protocol itself. Writing about a standard while it's still being defined is a strange, exhilarating thing, and I'm grateful to everyone working in the open and sharing what they learn. This book is a snapshot of their momentum as much as my own.

To everyone who picks this up and starts building: I hope it saves you some time, spares you a few dead ends, and leaves you a little more excited about what you can connect next. Our craft is changing fast; try not to be afraid of it, but embrace it. Learn everything there is to learn about it and become a 10x engineer, finally! I hope this book will help you with that.

Introduction

If you picked up this book, chances are you are a C# developer who has been watching the AI revolution unfold and wondering: "How do I actually build the thing that connects AI to my stuff?" You are not alone. I had that exact thought about a year ago, and it sent me down a rabbit hole that eventually became this book.

The Model Context Protocol is one of those technologies that makes you go "oh, obviously" once you understand it. Before MCP, connecting AI applications to external data sources and tools was a mess of custom integrations, each one slightly different, each one a maintenance headache. MCP provides a standardized way to do it. Build your server once, and any MCP-compatible client can use it. Simple as that.

This book is for C# developers who want to build MCP servers. Whether you are creating internal tools for your team, building something for the broader community, or just trying to make your AI-powered workflows less painful, you will find everything you need here. I wrote it to be the resource I wished existed when I started exploring MCP myself.

Who This Book Is For

You should be comfortable with C# and .NET. You do not need to be an expert. If you have built a web API or a console application, you are good to go. Some familiarity with concepts like dependency injection and async/await will help, but I explain things as we go. No prior experience with MCP or AI protocols is required. That is literally what this book is here to teach you.

What You Will Learn

By the end of this book, you will be able to build production-ready MCP servers in C# from scratch. Specifically, you will learn

- How the MCP protocol works under the hood and why it matters
- How to create tools, resources, and prompts—the three core building blocks

- How to handle different transport mechanisms (stdio and HTTP)
- How to integrate your MCP servers with real services using dependency injection
- How to build an MCP client
- How to properly test your servers
- How to secure and deploy your servers to production
- How to publish your servers as NuGet packages for others to use

How This Book Is Structured

The book follows a progressive path. We start with the fundamentals and build up to real-world applications.

Chapters 1 and 2 give you the conceptual foundation. You will understand what MCP is, why it was created, and how it works at an architectural level.

Chapter 3 gets your development environment set up—.NET 10, the MCP SDK, and the tools you will use throughout the book.

Chapters 4–7 are the core building chapters. You will build your first MCP server, then dive deep into tools, resources, and prompts, the three primitives that make MCP useful.

Chapter 8 covers transport layers—how your server actually communicates with clients over stdio and HTTP.

Chapters 9 and 10 expand your horizons with dependency injection, service integration, and building your own MCP client.

Chapter 11 teaches you to test your servers properly, because shipping untested code is not something we do around here.

Chapters 12 and 13 bring everything together. You will build a fun, complete MCP server (involving space pizza, because why not) and then apply enterprise patterns like authentication, observability, and rate limiting.

Chapter 14 takes you from "it works on my machine" to published, deployed, and available for the world to use.

Prerequisites

To follow along with the examples in this book, you will need

- .NET 10 SDK (or later)
- A code editor: Visual Studio or Visual Studio Code work great
- Basic familiarity with the command line
- An MCP-compatible client for testing (I use Visual Studio Code with GitHub Copilot, but any MCP client works)

All source code is available in the book's GitHub repository. Each chapter has its own folder with complete, runnable examples.

Conventions Used in This Book

Code listings are numbered and referenced in the text. When I show a code snippet inline, I use monospace formatting. Terminal commands you need to run are prefixed with a dollar sign ($), which you should not type; it just indicates a command prompt.

Throughout the book, you will see Note and Tip blocks that call out important details or helpful shortcuts. Pay attention to those; they are there for a reason.

Download the Source Code

The complete source code for every example in this book is available on GitHub. You can clone the repository and follow along chapter by chapter or use the code as a starting point for your own projects.

I genuinely had fun writing this book, and I hope that comes through as you read it. MCP is still early, the ecosystem is growing fast, and there is a real opportunity to build something useful. Let's get started.

CHAPTER 1

The Model Context Protocol

I still remember the first time I tried to connect an AI model to a database. I had this brilliant plan: take a large language model (LLM), hook it up to our product catalog, and let users ask natural-language questions about inventory. Simple, right? It was... not pretty. I spent an entire weekend writing glue code, parsing free-form text responses, and praying the model would return something my code could actually work with. By Sunday evening, I had something that worked about 60% of the time. Not great for a demo on Monday morning.

If you have been working in the software industry for any length of time, you know the pattern. Every few years, a new technology comes along that fundamentally changes how we build applications. The introduction of REST APIs. The rise of containerization with Docker. The shift to cloud-native development. Each of these moments changed the rules. And I think we're right in the middle of another such moment with the coming of AI, Copilot, LLMs, all those things. This is the biggest transformation yet if you ask me. At the time of writing this book, I can't remember when I last had Visual Studio open, and I'm a software engineer!

The way we are doing our work is drastically changing; you do not have to write all the code yourself anymore or even write any code at all if you don't want to. Agents can now do it for you, probably better than you, and if you give them all the tools, they can also take your code to the cloud, verify if everything works through Playwright or Appium, implement a design through Figma... Your imagination is the only limit.

While the agents are pretty good at finding ways to do all the things themselves, you can make them much more efficient if you provide them with the proper tools. Just like you would work more effectively when you had the right code editor, with the right extensions and a good coffee. This is where Model Context Protocol comes in, or

G. Versluis, *Building MCP Servers with C#*, https://doi.org/10.1007/979-8-8688-3010-5_1

MCP for short. I think we will see a big increase of command-line interface (CLI) tools together with MCP tools, and they will support how well AI-driven software development will work for you.

However, it doesn't stop at software development. I am a software engineer (at least that was my title in the "before times"; we probably need to come up with something new now), so that's where my mind immediately goes, but with MCP, you can also support all kinds of other users and scenarios. Like the scenario I described just above: query a database through natural language, analyze a medical X-ray for anomalies, check documents for compliance in a law firm, etc. The core theme across all of these is the same: MCP eliminates the "swivel chair" problem, where a person must manually pull information from five different systems to answer one question. And while that is a very helpful scenario that will already make a lot of jobs much more efficient, that is only the tip of the iceberg of what you can do with this, as we will learn in this book.

By the time you finish this chapter, you will have a solid understanding of the problem MCP solves and why the industry is rallying behind it. Here is what we will cover:

- Where MCP came from and the problem it was designed to fix
- How MCP works at a high level: tools, resources, and prompts
- Why C# is a fantastic choice for building MCP servers
- What you will build throughout this book (spoiler: space pizza is involved)

Think of this chapter as the foundation for everything else in the book. No code yet, just the mental model you need before we start building things.

The AI Integration Problem

Before we get into MCP itself, picture this scenario. You are building a chat application powered by a large language model. Your users love it. They can ask questions, generate text, and get creative help. Life is good. But then someone asks a perfectly reasonable question: "What is the current weather in Amsterdam?" And your brilliant AI assistant has absolutely no idea, because it is trapped inside its own training data with no way to reach the outside world.

So you do what any reasonable developer would do: you write some custom code to intercept weather-related questions, call a weather API, and feed the results back into the model. It works! Your users are happy. For about a week. Then they start asking for stock prices, calendar events, and database queries. Each new integration means more custom code, more maintenance, and more things that can break.

I have lived through this exact scenario. At one point I had a Frankenstein of adapters: one for a weather service, one for a database, one for a calendar API. Each one had its own authentication flow, its own error handling, its own data format. Every time the AI model changed, I had to update all of them. Every time a data source changed its API, I had to update the adapter and retest everything. It was exhausting, and honestly a little demoralizing when it broke in production for the third time in a month.

Now multiply that across thousands of AI applications and thousands of data sources. Every team is solving the same problem in slightly different ways. There is no standard way for an AI application to discover what tools are available, how to call them, or what kind of data they return. It is a mess. And it is the exact same kind of mess the industry faced before REST APIs standardized how web services communicate.

This is what people call the N-times-M problem. If you have N AI applications and M data sources, you end up with N times M custom integrations. Each one is a snowflake, lovingly handcrafted and impossible to reuse. The cost of maintaining all these integrations grows exponentially, and quality suffers because nobody has time to do it right when there are so many to build. Not great for maintainability.

Enter the Model Context Protocol

The Model Context Protocol, commonly referred to as MCP, is an open protocol that standardizes how AI applications connect to external data sources and tools. It was introduced by Anthropic, the company behind the Claude family of AI models, in November 2024. The goal is dead simple: define a universal way for AI applications to discover and use external capabilities.

You may have heard MCP described as the "USB-C for AI." If you are anything like me, you probably have a drawer full of cables from the pre-USB-C era. Micro-USB for the phone, a proprietary connector for the laptop, some weird barrel plug for the portable speaker. Then USB-C came along, and suddenly one cable worked for almost everything. That little moment of joy when you realize you can charge your laptop, your phone, and your headphones with the same cable? That is what MCP feels like for AI integrations.

Instead of building custom integrations for every combination of AI application and data source, you build an MCP server once, and any MCP-compatible client can use it. Build a weather tool as an MCP server, and it works with Claude Desktop, Visual Studio Code, GitHub Copilot, and any other application that speaks MCP. Build it once, use it everywhere. Pretty neat if you ask me.

Note Throughout this book, when I refer to "AI applications" or "LLM applications," I mean any software that uses a large language model as part of its functionality. This includes chat interfaces, code assistants, autonomous agents, and any other application that benefits from AI-powered capabilities.

A Brief History of MCP

To really appreciate MCP, it helps to understand the context in which it was born. The story starts with the rapid evolution of AI tooling in 2023 and 2024.

The Function Calling Era

When OpenAI introduced function calling in June 2023, it was a game changer. For the first time, AI models could express intent to call external functions in a structured way. Instead of generating free-form text that you had to parse and hope for the best, the model could say "I want to call the `get_weather` function with the argument city set to Amsterdam." Developers could then execute that function and feed the result back to the model.

I was genuinely surprised by how much this changed the developer experience. Before function calling, connecting an AI to external services felt like duct-taping two systems together. After function calling, it felt more like a proper integration. But it still had real limitations. Function calling was specific to OpenAI's API. Switch to a different model provider and you had to rewrite your integration code. There was no standard discovery mechanism; you had to tell the model exactly what functions were available by including their schemas in every request. And there was no protocol for managing the lifecycle of these interactions.

The Birth of MCP

Anthropic recognized these limitations and set out to build something better. In November 2024, they publicly released the Model Context Protocol as an open specification. The timing was not accidental. By late 2024, the AI ecosystem had matured enough that the pain of fragmented integrations was being felt by everyone, from individual developers to large enterprises.

What made MCP different from previous approaches was its scope and ambition. It was not just about function calling. MCP defines a complete protocol for three types of capabilities that a server can expose to an AI application: tools (actions the AI can take), resources (data the AI can read), and prompts (templates that guide the AI's behavior). We will explore each of these in detail throughout this book.

Anthropic also made a smart strategic decision by releasing MCP as a fully open specification with permissive licensing. This meant that anyone could implement it, and they did. Within months of its release, MCP had gained support from major players across the industry.

If you are interested in the full specification, and the latest state, you can always refer to `https://modelcontextprotocol.io/` where everything is described in great detail. Or, you know, let Copilot look at it and summarize it for you.

Industry Adoption

The adoption of MCP has been remarkably fast. Microsoft embraced it for Visual Studio Code, GitHub Copilot, and the broader .NET ecosystem. The official C# SDK became a Tier 1 project, meaning it receives the same level of attention and maintenance as the TypeScript and Python SDKs. That is a strong signal of commitment. If you are interested in MCP for other stacks as well, check out the other SDKs and their status at `https://modelcontextprotocol.io/docs/sdk`.

Beyond Microsoft, MCP support has been added to development tools like JetBrains IDEs and Zed, AI platforms like Claude Desktop, and enterprise tools across the industry. The ecosystem of pre-built MCP servers is growing rapidly, with servers available for everything from GitHub and Slack to Google Drive and PostgreSQL.

For us as C# developers, the timing could not be better. At the time of writing, the official MCP C# SDK reached version 1.0, providing a mature, production-ready foundation for building MCP servers and clients. It plugs right into the patterns we already know and love: dependency injection, the hosting model, and ASP.NET Core.

What MCP Provides

Now that you know where MCP came from, here is a high-level overview of what it actually provides. Think of MCP as defining a contract between two parties: the AI application that wants to use external capabilities and the server that provides those capabilities. The protocol covers three main areas.

Tools

Tools are the most commonly used feature of MCP, and they are probably what brought you to this book. A tool is an action that the AI can invoke. Think of it as a function that the AI model can call when it needs to do something in the real world. Checking the weather, querying a database, sending an email, creating a calendar event: these are all examples of tools.

Each tool has a name, a description (so the AI knows when to use it; it's still powered by a large *language* model), and a schema that defines its input parameters and output format. The beauty of MCP is that the AI application discovers these tools automatically. You do not need to hardcode anything on the client side. The server announces what it can do, and the client figures out the rest.

Resources

Resources represent data that the AI can read for context. While tools are about taking actions, resources are about providing information. A resource might be a file, a database record, a configuration setting, or any other piece of data that helps the AI understand the current context.

Resources can be static (a fixed piece of data) or dynamic (generated on demand based on a template). They have URIs for identification and can include metadata that helps the AI understand what it is looking at. If you have worked with REST APIs before, the concept of addressable resources will feel very familiar.

Prompts

Prompts are reusable templates that guide the AI's behavior. They allow the server to provide structured instructions that the AI can follow. Think of them as recipes: a prompt might define a specific workflow, like "analyze this code and suggest improvements" or "translate this document while preserving technical terminology."

Prompts can include parameters, making them dynamic and adaptable to different situations. They are a powerful way to encapsulate domain expertise and make it available to AI applications without requiring the client to know the details. You get to define the what and the how, and the AI takes care of the rest.

Why Build MCP Servers with C#?

You might be thinking: "Why C#? There are SDKs for TypeScript, Python, Java, and other languages." Here is the thing: as someone who edits text files for a living at Microsoft (trying out those new job titles right away), I may be a tiny bit biased. But I genuinely think there are compelling reasons to reach for C# here, and not just because it is what I know best.

First, as mentioned, the C# SDK is a Tier 1 implementation. That means it is developed in close collaboration with Anthropic and receives the same level of support as the TypeScript SDK. You are not working with a community port or a second-class citizen. This is a first-class implementation of the MCP specification, maintained by the same people who build the .NET runtime and libraries.

Second, the SDK is built on patterns that .NET developers already know. It uses the `Microsoft.Extensions.Hosting` model for application lifecycle management. It integrates with `Microsoft.Extensions.DependencyInjection` for service registration. It supports ASP.NET Core for HTTP-based transport. If you have built a .NET application in the last few years, you will feel right at home. No learning a whole new framework just to get started.

Third, C# gives you the performance and type safety that matter for production workloads. MCP servers in enterprise environments need to handle concurrent requests efficiently, integrate with existing .NET infrastructure, and be maintainable over time. C# excels at all of these things. The compiler catches mistakes before your users do, and the runtime performance is excellent out of the box.

Finally, if you are already working in a .NET shop, adding MCP servers to your existing codebase is straightforward. You can expose your existing services and APIs as MCP tools without rewriting anything. That is a huge advantage when you want to bring AI capabilities to an established application. Wrap what you already have, and you are up and running in no time.

What You Will Build in This Book

Throughout this book, we will build several MCP servers of increasing complexity. We start with the basics: a simple server that does nothing more than echo back what you say. From there, we gradually work our way up to real-world scenarios.

And then there is Cosmic Pizza. Why should learning be boring? I always try to add a little bit of fun and humor in my content and examples. I am convinced that keeping things fun will help you get through a technical book, and you'll learn better that way. So, we will build a fun, fictional pizza ordering system set in outer space, because why not. We have AI now; next stop is space; we'd better be prepared!

The Cosmic Pizza server will let AI assistants browse a menu of planetary pizzas, place orders, get space-themed dad jokes, and look up fascinating space facts. It sounds silly, and it absolutely is, but it will teach you every important concept in the MCP SDK while keeping things entertaining. I had way too much fun coming up with the menu.

Beyond the fun examples, we also tackle serious enterprise (no Star Trek pun intended) scenarios. You will learn how to build MCP servers that wrap database access, integrate with external APIs, handle authentication, and scale to production workloads. By the time you finish this book, you will have the knowledge and confidence to build MCP servers for any scenario you can imagine. I would love to see what you build with it!

Tip All the source code for the examples in this book is available on GitHub. You can find the repository URL here: `https://github.com/Apress/Building-MCP-Servers-with-C-Sharp`. I recommend cloning it and following along as you read each chapter.

Prerequisites

This book assumes you have a working knowledge of C# and .NET development. You do not need to be an expert, but you should be comfortable with concepts like classes, interfaces, async/await, and dependency injection. If you have built a web API or console application with .NET, you have everything you need to get started.

You do not need any prior experience with AI, machine learning, or large language models. I will explain everything you need to know as we go. If terms like "function calling" or "token window" sound unfamiliar, do not worry. By the end of the first few chapters, they will feel like old friends. Similarly, you do not need to understand the MCP protocol specification in detail. That is what the next chapter is for.

In terms of tooling, you will need the .NET 10.0 SDK and an editor or IDE of your choice. For the screenshots in this book, I will use Visual Studio Code on macOS, but you can also use Visual Studio on Windows or Rider on Linux; the code and working of the MCP solutions we will build will be exactly the same. I will cover the complete setup in detail in Chapter 3, so you do not need to install anything just yet.

Summary

I hope I have convinced you that MCP is worth your time. The problem it solves is real: the N-times-M integration mess that every developer working with AI has experienced, or will experience soon enough. MCP brings order to that chaos with a standardized protocol for tools, resources, and prompts.

You saw how MCP's "USB-C for AI" approach replaces a drawer full of incompatible connectors with a single universal standard. You learned how it grew out of the function calling era and was quickly adopted across the industry, with strong support from Microsoft and the .NET ecosystem.

You also got a taste of why C# is an excellent choice for building MCP servers: a first-class SDK, familiar .NET patterns, strong performance, and easy integration with existing codebases. And you got a preview of the fun (Cosmic Pizza!) and serious projects we will build together.

In the next chapter, we dig into the MCP architecture. You will learn about hosts, clients, servers, and the JSON-RPC protocol that ties everything together. Understanding the architecture will give you the mental model you need to build effective MCP servers throughout the rest of this book. Let's get started!

CHAPTER 2

MCP Architecture Under the Hood

In Chapter 1, we explored what the Model Context Protocol is and why it matters. You saw how the lack of a shared standard left every AI integration feeling like a one-off science project, and how MCP steps in to fix that. Now it is time to pop the hood and look at how MCP actually works under the surface. Understanding the architecture is not just an academic exercise. When you start building your own MCP servers in C# later in this book, every design decision you make will trace back to the concepts we cover in this chapter.

I will walk you through the three layers that make up every MCP interaction, the message format that carries information between them, and the lifecycle that governs how a connection is born, lives, and eventually shuts down. Along the way, I will sprinkle in real JSON examples so you can see exactly what travels over the wire. By the end of this chapter, you will have a mental model solid enough to make the hands-on chapters that follow feel almost intuitive.

The Three-Layer Architecture

MCP organizes every interaction into three distinct layers: the host, the client, and the server. If you have ever worked with layered architectures, where your UI talks to a service layer that talks to a data layer, then you already have a good intuition for this pattern. Your application (the host) does not talk directly to the external service. Instead, it uses a client layer that knows how to open connections, send requests, and translate responses back into something your code understands. MCP follows the same separation of concerns, and each layer has a clear, well-defined job.

G. Versluis, *Building MCP Servers with C#*, https://doi.org/10.1007/979-8-8688-3010-5_2

The Host

The host is the AI application that the end user actually interacts with. Think of Claude Desktop, GitHub Copilot in VS Code, or any custom chat interface your company might build. The host is responsible for the overall user experience: it renders the conversation, manages the language model, enforces security policies, and decides which MCP servers to connect to. A single host can maintain connections to many servers at the same time, which is exactly what happens when you configure GitHub Copilot with a file-system server, a database server, and a web-search server all at once.

One important detail is that the host never speaks the MCP wire protocol directly. It delegates that job to one or more MCP clients that live inside it. This keeps the host code clean and focused on user-facing concerns, while all the protocol plumbing stays neatly encapsulated.

The Client

The client is the MCP-aware connector that lives inside the host. For every server the host wants to talk to, it spins up a dedicated client instance. That client is responsible for opening the transport, performing the initialization handshake, sending requests, and routing responses back to the host. If the host is a restaurant manager, the client is the waiter who takes orders to the kitchen and brings dishes back to the table.

Each client maintains a one-to-one relationship with a single server. This design keeps things simple and predictable: if a server crashes, only the client connected to it is affected, while the rest of the host continues running. The client also handles capability negotiation, which we will look at later in this chapter. It makes sure the client and server agree on which features they both support before any real work begins.

The Server

The server is the component you will spend most of your time building throughout this book. An MCP server exposes one or more of three primitives to clients: tools, resources, and prompts. Tools let the AI call functions, like querying a database or sending an email. Resources provide read access to data, much like a GET endpoint in a REST API. Prompts offer reusable templates that guide how the AI interacts with the server's domain. We will explore each of these in depth: tools in Chapter 5, resources in Chapter 6, and prompts in Chapter 7.

A server can be as simple as a single tool that returns the current weather, or as complex as a full enterprise integration that exposes dozens of tools and resources. What is great about MCP is that the protocol does not care. Whether your server wraps a legacy SOAP (Simple Object Access Protocol) service or a shiny new gRPC (Google Remote Procedure Call) microservice, the client sees the same clean interface.

Figure 2-1 illustrates how these layers relate. Notice that the host sits at the top, closest to the user. Inside it, you find one client per server connection. Each client talks to exactly one server over a transport, and the server exposes its capabilities back through that same channel. This clean layering is what makes MCP servers so easy to develop and test in isolation. You do not need a full AI application running just to verify that your server returns the right data.

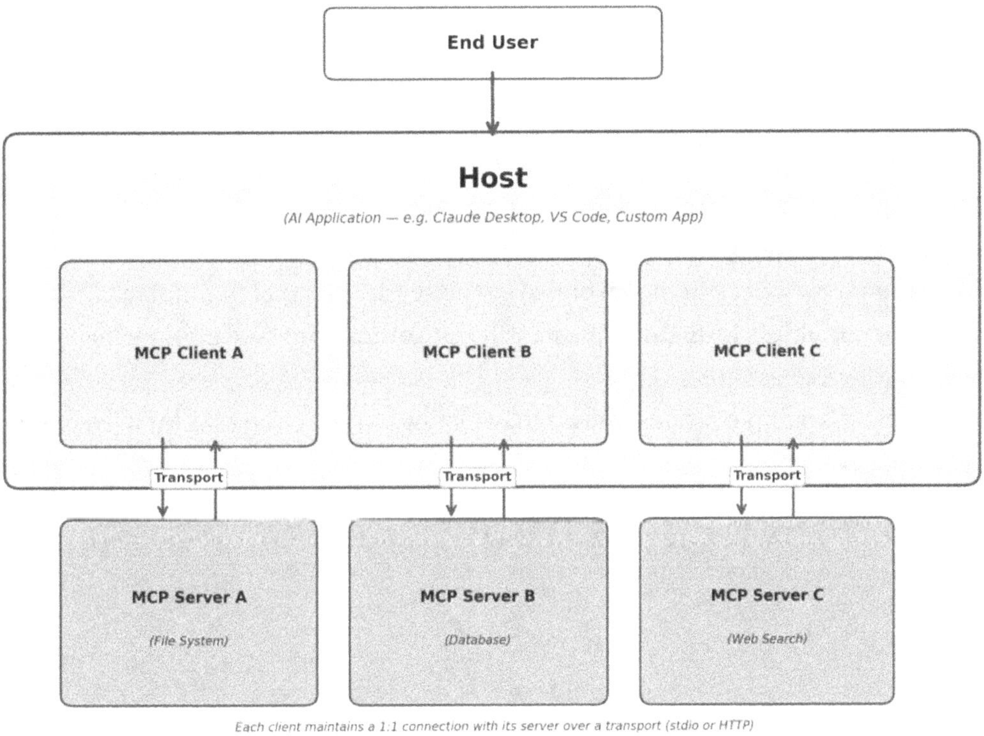

***Figure 2-1.** The three-layer MCP architecture showing how the host contains one or more clients, each connected to a separate server*

The JSON-RPC 2.0 Foundation

Every message that flows between an MCP client and server is a JSON-RPC 2.0 message. If you have not encountered JSON-RPC before, do not worry. It is one of the simplest remote procedure call protocols ever designed, and that simplicity is exactly why the MCP designers chose it. Unlike REST, which is built around resources and HTTP verbs, JSON-RPC is built around method calls. You send a JSON object that says, "Please call this method with these parameters," and you get back a JSON object with the result. There are no URLs to design, no status codes to memorize, and no content negotiation to worry about.

JSON-RPC defines three kinds of messages: requests, responses, and notifications. Let us look at each one.

Requests

A request is a message that expects a response. It contains four fields: the JSON-RPC version string (always "2.0", at least for now), an id that the sender chooses, the method name, and an optional params object. The id can be a string or a number, and the receiver must echo it back in the response so the sender can match them up. This is how MCP supports multiple in-flight requests without getting confused about which answer belongs to which question.

You can see a sample request message in Listing 2-1; this one asks for a list of the tools that are available.

Listing 2-1. A JSON-RPC request message calling the tools/list method

```
{
    "jsonrpc": "2.0",
    "id": 1,
    "method": "tools/list",
    "params": {}
}
```

Responses

A response is the answer to a request. It always includes the same id that was sent in the request, plus either a result field on success or an error field on failure. You will never see both result and error in the same response. This either-or rule makes it easy to handle responses in code: check for an error first, and if there is none, process the result.

In Listing 2-2, you can see the response to the request in Listing 2-1, with a list of all the available tools, in this case only one; get the current weather for a city.

Listing 2-2. A successful JSON-RPC response returning a list of tools

```
{
    "jsonrpc": "2.0",
    "id": 1,
    "result": {
        "tools": [
            {
                "name": "get_weather",
                "description":
                "Returns the current weather"
                + " for a city",
                "inputSchema": {
                    "type": "object",
                    "properties": {
                        "city": {
                            "type": "string"
                        }
                    },
                    "required": ["city"]
                }
            }
        ]
    }
}
```

Notifications

Notifications are fire-and-forget messages. They look like requests but they have no id field, which signals that the sender does not expect a response. MCP uses notifications for events like progress updates and cancellation signals. Because notifications do not require a round trip, they keep the protocol efficient for situations where an acknowledgment is not needed.

In Listing 2-3, you can see a sample notification message.

Listing 2-3. A JSON-RPC notification sent when initialization is complete

```
{
    "jsonrpc": "2.0",
    "method":
    "notifications/initialized"
}
```

Table 2-1 summarizes the three message types and their key characteristics.

Table 2-1. *JSON-RPC 2.0 message types used in MCP*

Message Type	Has id?	Expects Response?	Direction
Request	Yes	Yes	Client ➤ Server or Server ➤ Client
Response	Yes (echoes request id)	No	Reply to a request
Notification	No	No	Client ➤ Server or Server ➤ Client

Capability Negotiation

Before a client and server can do anything useful, they need to agree on what each side supports. Not every server implements every feature of the protocol, and not every client knows how to handle every feature a server might offer. MCP solves this with a capability negotiation step that happens right at the start of every connection.

Think of it like two people meeting for the first time at a conference. Before they jump into a deep technical discussion, they quickly establish common ground: "I work with .NET." "Great, me too! Do you do Blazor?" "No, mostly APIs." Now both sides know exactly what topics are on the table. MCP does the same thing, just with JSON instead of small talk.

The Initialization Handshake

The handshake is a two-step dance. First, the client sends an initialize request that advertises the protocol version it speaks and the capabilities it supports. The server replies with its own protocol version and capabilities. Second, if the versions are compatible, both sides are happy and the client sends an initialized notification to signal that it is ready to start working. If the versions are incompatible, the connection is closed before any damage can be done.

Note At the time of writing, the latest stable specification revision is 2025-11-25. The protocol version negotiated during the handshake ensures that clients and servers can evolve independently while remaining compatible. You can always find the current specification at `https://modelcontextprotocol.io/specification`.

In Listing 2-4 and Listing 2-5, you can see the request and response for this handshake.

Listing 2-4. The client sends an initialize request advertising its capabilities

```
{
    "jsonrpc": "2.0",
        "id": 1,
        "method": "initialize",
        "params": {
            "protocolVersion": "2025-03-26",
                "capabilities": {
                    "roots": {
                        "listChanged": true
                    },
```

```
                    "sampling": {}
                },
                "clientInfo": {
                    "name": "MyAIApp",
                        "version": "1.0.0"
                }
        }
}
```

Listing 2-5. The server responds with its own capabilities

```
{
    "jsonrpc": "2.0",
        "id": 1,
        "result": {
            "protocolVersion": "2025-03-26",
                "capabilities": {
                    "tools": {
                        "listChanged": true
                    },
                        "resources": {
                            "subscribe": true,
                                "listChanged": true
                        },
                        "prompts": {
                            "listChanged": true
                        }
                },
                "serverInfo": {
                    "name": "WeatherServer",
                        "version": "0.1.0"
                }
        }
}
```

Notice the structure of the capabilities objects. The client in Listing 2-4 is telling the server that it supports the roots feature with change notifications and that it can handle sampling requests. The server in Listing 2-5 responds by saying it offers tools, resources, and prompts, all with change-notification support. This exchange ensures that neither side tries to use a feature the other does not understand.

Note The `protocolVersion` field uses a date-based versioning scheme. Both client and server must agree on the same version. If your client sends a version the server does not recognize, the initialization will fail cleanly instead of producing mysterious errors later.

The Protocol Lifecycle

Every MCP connection follows a well-defined lifecycle with four phases: connection, initialization, operation, and shutdown. Understanding this lifecycle will save you hours of debugging when you start building your own servers, because most confusing errors happen when code tries to do something in the wrong phase.

Phase 1: Connection

In this phase, the transport layer establishes a raw communication channel between the client and the server. For a stdio transport, this means launching the server process and connecting to its standard input and output streams. For an HTTP-based transport, it means opening a network connection to the server's endpoint. At this point, no MCP messages have been exchanged yet. The two sides can send bytes to each other, but they have not agreed on anything.

Phase 2: Initialization

This is where the capability negotiation we just discussed takes place. The client sends the initialize request, the server responds, and the client confirms with an initialized notification. During this phase, neither side should send any other requests. The protocol specification is strict about this: if a server receives a tools/list request before initialization is complete, it should reject it. This rule prevents race conditions and ensures both sides have a consistent view of each other's capabilities before any real work begins.

Phase 3: Operation

Once initialization succeeds, the connection enters the operation phase. This is where the interesting stuff happens. The client can now call tools, read resources, and fetch prompt templates. The server can send notifications to inform the client about changes, like a new tool becoming available or an existing resource being updated. Both sides can send requests and responses freely, and multiple requests can be in flight at the same time.

The operation phase lasts as long as the connection is open. For a stdio server, that might be the entire lifetime of the host application. For an HTTP server, it could be a single session that ends when the user closes their browser tab. The protocol does not dictate how long the operation phase should last. It simply provides the rules for how messages flow while it is active.

Phase 4: Shutdown

When the host decides it is done with a server, the client initiates a graceful shutdown. For stdio servers, the client simply closes the server's input stream; for HTTP-based servers, the client disconnects. There is no formal shutdown message in the protocol. The server should finish any in-progress work, release resources, and exit cleanly. A well-behaved server never leaves temporary files lying around or database connections dangling after a shutdown.

Tip When developing your own MCP servers, always test the shutdown path. It is easy to focus on the happy path during development and forget that your server needs to clean up after itself. A simple integration test that starts the server, calls a tool, and then shuts down can catch resource leaks early.

Figure 2-2 shows how these four phases flow from left to right. A connection that fails during initialization never reaches the operation phase, which is why getting the capability handshake right matters.

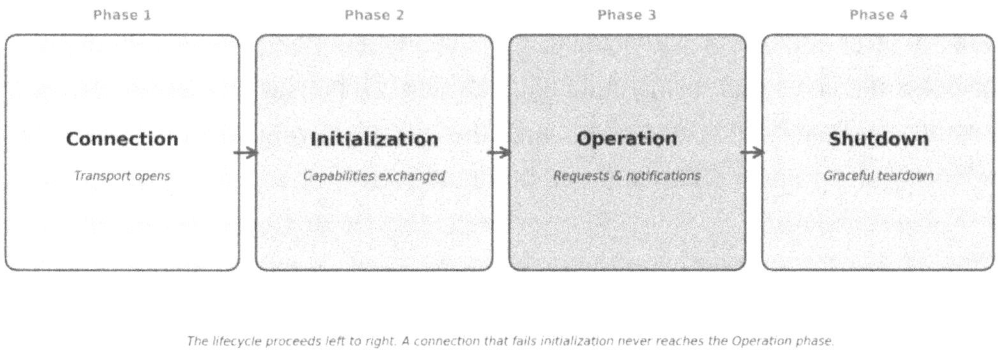

Figure 2-2. *The four phases of the MCP connection lifecycle*

Transport Layer

The transport layer is the plumbing that carries JSON-RPC messages between client and server. MCP does not force you to use a single transport. Instead, it defines a transport interface and provides several implementations. This keeps the protocol flexible: you can pick the transport that best fits your deployment scenario. The three transports you will encounter most often are stdio, Server-Sent Events (SSE), and Streamable HTTP.

Standard I/O (stdio)

The stdio transport is the simplest option and the one you will use most often during development. The host launches the server as a child process and communicates by writing JSON-RPC messages to the server's standard input and reading responses from its standard output. There is no networking involved, no ports to configure, and no TLS certificates to manage. This makes stdio perfect for local development and for scenarios where the server runs on the same machine as the host.

Note If the term "standard input and output" is new to you, here is the short version. Every process your operating system starts gets three streams: standard input (stdin) for data coming in, standard output (stdout) for data going out, and standard error (stderr) for diagnostics. When you type a command in a terminal and see a result, you are using stdin and stdout. MCP borrows these same streams to shuttle JSON-RPC messages back and forth, which is why an MCP server looks and feels like a regular command-line program.

The downside is that stdio only works when the host can directly spawn the server process. If you need your server to run on a different machine or be shared by multiple clients, you will need a network transport.

Server-Sent Events (SSE)

The SSE transport uses HTTP to carry messages. The client opens a long-lived HTTP connection to the server, and the server pushes messages to the client as server-sent events. The client sends messages to the server via regular HTTP POST requests. SSE was the original network transport for MCP and you may still encounter it in older implementations.

Note While SSE still works, at the time of writing, the MCP specification now recommends using the newer Streamable HTTP transport for new deployments. SSE support may eventually be deprecated, so keep that in mind when choosing a transport for production use.

Streamable HTTP

Streamable HTTP is the recommended network transport for MCP going forward. It builds on standard HTTP and supports both request-response and streaming patterns in a single, unified protocol. Unlike SSE, Streamable HTTP does not require a persistent connection. Clients send requests as HTTP POST messages and can optionally upgrade to a streaming connection when they need to receive server-initiated messages like progress updates or change notifications.

This flexibility makes Streamable HTTP a great fit for production deployments. It works well with load balancers, proxies, and container orchestrators that might not handle long-lived connections gracefully. We will explore transport configuration in much greater detail in Chapter 8, where you will learn how to set up both local and remote transports for your C# MCP servers.

Security Model

Connecting an AI model to external tools is powerful, but it also introduces real risk. An MCP server that can read files, query databases, or call APIs could do serious damage if misused. The MCP specification takes security seriously and bakes several protective measures directly into the protocol.

User Consent and Control

The most fundamental security principle in MCP is that the user must remain in control. When an AI model decides it wants to call a tool, the host application should present that request to the user and ask for confirmation before the call actually happens. You have probably seen this pattern in GitHub Copilot or Claude Desktop, where a tool call appears in the conversation with an "Allow" button. This is not optional politeness. The specification explicitly states that hosts should obtain user approval before executing tool calls, especially for operations that have side effects.

This consent model exists because the AI model is not always right. It might misunderstand the user's intent and try to delete a file when the user only wanted to read it. By putting a human in the loop, MCP ensures that no destructive action happens without explicit approval.

Trust Boundaries

MCP defines clear trust boundaries between the three layers. The host trusts the client because the client is part of the host's own code. But neither the host nor the client should blindly trust the server. The server is external code that could come from anywhere, and its output should always be treated as untrusted input. This means the host should validate and sanitize data received from the server before displaying it to the user or passing it to the AI model.

Similarly, the server should not blindly trust the client. Even though the client authenticated during initialization, the server should still validate all incoming parameters and enforce its own authorization rules. Defense in depth is the name of the game: every layer protects itself, and no layer assumes the others are doing their job perfectly.

Data Privacy

MCP servers often handle sensitive data, from database records to file contents to API keys. The protocol's security model asks server developers to be thoughtful about what data they expose. Just because a server can read an entire database does not mean it should return every row to the AI model. Servers should implement proper access controls, filter sensitive fields, and log access for audit purposes.

The host also plays a role in data privacy. It should never send user data to a server that the user has not explicitly authorized. If a user configures a server for weather lookups, the host should not start sending the user's email content to that server just because the AI thinks it might be relevant.

Caution Never store API keys, passwords, or other secrets directly in your MCP server code. Use environment variables or a secrets manager instead. When we start building servers in Chapter 4, I will show you how to handle configuration securely.

Putting It All Together

Let us trace a complete interaction from start to finish so you can see how all these pieces work together. Imagine a user is chatting with an AI assistant in Claude Desktop and asks: "What is the weather in Seattle?"

First, Claude Desktop (the host) started a weather MCP server when it launched, using the stdio transport. Its internal MCP client already completed the initialization handshake, so the connection is in the operation phase. The client knows the server supports a tool called `get_weather` because it received that information during capability negotiation.

When the user asks about the weather, Claude's language model sees the available tools and decides it should call `get_weather` with the parameter city set to "Seattle." Claude Desktop shows the user a confirmation prompt: "The assistant wants to call `get_weather` with city: Seattle. Allow?" The user clicks Allow.

Now the MCP client sends a tools/call request to the server with the appropriate parameters. The server receives the request, calls a weather API internally, and returns the result as a JSON-RPC response. The client hands the result back to Claude Desktop, which feeds it into the language model. The model uses the weather data to compose a natural-language answer: "It is currently 58°F and cloudy in Seattle."

Have a look at Listing 2-6 and Listing 2-7 to see what that looks like in JSON requests and responses.

Listing 2-6. The complete tools/call request the client sends to the weather server

```
{
    "jsonrpc": "2.0",
        "id": 42,
        "method": "tools/call",
        "params": {
            "name": "get_weather",
                "arguments": {
                    "city": "Seattle"
                }
        }
}
```

Listing 2-7. The server's response with the weather data

```
{
    "jsonrpc": "2.0",
        "id": 42,
        "result": {
            "content": [
            {
                "type": "text",
                    "text":
```

```
                "Current weather in Seattle:"
                    + " 58°F, cloudy,"
                    + " humidity 72%"
            }
            ]
        }
}
```

This entire flow, from user question to natural-language answer, happens in a fraction of a second. The cool thing about MCP is that none of the participants need to know anything about the others' internals. The host does not know how the server gets weather data. The server does not know which AI model the host is using. And the user does not need to know that any of this protocol machinery exists at all. They just get a helpful answer to their question.

Beyond the Basics

So far, we have focused on the core building blocks: hosts, clients, servers, tools, resources, and prompts. Those are the features you will use every day, and they cover the majority of what MCP can do. But the protocol has a few more tricks up its sleeve that are worth knowing about, even if you will not use all of them right away.

Sampling

The protocol also supports something called sampling, where the server can ask the client to use the AI model on its behalf. Think of it as the server saying, "Hey, I need the AI to analyze this data for me." Instead of the usual flow where the AI calls a tool on the server, sampling flips the direction. The server sends a request to the client with a prompt and some context, and the client runs that through the AI model and sends the result back. Not bad, right?

This opens up some interesting possibilities. A server could ask the AI to summarize a large document, classify incoming data, or even generate code as part of a larger workflow. The key constraint is that the host remains in control. The user can see the sampling request and approve or reject it, just like with tool calls. It is a powerful concept, though not all clients support it yet.

Roots

Roots let the client tell the server about the project context. If you are using VS Code, roots might include the files and folders in your workspace. The idea is that the server sometimes needs to know what the user is working on so it can scope its behavior accordingly. For example, a code analysis server might only want to scan the files that are actually part of the current project, not every file on the hard drive.

During capability negotiation, the client can advertise that it supports roots and even that it will send notifications when the root list changes. The server can then request the list of roots and use that information to tailor its responses. It is a small feature, but it makes a big difference for servers that need project awareness.

Notifications

We touched on notifications earlier when we discussed JSON-RPC message types, but there is more to the story. Both client and server can send notifications to each other throughout the operation phase. The server might say, "Hey, my list of tools just changed," and the client can update accordingly. The client might notify the server that the root list has been modified. These are one-way messages with no response expected, which keeps them lightweight and fast.

The MCP specification defines several standard notification types, including notifications for tool list changes, resource list changes, resource updates, and progress reporting. You already saw progress notifications in action when we discussed the protocol lifecycle. The important thing to remember is that notifications are optional. A server can send them, but the client is not required to act on them. Well-behaved clients will update their state when they receive a change notification, but the protocol does not break if they ignore one.

Elicitation

Elicitation is a newer addition that lets the server ask the user questions directly through the client. Think of it as a dialog box but triggered by the server. Say your server needs a piece of information that the AI cannot figure out on its own, like which database environment to connect to. Instead of guessing or failing, the server can send an elicitation request to the client, which pops up a prompt for the user to answer.

This is different from tool calls because the question goes to the human, not the AI. The client presents the server's question to the user, collects the answer, and sends it back. It is a clean way to handle those situations where a bit of human input makes all the difference. Like the other features in this section, elicitation support varies by client, so check your target client's documentation before relying on it.

These features are evolving rapidly. For the latest on what is supported in the C# SDK, check out `https://csharp.sdk.modelcontextprotocol.io/`.

Summary

In this chapter, you took a close look at the architecture that powers the Model Context Protocol. You learned that MCP uses a three-layer architecture with hosts, clients, and servers, each with a clear responsibility. You saw that JSON-RPC 2.0 provides the simple but powerful message format that ties everything together, supporting requests, responses, and notifications. You walked through capability negotiation and understood why it is critical for clients and servers to agree on features before doing any real work.

You also explored the four-phase protocol lifecycle and saw how a connection moves from raw transport to fully operational, and eventually to a clean shutdown. We touched on the three transport options, stdio, SSE, and Streamable HTTP, and noted which scenarios each one fits best. Finally, you learned about the security model that protects users, data, and systems by keeping humans in the loop and enforcing trust boundaries between layers.

With this architectural foundation in place, you are ready to get your hands dirty. In Chapter 3, we will set up your development environment with all the tools you need to build MCP servers in C#. You will install the .NET SDK, configure your IDE, and create a skeleton project that we will keep building on throughout the rest of the book.

CHAPTER 3

Setting Up Your Development Environment

Before we can build anything, we need to make sure our development environment is ready to go. Here's what we'll cover: installing the .NET SDK, picking an editor, pulling in the right NuGet packages, and wiring up a test client so you can actually talk to the servers you build. By the end of the chapter, you will have a fully working setup and a tiny project that proves it.

Installing the .NET SDK

The MCP SDK for C# targets .NET 10.0 and later. If you already have a recent .NET SDK on your machine, you are probably fine, but here is how to check and, if needed, how to get the latest bits installed.

Head over to `https://dot.net` and download the SDK installer for your operating system. The site auto-detects whether you are on Windows, macOS, or Linux and offers the right download.

Once the installer finishes, open a terminal and verify the installation. In Figure 3-1, you can see a terminal window on macOS that ran the `dotnet --info` command and shows that I have .NET 10.0.201 installed.

G. Versluis, *Building MCP Servers with C#*, https://doi.org/10.1007/979-8-8688-3010-5_3

Figure 3-1. *Verifying the .NET SDK installation*

As long as the major version is 10 or higher, you are good. That's it! If you see an older version, make sure the new SDK is on your PATH. On Windows, the installer usually takes care of that, but on macOS and Linux, you may need to add the dotnet directory to your shell profile. Typically, the installer will take care of that though.

You can also run `dotnet --list-sdks` to see every SDK version that is installed side by side. This is handy when you work on projects that target different .NET versions. In Listing 3-1, you can see the example output when you have a .NET 9 and .NET 10 SDK installation side-by-side.

Listing 3-1. Listing all installed .NET SDKs

```
$ dotnet --list-sdks
9.0.200 [/usr/local/share/dotnet/sdk]
10.0.100 [/usr/local/share/dotnet/sdk]
```

Having multiple SDKs installed is perfectly normal. The tooling will pick the right one based on the `global.json` file in your project or fall back to the newest version.

Choosing Your IDE

You have several excellent options for writing C# code these days. Here is a quick tour of the three most popular ones. I will explain why I will be using Visual Studio Code for the examples in this book.

Visual Studio 2026

Visual Studio 2026 is the heavyweight champion of .NET development and the IDE most C# developers know inside and out. It comes packed with a world-class debugger, built-in profilers, designers for UI frameworks, and first-party project templates for virtually every .NET workload. If you are building enterprise applications or working with .NET MAUI, WPF, or ASP.NET, Visual Studio 2026 is hard to beat. If you are still on Visual Studio 2022, most of the code will work just fine, but I recommend upgrading to 2026 to get the latest .NET 10 tooling and MCP-related features.

The Community edition is free for individuals, open-source projects, and small teams. Professional and Enterprise editions add collaboration and compliance features aimed at larger organizations. One thing to keep in mind is that Visual Studio 2026 only runs on Windows. There used to be a Mac version, but Microsoft retired it and now points Mac users to Visual Studio Code or the C# Dev Kit.

Visual Studio Code with C# Dev Kit

Visual Studio Code is a lightweight, cross-platform editor that has taken the developer world by storm. On its own, it is a fast text editor, but once you install the C# Dev Kit extension, it gains IntelliSense, debugging, test discovery, and a solution explorer that feels surprisingly close to the full Visual Studio experience.

I will be using Visual Studio Code throughout this book for several reasons. First, it runs on Windows, macOS, and Linux, so every reader can follow along regardless of their operating system. Second, it starts up fast and stays out of the way, which is perfect for the small, focused projects we will be building. Third, the integrated terminal makes it easy to run dotnet commands and test our MCP servers without switching windows. And it also has excellent support for MCP itself, making it easy to use an MCP server directly from within the editor.

Note You do not have to use Visual Studio Code. Every command and code sample in this book works with any editor. I just happen to think VS Code offers the best balance of power and simplicity for the kind of work we will be doing.

JetBrains Rider

JetBrains Rider is a cross-platform .NET IDE from the same company that makes IntelliJ IDEA and ReSharper. It combines a fast editor with deep code analysis, refactoring tools, and built-in database and Docker support. If you are coming from the JetBrains ecosystem, you will feel right at home.

Rider requires a paid subscription after the trial period, which is worth mentioning. That said, many professional developers consider it the most productive .NET IDE available, especially on macOS and Linux where Visual Studio is not an option. For this book, any of the three editors will work just fine, so use whatever you are most comfortable with.

The MCP NuGet Packages

The official MCP SDK for .NET is published as a set of NuGet packages. Understanding which package to reference in your project is important because choosing the wrong one can pull in dependencies you do not need or, worse, leave out functionality you do need.

ModelContextProtocol

This is the main package and the one I recommend for most projects. It includes everything you need to build both MCP servers and clients over the stdio transport. Under the hood, it depends on `ModelContextProtocol.Core`, so you get the full type system, serialization, and protocol handling out of the box. For the majority of this book, we will reference this package.

ModelContextProtocol.Core

If you want the lightest possible footprint, `ModelContextProtocol`.Core gives you the protocol types, interfaces, and base classes without the higher-level hosting helpers. You would typically use this package when you are integrating MCP into an existing application framework and want full control over the server lifecycle. Unless you have a specific reason to go minimal, I suggest starting with the main package instead.

ModelContextProtocol.AspNetCore

When you want to expose your MCP server over HTTP instead of stdio, this package is what you need. It integrates with ASP.NET Core and adds support for the Streamable HTTP transport as well as Server-Sent Events (SSE). We will explore HTTP-based MCP servers in detail in a later chapter, so for now, just know it exists.

Table 3-1 summarizes when to reach for each package.

Table 3-1. *MCP NuGet packages at a glance*

Package	When to Use
ModelContextProtocol	Most projects. Full server and client support over stdio, including hosting helpers.
ModelContextProtocol.Core	Lightweight integration. Protocol types and interfaces only, for embedding MCP into existing frameworks.
ModelContextProtocol.AspNetCore	HTTP transport. Adds Streamable HTTP and SSE support via ASP.NET Core middleware.

All three packages are available on NuGet.org and follow the same versioning scheme. At the time of writing, the latest stable version is 1.3.0. Newer versions may be available by the time you read this, but the APIs covered in this book should remain stable across minor releases.

Note Always check NuGet.org for the latest version before adding the package to your project. Newer minor versions should be backward compatible.

Setting Up an MCP Client for Testing

Building an MCP server is only half the story. You also need a client that can connect to it so you can verify that your tools, resources, and prompts actually work. I want to walk you through three client options that you will use throughout this book. Because MCP is an open standard, the servers you build will work with any client that supports the protocol. These three just happen to be the ones I reach for during development.

Claude Desktop

Claude Desktop from Anthropic was one of the first applications to support MCP, which makes sense because Anthropic created the protocol in the first place. It is a desktop app that gives you a chat interface to Claude and lets you connect to local MCP servers through a JSON configuration file.

To configure Claude Desktop to talk to one of our servers, you need to edit the configuration file. On macOS, this file lives at `~/Library/Application Support/Claude/claude_desktop_config.json`, and on Windows, you can find it at `%APPDATA%\Claude\claude_desktop_config.json`. In Listing 3-2, you can see what a typical configuration looks like.

Listing 3-2. Claude Desktop MCP configuration

```
{
    "mcpServers": {
        "my-mcp-server": {
            "command": "dotnet",
            "args": [
                "run",
                "--project",
                "/path/to/your/McpServer.csproj"
            ]
        }
    }
}
```

The command field tells Claude Desktop which executable to launch, and `args` provides the arguments. In our case, we use `dotnet run` with a `--project` flag pointing to the `.csproj` file. Claude Desktop will start the process, connect to it over stdio, and you can immediately start chatting with Claude while it uses your server's tools.

Tip If you do not have a Claude Desktop subscription, do not worry. The other two client options I describe next are completely free.

Visual Studio Code

Visual Studio Code has built-in MCP support through GitHub Copilot. If you already use Copilot chat in VS Code, adding an MCP server is just a matter of creating a small configuration file in your workspace.

Create a file called `.vscode/mcp.json` in the root of your project with the following content as seen in Listing 3-3. We will create the actual project in the next section, but you can already prepare this configuration file in any folder.

Listing 3-3. VS Code MCP server configuration

```
{
    "servers": {
        "my-mcp-server": {
            "type": "stdio",
                "command": "dotnet",
                "args": [
                "run",
                "--project",
                "/path/to/your/McpServer.csproj"
            ]
        }
    }
}
```

After saving the file, open the Copilot chat panel and you should see your server listed. VS Code will start the process for you and route tool calls through the stdio transport, exactly like Claude Desktop does. This is the setup I will use most often in the book because it keeps everything inside a single editor window.

MCP Inspector

The MCP Inspector is a browser-based debugging tool maintained by the MCP project itself. It gives you a clean UI to connect to any MCP server, browse its capabilities, and invoke tools or read resources manually. Think of it as Postman or Swagger UI, but for MCP.

You can launch the Inspector directly with npx without installing anything globally. In Listing 3-4, you can see the terminal command for that.

Listing 3-4. Launching the MCP Inspector

```
$ npx @modelcontextprotocol/inspector dotnet run \
--project /path/to/your/McpServer.csproj
```

This command starts your MCP server and opens a web page where you can see every tool, resource, and prompt that the server exposes. You can then call tools interactively and inspect the JSON payloads going back and forth. The Inspector is invaluable when you are debugging protocol issues or just want to poke around without firing up a full chat client. We will take a proper guided tour of the Inspector in Chapter 11. Figure 3-2 shows what the interface looks like.

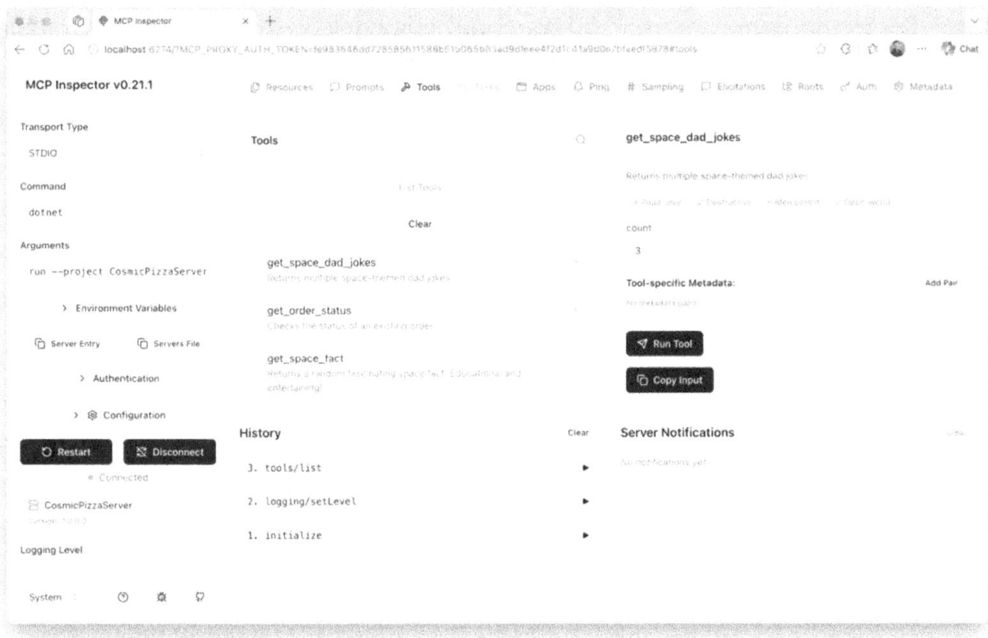

Figure 3-2. *The MCP Inspector web interface showing the connection panel and tabs for Tools, Resources, and Prompts*

Note The MCP Inspector requires Node.js to be installed because it uses npx. If you do not have Node.js yet, grab it from `https://nodejs.org`.

Creating Your First Project

With the SDK installed, an editor chosen, and a test client ready, let us create our first .NET project that references the MCP NuGet package. We are not building a real server yet (that is the job of Chapter 4), but we will make sure the package installs correctly and that we can resolve types from it.

Open a terminal, navigate to a folder where you keep your projects, and run the following commands, as seen in Listing 3-5.

Note For the terminal command throughout this book, like below, the $ symbol at the start of each line represents the terminal prompt and is not part of the command. On Windows, your prompt might look like > or C:\> instead. The actual commands should work on Windows, macOS, and Linux.

Listing 3-5. Creating a new console project and adding the MCP package

```
$ mkdir EnvironmentCheck
$ cd EnvironmentCheck
$ dotnet new console
$ dotnet add package ModelContextProtocol
```

The first command creates a new directory. The second command scaffolds a minimal console application with a `Program.cs` and a `.csproj` file. The third command pulls in the `ModelContextProtocol` NuGet package and adds a `PackageReference` to the project file.

Tip At the time of writing, Microsoft offers preview project templates for MCP servers. Run `dotnet new install Microsoft.McpServer.ProjectTemplates` to install them, then `dotnet new mcpserver` to scaffold a server with stdio or HTTP transport already wired up. We set everything up by hand in this book because understanding each piece matters more than saving a few keystrokes, but once you are comfortable with the fundamentals, these templates are a nice shortcut.

After running these commands, open the `.csproj` file. The contents should look like Listing 3-6, although slight variations might be possible.

Listing 3-6. The project file after adding the MCP package

```
<Project Sdk="Microsoft.NET.Sdk">
    <PropertyGroup>
        <OutputType>Exe</OutputType>
        <TargetFramework>net10.0</TargetFramework>
        <ImplicitUsings>enable</ImplicitUsings>
```

```
        <Nullable>enable</Nullable>
    </PropertyGroup>
    <ItemGroup>
        <PackageReference Include="ModelContextProtocol" Version="1.3.0" />
    </ItemGroup>
</Project>
```

The exact version number may differ depending on when you read this. The important thing is that the PackageReference element is present and that the package restores without errors.

Tip If you want to try the very latest bits, add the `--prerelease` flag: `dotnet add package ModelContextProtocol --prerelease`. For this book, the stable release is all you need.

Verifying Everything Works

Let us write a tiny smoke test to confirm that the SDK is properly installed and that we can reference types from the MCP package. Open `Program.cs` and replace its contents with the following code from Listing 3-7.

Listing 3-7. A simple environment check (Program.cs)

```
using System.Reflection;
using System.Runtime.InteropServices;

Console.WriteLine("=== MCP Development Environment Check ===");
Console.WriteLine();

// .NET runtime info
Console.WriteLine($"  .NET Version:   {RuntimeInformation.
FrameworkDescription}");
Console.WriteLine($"  OS:             {RuntimeInformation.OSDescription}");
Console.WriteLine($"  Architecture:   {RuntimeInformation.OSArchitecture}");
Console.WriteLine();
```

```
// Try to load the MCP assembly
try
{
    var asm = Assembly.Load("ModelContextProtocol");
    Console.WriteLine($"  MCP SDK loaded:  {asm.GetName().Version}");
    Console.WriteLine("  Status:          All good!");
}
catch (Exception ex)
{
    Console.WriteLine($"  MCP SDK:          NOT FOUND ({ex.Message})");
    Console.WriteLine("  Status:          Please install the
    ModelContextProtocol NuGet package.");
}
Console.WriteLine();
Console.WriteLine("Environment check complete.");
```

This program does two things.

First, it prints information about the .NET runtime and the operating system. Second, it tries to load the `ModelContextProtocol` assembly at runtime. If the load succeeds, it prints the assembly version, confirming that the NuGet package is properly installed. If it fails, it prints a helpful error message.

Run the project to see the output; an example is seen in Listing 3-8.

Listing 3-8. Running the environment check

```
$ dotnet run
=== MCP Development Environment Check ===
.NET Version:    .NET 10.0.0
OS:              Darwin 24.3.0
Architecture:    Arm64
MCP SDK loaded:  1.0.0.0
Status:          All good!
Environment check complete.
```

If your output looks similar to Listing 3-8, congratulations! Your development environment is fully set up and the MCP SDK is ready to use. The exact version numbers and OS details will of course vary depending on your machine, but the important line is the one that says, "All good!" which tells you the SDK assembly loaded successfully.

If the assembly fails to load, double-check that you ran `dotnet add package ModelContextProtocol` in the project directory and that the package restored without errors. You can also run `dotnet restore` explicitly to force a fresh package restore.

Summary

Here's what we covered: We set up everything you need to follow along with the rest of this book. We installed the .NET 10 SDK, explored the three most popular editors for C# development, and discussed the NuGet packages that make up the official MCP SDK. We also configured three different MCP clients (Claude Desktop, VS Code, and the MCP Inspector) so that you have options for testing the servers you build.

Finally, we created a small console project, added the `ModelContextProtocol` package, and ran a quick smoke test to confirm everything is wired up correctly. With your environment ready to go, it is time to build something real.

In Chapter 4, you will create your first MCP server from scratch. We will register tools, handle requests, and connect a client to see the whole round trip in action. Let's go!

CHAPTER 4

Your First MCP Server

If you have been reading the previous chapters and are itching to write some code, I have good news: this is the chapter where theory meets practice. We are going to build an actual, working MCP server from scratch. By the end of this chapter, you will have a server that exposes tools, connects to a real AI client, and does something you can see with your own eyes. Nothing motivates quite like watching your code come alive.

The approach I am going to take here is deliberately simple. We will start with the absolute minimum amount of code required to get a server running, prove that it works, and then layer on a second tool to see how the system scales. Along the way I will explain every moving part, so you understand not just what to type, but why it works the way it does.

Creating the Project

Let's kick things off with a plain .NET console application. Just like we did at the end of Chapter 3, but let's start fresh. Open your terminal, navigate to the folder where you want your project to live, and run the following command:

```
dotnet new console -n FirstMcpServer
```

That gives us the familiar Hello World starter. Before we touch any code, we need the official MCP NuGet package. The C# SDK lives in a package called `ModelContextProtocol`. The C# SDK is available as a stable 1.3.0 release at the time of writing. This package is maintained by Microsoft and Anthropic together. Add it together with the hosting package:

```
$ cd FirstMcpServer
$ dotnet add package ModelContextProtocol
$ dotnet add package Microsoft.Extensions.Hosting
```


G. Versluis, *Building MCP Servers with C#*, https://doi.org/10.1007/979-8-8688-3010-5_4

The ModelContextProtocol package brings in everything we need: the transport layer, the JSON-RPC plumbing, tool discovery, and the attributes we will use to mark our tools. The Microsoft.Extensions.Hosting package gives us the generic host that manages the lifetime of our server. After running these commands, your project file should look similar to what is shown in Listing 4-1:

Listing 4-1. The FirstMcpServer.csproj project file

```
<Project Sdk="Microsoft.NET.Sdk">
    <PropertyGroup>
        <OutputType>Exe</OutputType>
        <TargetFramework>net10.0</TargetFramework>
        <ImplicitUsings>enable</ImplicitUsings>
        <Nullable>enable</Nullable>
    </PropertyGroup>
    <ItemGroup>
        <PackageReference Include="Microsoft.Extensions.Hosting"
        Version="10.0.3" />
        <PackageReference Include="ModelContextProtocol" Version="1.3.0" />
    </ItemGroup>
</Project>
```

Nothing exotic here. It is a standard console app with two NuGet references. The target framework is net10.0, which is required by the ModelContextProtocol 1.3.0 package.

The Minimal MCP Server

Now let's replace the generated Program.cs with our MCP server code. If you have worked with ASP.NET Core or any other .NET application that uses the generic host, the structure will feel familiar. We use Host.CreateEmptyApplicationBuilder to set up a host, configure the MCP server as a hosted service, and then run it.

You might wonder why we use CreateEmptyApplicationBuilder instead of the more common CreateApplicationBuilder. The reason is the stdio transport. Our MCP server communicates with the client through stdin and stdout, and the regular CreateApplicationBuilder registers a console logger that writes to stdout by default.

That logging output would mix with the JSON-RPC messages and break the protocol stream. `CreateEmptyApplicationBuilder` starts with a clean slate, no default logging providers, no surprise output on stdout, which is exactly what we need for a well-behaved stdio server.

The key extension methods are provided as `Microsoft.Extensions.DependencyInjection` extensions by the SDK package. `AddMcpServer` registers the MCP server with the dependency injection container. `WithStdioServerTransport` tells the server to communicate over standard input and output, which is the transport that most desktop AI clients like Claude Desktop and GitHub Copilot in VS Code expect. Finally, `WithToolsFromAssembly` scans the current assembly for any classes decorated with the right attributes and registers them as tools automatically.

Here is the complete `Program.cs` for our first iteration. I am keeping the echo tool and the server setup in the same file for simplicity. As your projects grow, you will probably want to move tools into their own files, but for a first example, this approach keeps everything visible at a glance. Have a look at Listing 4-2 for the full code.

Listing 4-2. The complete Program.cs with hosting and EchoTool

```
using Microsoft.Extensions.DependencyInjection;
using Microsoft.Extensions.Hosting;
using ModelContextProtocol;
using ModelContextProtocol.Server;
using System.ComponentModel;

var builder = Host.CreateEmptyApplicationBuilder(null);

builder.Services
    .AddMcpServer()
    .WithStdioServerTransport()
    .WithToolsFromAssembly();

await builder.Build().RunAsync();

[McpServerToolType]
public static class EchoTool
{
    [McpServerTool]
    [Description("Echoes the input back.")]
```

```
    public static string Echo([Description("Message to echo")] string
    message)
    {
        return $"Echo: {message}";
    }
}
```

Take a look at the important pieces. The first couple of lines bring in the namespaces we need to turn this command-line application into an MCP server. The `ModelContextProtocol` namespace provides the types we need.

The `AddMcpServer` and `WithStdioServerTransport` methods are dependency injection extensions provided by the SDK package. The `ModelContextProtocol.Server` namespace has the attributes `McpServerToolType` and `McpServerTool`. And `System.ComponentModel` gives us the Description attribute, which the SDK reads to generate human-readable descriptions for AI clients.

The builder setup is three lines of fluent API. `AddMcpServer` hooks the MCP server into the dependency injection system. `WithStdioServerTransport` configures the server to read JSON-RPC messages from `stdin` and write responses to `stdout`.

`WithToolsFromAssembly` uses reflection to find every class marked with the `McpServerToolType` attribute (that you can see a little below that) and registers each method marked with `McpServerTool` as a callable tool. After the configuration is done, `Build` and `RunAsync` start the host and keep it alive until it receives a shutdown signal.

Don't worry if all that seems to go a little fast and you didn't get all of that yet. We will go over the different moving parts in a bit more detail.

Your First Tool: Echo

The `EchoTool` class is where things get interesting. If you look at it closely, you will notice that it is remarkably simple: a static class with a static method that takes a string and returns a string. There is no base class to inherit from, no interface to implement, and no complex registration ceremony. The attributes do all the heavy lifting.

The `McpServerToolType` attribute on the class tells the SDK that this class contains one or more MCP tools. Think of it as a marker that says, "Look inside me for tool methods." The `McpServerTool` attribute on the method marks it as an individual tool that should be exposed to AI clients. The `Description` attribute, which comes from the standard `System.ComponentModel` namespace, provides the human-readable text that AI clients display when they list available tools. The AI model uses this description to decide when to call your tool, so writing a clear and accurate description is important.

Notice that the method parameter also has a `Description` attribute. This tells the AI client what the parameter is for, and the SDK uses it to generate the JSON Schema that describes the tool's input. When an AI model decides to call your tool, it will construct a JSON object that matches this schema, and the SDK handles deserializing it into the correct .NET types.

The return type is a plain string. Under the hood, the SDK wraps this string into the proper MCP response format and sends it back through the JSON-RPC channel. You can also return more complex types, but for now, a string is all we need.

Note For simple tools without dependencies, static classes with static methods are the easiest approach. The SDK also supports instance methods on non-static classes, which enables dependency injection. We will cover that in the next chapter.

Running the Server

With the code in place, let's see if it actually runs. Open a terminal in your project folder and type

```
dotnet run
```

And then… nothing happens. Or at least, nothing visible. The terminal just sits there with a blinking cursor, and you might wonder if something went wrong. But this is exactly the correct behavior. Remember, our server communicates over stdio. It is sitting there, patiently reading from `stdin`, waiting for a JSON-RPC message to arrive. It does not print a welcome banner or a "server started" message because `stdout` is reserved for JSON-RPC responses. Any text that is not valid JSON-RPC would confuse the client on the other end.

This is one of the things that trips up developers new to MCP. With a web API, you get a nice "Now listening on https://localhost:5000" message. With an MCP stdio server, silence is golden. The server is running, it is healthy, and it is ready. It just cannot tell you that without breaking the protocol.

Tip If you want to verify that the server starts correctly during development, you can add logging to a file or to `stderr`. The MCP specification reserves `stdout` for protocol messages, but `stderr` is fair game for diagnostics.

One gotcha worth knowing: if you add logging later, make sure it goes to `stderr`, not `stdout`. Any output on `stdout` will corrupt the JSON-RPC message stream. The hosting framework in the SDK handles this for you when you use `WithStdioServerTransport`, but keep it in mind if you ever configure logging manually.

Press Ctrl+C to stop the server. Now let's connect it to something that actually speaks MCP and verify that it is in fact working.

Connecting to Claude Desktop

Claude Desktop was one of the first AI clients to support MCP, and it remains one of the easiest ways to test your servers. To connect our echo server, we need to edit Claude Desktop's configuration file. On macOS, this file lives at `~/Library/Application Support/Claude/claude_desktop_config.json`, and on Windows, you can find it at `%APPDATA%/Claude/claude_desktop_config.json`. You can also open it by going to the settings of Claude Desktop, then Developer, and under the Local MCP Servers section, click the Edit Config button.

Create or edit the file so it contains the configuration as seen in Listing 4-3. The part in bold is the actual MCP server we are adding; if there are already multiple MCP servers listed, make sure to add a comma and then add the entry in bold.

There might already be other sections in the config file like `preferences`. Just add the `mcpServers` section in the same block and again make sure to note the comma. It just needs to be a valid JSON file when you save it.

Listing 4-3. Claude Desktop MCP server configuration

```
{
    "preferences": {
        "somePreference": true
   },
```

```
    "mcpServers": {
        "FirstMcpServer": {
            "command": "dotnet",
            "args": [
                "run",
                "--project",
                "/full/path/to/FirstMcpServer"
            ]
        }
    }
}
```

Replace the path in the args array with the actual path to your project folder. The command tells Claude Desktop to run dotnet, and the args tell it to run your project. When Claude Desktop starts, it will launch your server as a child process and communicate with it over stdin and stdout. Simply put, it will just run `dotnet run --project /full/path/to/FirstMcpServer` for you when it's loading the available MCP servers.

After saving the configuration file, restart Claude Desktop. If something went wrong with parsing the configuration file or loading the actual MCP server we added, there will be an error message. If after a couple of seconds nothing pops up, you can be safe to assume that everything is working so far. You can double-check to see if your MCP server is loaded by clicking on the + sign in the text entry field and navigate to Connectors. Under there, you will see the FirstMcpServer (or the different name you might have chosen). You can see this depicted in Figure 4-1.

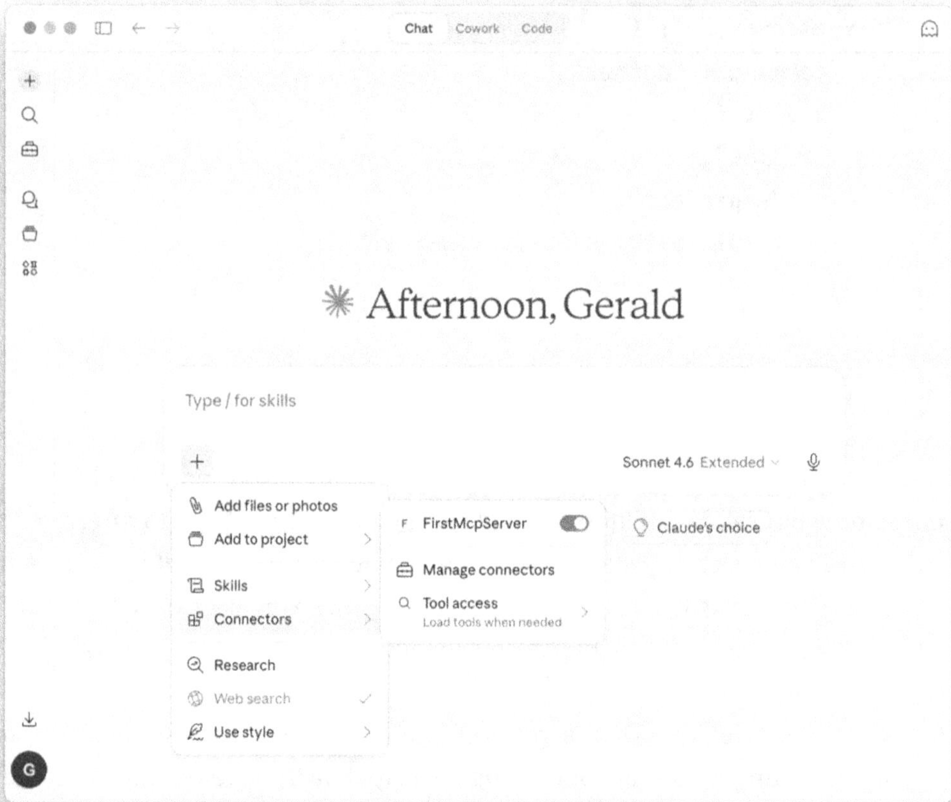

***Figure 4-1.** Our very first MCP server loaded in Claude Desktop*

Now type something like "Can you echo the message Hello MCP for me?" into the chat. Claude will recognize that it has an echo tool available, decide to use it, and send a tool call to your server. Your server processes the request and returns the echoed string. Claude then incorporates the result into its response. The whole round trip happens in a fraction of a second. Since tools can do all kinds of things, including destructive operations, depending on your settings, Claude Desktop (and any other tool that invokes tools) might ask you for permission first. In Figure 4-2, you can see that it detected our echo tool and asks us for permission to actually invoke it.

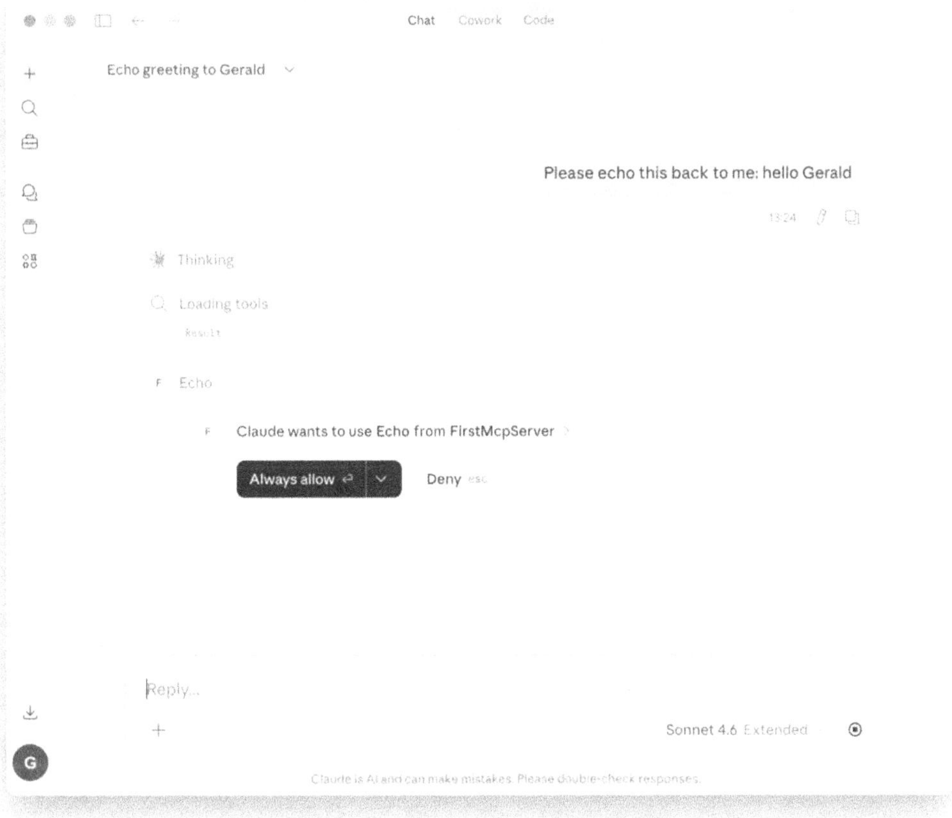

Figure 4-2. *Claude Desktop is asking permission to invoke our Echo tool from the FirstMcpServer*

What makes this moment special is that you just extended an AI model's capabilities with your own code. The model did not know how to echo messages before; you taught it by writing a five-line method. And what I like about MCP is that the model figured out when and how to call your tool based solely on the descriptions you provided.

I still remember the first time one of my tools showed up in Claude Desktop. I may have done a little fist pump. Nobody was around to witness it, so it definitely happened.

Tip If the tool does not appear in Claude Desktop, check that the path in your configuration is correct and that `dotnet` is available on your system PATH. You can test this by opening a terminal and running `dotnet --version`. Also make sure you fully restart Claude Desktop after changing the configuration.

In some cases, Claude Desktop does not find the `dotnet` command. In that case, you can fully qualify the path to the dotnet executable in the `command` field in the configuration JSON file. Or… ask Claude how to fix it!

Connecting to Visual Studio Code

Claude Desktop is great for quick testing, but many of us spend most of our time in Visual Studio Code. The good news is that VS Code also supports MCP servers, and the setup is straightforward.

In VS Code, open the Command Palette with Ctrl+Shift+P (or Cmd+Shift+P on macOS) and search for "MCP: Add Server." VS Code will first ask whether this should be a User (global) or Workspace (local) configuration. For now, choose Workspace so the configuration stays with your project. Next, it will prompt you for the server type; choose "stdio." Then it will ask for the command to run. Here, we can just enter the full command we want to run including parameters, so: `dotnet run -project /full/path/to/FirstMcpServer`. Finally, it will ask for a name (or server id). This can be anything you want; let's just go with FirstMcpServer again. After you entered everything, VS Code will open the configuration JSON file so you can inspect the result and see the status of your MCP server. You can see this happening in Figure 4-3.

Note how there are little helpers just about the "FirstMcpServer" line that indicates the server is running and some actions to Stop, Restart and inspect the number of tools included in this MCP server, in our case just one.

If something went wrong, it will say Error instead of Running and you can click on that to open the Output pane that we see in the bottom with the logging from our MCP server.

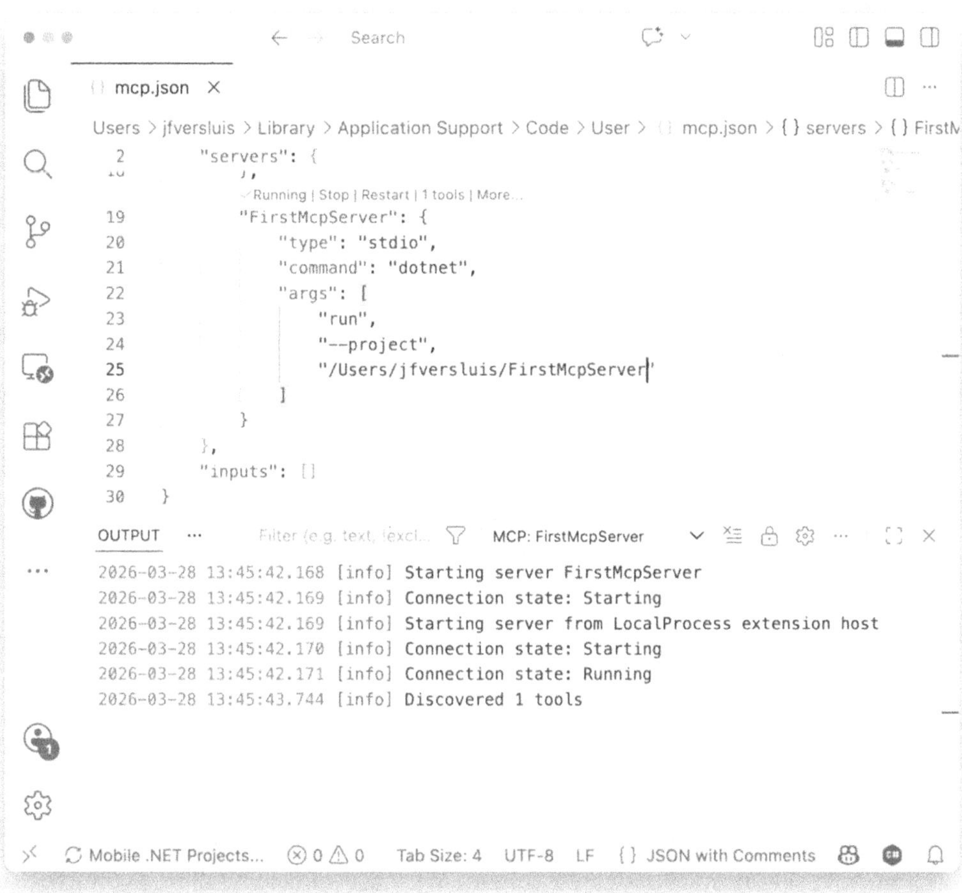

Figure 4-3. *Our MCP server added to the VS Code configuration*

Note Closely inspect the output from adding the MCP server through the Command Palette. Because you enter the full command to execute as one line, VS Code tries to parse the command and the arguments. It doesn't always get it 100% right. For instance, if you have a space in the path to your MCP server, it might see that as two arguments and wrongfully split that up.

Alternatively, you can add the configuration manually. Open your VS Code settings JSON file and add the following like Listing 4-4.

Listing 4-4. VS Code MCP server configuration

```
{
    "mcp": {
        "servers": {
            "FirstMcpServer": {
                "type": "stdio",
                "command": "dotnet",
                "args": [
                    "run",
                    "--project",
                    "/full/path/to/FirstMcpServer"
                ]
            }
        }
    }
}
```

Once configured, you can interact with your MCP server through GitHub Copilot Chat in VS Code. When Copilot detects that an MCP server is available, it will use the tools you defined just like Claude Desktop does. Ask it to echo a message and watch it call your tool.

You can also put this configuration in a .vscode/`mcp.json` file inside your project folder. This is especially useful when you want to share the MCP server configuration with your team through source control.

To verify if it works, click the speech balloon with sparkles (sparkles seem to be the universal sign for AI) to open the Copilot Chat pane. Open a new session and click the Configure Tools icon in the text entry field. That's the icon with the two horizontal lines with circles on them. Can you see it in Figure 4-4 indicated by the arrow? That will open the Configure Tools pane in the top that shows all the available tools, including our FirstMcpServer with the Echo tool!

If you now ask in the chat to echo your message, it should detect the tool, potentially request permission to invoke it, execute it, and then send the message back to you similar to what we have seen in Claude Desktop.

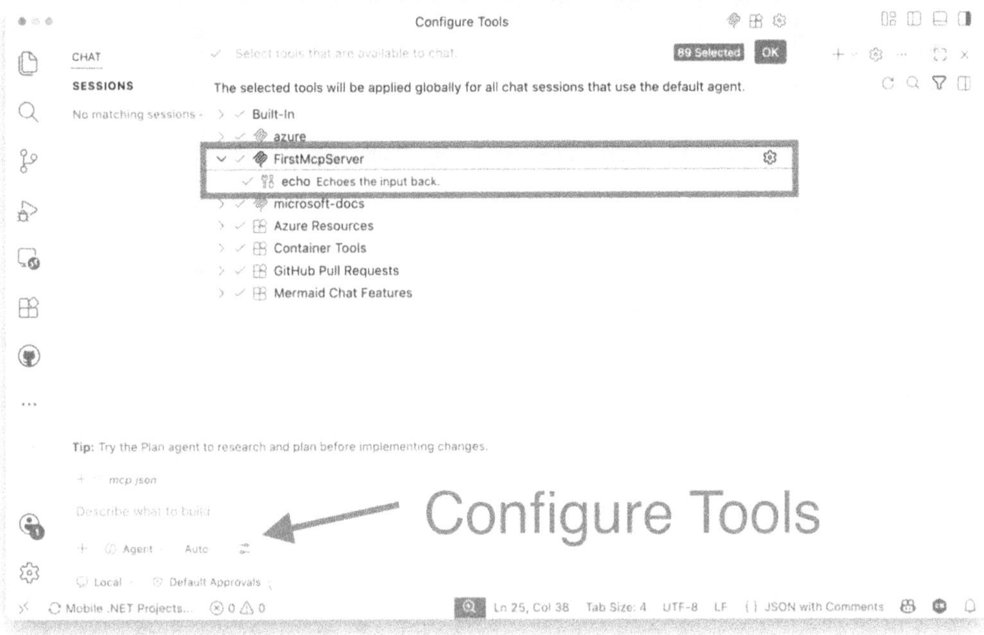

Figure 4-4. *Verifying our MCP server configuration in VS Code*

Understanding What Just Happened

Now that you have seen the server work end to end, let's walk through what happened behind the scenes. When an AI client launches your server, a carefully choreographed sequence of events takes place.

The Initialization Handshake

The very first thing that happens when the client starts your server is the initialization handshake. The client sends an "initialize" request that includes its own capabilities and the protocol version it supports. Your server responds with its capabilities, which include things like "I support tools" or "I support resources." This handshake ensures that both sides agree on what features are available before any real work begins.

You do not have to write any code for this. The SDK handles the entire handshake automatically. It advertises tool support because we called `WithToolsFromAssembly`, and it negotiates the protocol version behind the scenes.

Tool Discovery

After initialization, the client sends a "tools/list" request. Your server responds with a JSON array describing every tool it offers. For our echo tool, the response includes the tool name, the description from our `Description` attribute, and a JSON Schema that describes the expected input parameters. The client uses this information to present the tools to the user and, more importantly, to tell the AI model what tools are available.

This is where the `Description` attributes really earn their keep. The AI model reads these descriptions to decide which tool to call for a given user request. A vague description leads to the model guessing wrong or not using your tool at all. A clear, specific description helps the model make the right choice.

Let us look at what the server actually sends back. When the client sends a `tools/list` request, the server responds with a JSON-RPC message containing the tool name, description, and a JSON Schema describing the expected input. Listing 4-5 is the exact response our server returns for the `EchoTool`.

Listing 4-5. The tools/list response describing the EchoTool

```
{
    "jsonrpc": "2.0",
    "id": 2,
    "result": {
        "tools": [
            {
                "name": "Echo",
                "description": "Echoes the input back.",
                "inputSchema": {
                    "type": "object",
                    "properties": {
                        "message": {
                            "type": "string",
                            "description": "Message to echo"
```

```
                        }
                    },
                    "required": [
                        "message"
                    ]
                }
            }
        ]
    }
}
```

See how the `Description` attributes we wrote map directly to the description fields in the JSON? The `inputSchema` is a standard JSON Schema object that tells the AI model exactly what parameters the tool expects, their types, and which ones are required. This is the contract between your code and the AI model. When you write good descriptions, you are literally writing the instructions that the model reads to decide when and how to call your tool.

Tool Invocation

When the user asks the AI to do something that matches one of your tools, the model generates a `tools/call` request. This request includes the tool name and the arguments as a JSON object. The SDK deserializes the arguments, calls your static method with the correct parameter values, takes the return value, wraps it in the proper MCP response format, and sends it back to the client.

Let's trace the complete flow for our echo example. The user types "echo hello world" in the chat. The AI model sees that an `Echo` tool is available and decides to call it with the message "hello world." The client sends a JSON-RPC request to your server. The SDK receives it, finds the `EchoTool.Echo` method, calls it with "hello world" as the argument, gets back "Echo: hello world," and returns that to the client. The AI model receives the result and weaves it into its response to the user. The entire exchange happens over `stdin` and `stdout` as a series of JSON-RPC messages.

Adding a Second Tool

One tool is great for proving the concept, but real servers typically expose multiple tools. Let's add a second tool that does something a bit more fun: returning random facts about space. This will also show you how effortless it is to add new capabilities to an existing server.

Create a new class called `SpaceFactTool`. Like our `EchoTool`, it is a static class decorated with `McpServerToolType`. The tool method does not take any parameters and returns a random string from a predefined list. Listing 4-6 is the complete updated `Program.cs` with both tools; you can of course also find this under Chapter 4 in the source files available with this book.

Listing 4-6. Program.cs with EchoTool and SpaceFactTool

```
using Microsoft.Extensions.DependencyInjection;
using Microsoft.Extensions.Hosting;
using ModelContextProtocol;
using ModelContextProtocol.Server;
using System.ComponentModel;

var builder =
    Host.CreateEmptyApplicationBuilder(null);
builder.Services
    .AddMcpServer()
    .WithStdioServerTransport()
    .WithToolsFromAssembly();
await builder.Build().RunAsync();

[McpServerToolType]
public static class EchoTool
{
    [McpServerTool,
        Description("Echoes the input back.")]
    public static string Echo(
        [Description("Message to echo")]
        string message)
    {
```

```
        return $"Echo: {message}";
    }
}

[McpServerToolType]
public static class SpaceFactTool
{
    private static readonly string[] Facts =
        [
    "A day on Venus is longer than "
        + "a year on Venus.",
        "Neutron stars are so dense that "
        + "a teaspoon would weigh about "
        + "6 billion tons.",
        "There are more stars in the "
        + "universe than grains of sand "
        + "on all of Earth's beaches.",
        "The footprints on the Moon will "
        + "be there for 100 million "
        + "years.",
        "One million Earths could fit "
        + "inside the Sun.",
        "Space is completely silent "
        + "because there is no "
        + "atmosphere to carry sound.",
        "The Milky Way galaxy is about "
        + "100,000 light-years in "
        + "diameter.",
        "A full NASA space suit costs "
        + "approximately $12 million.",
        "Saturn's density is low enough "
        + "that it would float in "
        + "water.",
        "The International Space Station "
```

```
            + "travels at about 28,000 "
            + "kilometers per hour."
    ];

    [McpServerTool, Description(
        "Returns a random fun fact about space.")]
    public static string GetSpaceFact()
    {
        return Facts[Random.Shared.Next(Facts.Length)];
    }
}
```

There are a few things worth calling out here. First, we did not have to change any of the server configuration code. Because we use `WithToolsFromAssembly`, any new class with the `McpServerToolType` attribute is automatically discovered and registered. Second, the `GetSpaceFact` method takes no parameters. Not every tool needs input. The AI model can call it with no arguments, and the SDK handles that case just fine.

If you rebuild and restart your server, then reload it in Claude Desktop or VS Code, you will see both tools listed. Try asking the AI, "Tell me a fun fact about space," and watch it call the `GetSpaceFact` tool. Then ask it to echo a message to confirm that the first tool still works. Both tools coexist happily in the same server.

This pattern of discovery through attributes is one of the things I really like about the C# SDK. It feels natural if you have used ASP.NET controllers or Minimal API endpoints before. You focus on writing the tool logic, and the framework takes care of the wiring.

Tip You can organize tools across multiple classes and even multiple files. As long as each class has the `McpServerToolType` attribute and each tool method has the `McpServerTool` attribute, `WithToolsFromAssembly` will find them all.

Debugging Your MCP Server

Before we wrap up, I want to address a practical concern: how do you debug an MCP server? Since the server communicates over stdio, you cannot just set a breakpoint and run it from your IDE the way you normally would. If you launch the server directly, there is no client sending requests, so your breakpoints will never be hit.

The easiest approach during development is to use the MCP Inspector. This is a web-based tool that connects to your server and lets you send requests manually. You can install it through npm and run it with the following command:

```
npx @modelcontextprotocol/inspector \
dotnet run --project /path/to/FirstMcpServer
```

The Inspector launches a web interface where you can see the tools your server exposes, send tool calls with custom arguments, and inspect the JSON-RPC messages flowing back and forth. It is an invaluable tool for development, and we will use it more in later chapters. You can see a first glimpse of this in Figure 4-5. We will explore the Inspector in detail in Chapter 11.

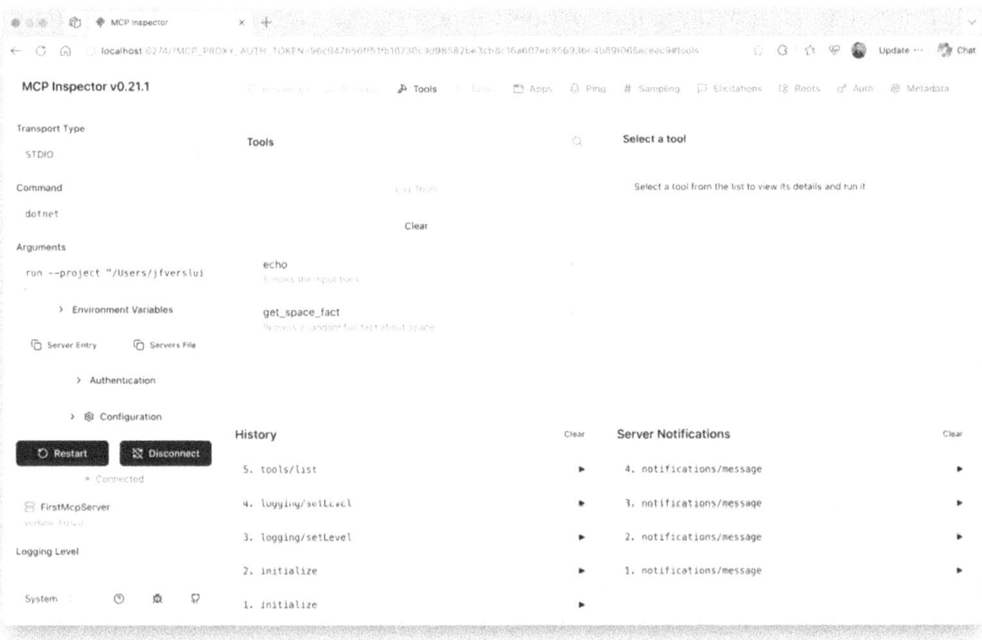

***Figure 4-5.** The MCP inspector tool with our FirstMcpServer project loaded and connected*

Another option is to attach a debugger to the running process. Start your server through Claude Desktop or VS Code, and then use "Attach to Process" in Visual Studio or VS Code to connect to the dotnet process. Once attached, your breakpoints will work as expected.

Summary

Here's what we covered: We went from an empty folder to a working MCP server with two tools. We created a console application, added the `ModelContextProtocol` NuGet package, and wrote a minimal server using the generic host pattern. We built an `EchoTool` that takes a string and returns it and a `SpaceFactTool` that returns random facts about the cosmos. We connected the server to both Claude Desktop and Visual Studio Code, and we traced the flow of a tool call from user request to server response. Pretty cool.

The key takeaways are that MCP servers in C# are built on familiar .NET patterns like the generic host and dependency injection. Tools are just static methods decorated with attributes, and the SDK handles all the protocol details. The Description attributes serve double duty as documentation and as the mechanism the AI uses to decide when to invoke your tools.

We deliberately kept things simple in this chapter. You might be thinking that real-world tools need more than this. You would be right. Our tools are stateless, take simple parameters, and return plain strings. In the next chapter, we will explore the tool system in detail. You will learn how to work with complex parameter types, return structured data, use dependency injection in your tools, handle errors gracefully, and apply the many options the SDK provides for customizing tool behavior. The echo and space fact tools were your first steps; now it is time to start running.

CHAPTER 5

Creating Tools

If resources are the eyes of your MCP server, then tools are its hands. They let an AI model reach out and actually do something in the world: run a calculation, query a database, place an order, or even scan a galaxy for anomalies (we will get to that one, I promise). In Chapter 4, you built your first MCP server and registered a simple tool. Now it is time to dig into the details and understand everything the C# MCP SDK offers when it comes to creating tools.

By the end of this chapter, you will know how to declare tools with attributes, return data in several different formats, accept every kind of parameter imaginable, run long-lived asynchronous work, report progress back to the client, handle errors gracefully, and organize your tools into a clean, maintainable code base. We will build up a sample project called `ToolShowcase` along the way, and every code listing you see maps directly to a file in the companion source code.

Anatomy of an MCP Tool

Before you start writing tools, it helps to understand what the SDK is doing on your behalf. As we've seen already, an MCP tool is nothing more than a static method decorated with the right attributes. The SDK inspects those attributes at startup, generates a JSON schema that describes every parameter, and registers the whole thing with the MCP server so that clients can discover and invoke it. Let's dig a bit deeper into the moving parts.

The McpServerToolType Attribute

The first attribute you need is `McpServerToolType`. You place it on a class to tell the SDK that this class contains one or more tool methods. Without it, the SDK will simply ignore the class during assembly scanning. The attribute takes no parameters; it is purely a marker:

G. Versluis, *Building MCP Servers with C#*, https://doi.org/10.1007/979-8-8688-3010-5_5

```
[McpServerToolType]
public static class MyTools
{
    // tool methods go here
}
```

You will notice that the class itself is declared as static. While not strictly required by the SDK, making tool classes static is the simplest approach. Keeping the class static makes the intent clear and prevents anyone from accidentally adding instance state.

The McpServerTool Attribute

Each method you want to expose as a tool gets the `McpServerTool` attribute. This attribute accepts several optional properties that control how the tool appears to clients.

The `Name` property sets the tool name that clients will use when they call it. If you omit it, the SDK uses the method name, which might not follow the snake_case convention that most MCP clients expect. I recommend always setting `Name` explicitly, so you have full control over the public contract.

Next is the `Description` property on the `System.ComponentModel`.Description attribute. You place this attribute on the method itself and it tells the AI model what the tool does. Write descriptions the way you would explain the tool to a colleague: clear, concise, and focused on what the tool accomplishes rather than how it works internally.

Finally, there is the `ReadOnly` property. When set to `true`, it signals to clients that this tool only reads data and never modifies anything. An AI model can use this hint to decide whether it is safe to call the tool without asking the user for confirmation first. The default is `false`.

Naming your tools is one of those things that seems trivial until you realize the AI model is literally reading these descriptions to decide what to call. It is still a large *language* model after all. I have spent more time wordsmithing tool descriptions than I care to admit. Of course, as with anything, you can ask Copilot to help you improve.

In Listing 5-1, you can see a simple greeting tool with all the attributes we just described.

Listing 5-1. The `McpServerTool` attribute used with its attributes, together with the `Description` attributes to describe methods and parameters

```
[McpServerTool(Name = "greet", ReadOnly = true)]
[Description("Greets the user by name.")]
public static string Greet([Description("The person's name")] string name)
{
    return $"Hello, {name}!";
}
```

The v1.0 SDK also introduces the `Title` and `IconSource` properties. `Title` provides a human-friendly display name for your tool, separate from the machine-readable `Name`. If your tool is called `get_server_metrics`, you could set `Title` to "Server Metrics" so the client shows something prettier in its UI.

`IconSource` is even more fun. You can point it to an SVG or PNG icon, and clients will display it alongside your tool. The value must be either an HTTP or HTTPS URL or a `data:` URI with base64-encoded image data. Local file paths are not supported. Here is how you might use both `Title` and `IconSource`:

```
[McpServerTool(Name = "get_weather", Title = "Current Weather",
    IconSource = "https://example.com/weather.svg")]
[Description("Gets the current weather for a city.")]
public static string GetWeather( [Description("City name")] string city)
{
    return $"Sunny and 25C in {city}!";
}
```

If you need more control over icons, say different icons for light and dark themes, or you want to specify MIME types and size hints, you can configure them programmatically through `McpServerToolCreateOptions.Icons` when using manual tool registration. For most tools though, a single `IconSource` URL on the attribute does the job.

You can also add metadata to your server as a whole. Remember the options lambda you can pass to `AddMcpServer`? It has a `ServerInfo` property of type `Implementation`. That is the class from the MCP specification that describes who built the server and which version it is. In Chapter 4, we called `AddMcpServer()` without any options, so the SDK filled in sensible defaults. Here, we pass a lambda to set `Icons` and `WebsiteUrl` so clients can display your server with a recognizable icon and a link to your documentation:

```
.AddMcpServer(options =>
{
    options.ServerInfo = new()
    {
        Name = "CosmicPizza",
        Version = "1.0.0",
        WebsiteUrl = "https://cosmicpizza.dev",
        Icons = [
            new Icon
            {
                Source = "https://cosmicpizza.dev/icon.svg",
                MimeType = "image/svg+xml"
            }
        ]
    };
})
```

Describing Parameters

Every parameter on a tool method should have a `Description` attribute of its own. The SDK uses these descriptions when it builds the JSON schema for the tool. That schema is what the AI model reads to understand which arguments to pass and what each one means. If you skip the description, the model has to guess from the parameter name alone, and let me tell you, models are not great at guessing.

How the SDK Generates JSON Schema

Under the hood, the SDK uses reflection to inspect your method signature at startup. It reads the parameter names, their .NET types, any default values, and the `Description` attributes you added. From all of that, it generates a JSON schema object that it sends to the client during tool discovery.

For example, a parameter of type `int` becomes `"type": "integer"` in the schema. A `string` becomes `"type": "string"`. An `enum` becomes `"type": "string"` with an "enum" array listing every value. Optional parameters, those with default values in your method signature, are not included in the required array of the schema. This means you rarely need to think about JSON schema directly; just write idiomatic C# and the SDK does the translation for you.

Tip If you want to see the exact JSON schema the SDK generates, send a `tools/list` request to your server. The response includes the full input schema for every registered tool. The MCP Inspector makes this easy with a visual interface; we will use it in Chapter 11.

Return Types

A tool method can return its result in three different ways, and the SDK will serialize each one correctly for the MCP protocol. Which approach you choose depends on how much control you need over the response. The good news is that the SDK makes all three feel natural, so you can start simple and upgrade when you need to.

Returning Strings

The simplest return type is a plain string. The SDK wraps it in a text content block and sends it back to the client. This is perfect for tools that produce human-readable output, and honestly, most tools fall into this category. If your tool's job is to greet someone, look up an answer, or format a quick summary, a string return is all you need. Have a look at Listing 5-2 to see how.

Listing 5-2. A tool that returns a simple string

```
[McpServerTool(Name = "greet")]
[Description("Greets the user by name.")]
public static string Greet [Description("The person's name")] string name)
{
    return $"Hello, {name}! Welcome to the ToolShowcase MCP server.";
}
```

As you can see, there is nothing special here. Return a string and the SDK handles the rest. The client receives a `CallToolResult` with a single text content block containing your string.

For simple tools, a plain string works great. But what happens when you need to return structured data that the AI model can parse and reason about programmatically? That is where things get interesting.

Returning Complex Objects

If you return an object instead of a string, the SDK serializes it to JSON automatically. This is useful when you want to return structured data that the AI model can parse and reason about. In Listing 5-3, you can see how we create a new anonymous object and return some information about the environment that we are running on.

Listing 5-3. Returning a complex object (auto-serialized to JSON)

```
[McpServerTool(Name = "get_system_info")]
[Description("Returns system information.")]
public static object GetSystemInfo()
{
    return new
    {
        MachineName = Environment.MachineName,
        OsVersion =Environment.OSVersion.ToString(),
        ProcessorCount = Environment.ProcessorCount,
            DotNetVersion = Environment.Version.ToString(),
            CurrentTime = DateTime.UtcNow.ToString("o")
    };
}
```

When the client receives this response, the text content block will contain a nicely formatted JSON string with all of the properties you included. Anonymous types work great here, but you can also return a named class or record if you prefer.

Both strings and objects cover the vast majority of use cases. But sometimes you need even more control. Maybe you want to flag an error, return multiple content blocks, or mix text with images. For those situations, you can go all the way and return the response object itself.

Returning CallToolResult

When the SDK wraps your return value, it is actually building a `CallToolResult` behind the scenes. That is the MCP protocol's response object for any tool call. Most of the time, you never see it because the SDK creates it for you. But you can return one yourself when you need control that a simple string or object cannot give you.

Think of scenarios like reporting that something went wrong without throwing an exception, sending back multiple content blocks in a single response, or mixing text with images and other media types. You will see the error side of this in the "Error Handling" section later in this chapter; for now, let us focus on the happy path.

Just for reference, in Listing 5-4, you can see how you would build and return such a result yourself.

Listing 5-4. Returning a CallToolResult for full control

```
[McpServerTool(Name = "get_server_status")]
[Description("Returns server status.")]
public static CallToolResult GetServerStatus()
    {
        var status = new
        {
            Status = "Healthy",
            Uptime = "3 hours, 42 minutes",
            ToolsLoaded = 8
        };
        var json = JsonSerializer.Serialize(
            status,
            new JsonSerializerOptions
            {
                WriteIndented = true
            });

        return new CallToolResult
        {
            Content =
            [
                new TextContentBlock
```

```
                {
                    Text = json,
                }
            ],
            IsError = false
        };
    }
```

The Content property is an `IList<ContentBlock>` where each item is a subclass like `TextContentBlock`, `ImageContentBlock`, or EmbeddedResourceBlock. For most tools, a single `TextContentBlock` block is all you need, but the option to return richer content is there when you need it.

So to recap: Start with a string return when your output is simple text. Graduate to an object return when you want automatic JSON serialization. And reach for `CallToolResult` when you need complete control over error flags, multiple content blocks, or mixed media. Pick the simplest option that gets the job done, and you will keep your tool code clean and readable.

Parameter Types

One of the nicest things about the C# MCP SDK is how naturally it maps .NET parameter types to the JSON schema that clients use. You do not have to write any schema by hand. Just declare your parameters the way you normally would in C#, and the SDK figures out the rest.

You might be wondering how the AI model actually knows what to pass to your tool. Here is how it works: The SDK inspects your method signature, translates each parameter into its JSON schema equivalent, and hands that schema to the client. The AI model reads the schema, sees the types, the names, and the descriptions you wrote, and uses all of that to construct the right arguments. You never have to parse raw JSON yourself.

Simple Types

`String`, `int`, `double`, `bool`, `DateTime`: all the types you reach for everyday work exactly as you would expect. The SDK maps them to their JSON schema equivalents and makes sure that the values the client sends are deserialized correctly before your method is called.

```
[McpServerTool(Name = "add_numbers")]
[Description("Adds two numbers together.")]
public static string AddNumbers([Description("The first number")] double a,
    [Description("The second number")] double b)
{
    var result = a + b;
    return $"The sum of {a} and {b} is {result}.";
}
```

Pretty straightforward, right? But real-world tools usually need more flexibility than just required strings and numbers. What about parameters that are optional, or values that must come from a fixed set of choices? That is where enums and defaults come in.

Optional Parameters and Enums

When a parameter has a default value in your method signature, the SDK marks it as optional in the JSON schema. The client can choose to pass it or leave it out, and your method will use the default. Enum parameters are particularly useful because the SDK automatically generates an enum array in the schema, which helps the AI model pick a valid value.

Let me show you something fun. Suppose you are building an MCP server for a pizza restaurant. You want a tool that lets the AI model place an order with full customization: size, crust, toppings, quantity, extra cheese, and delivery notes. Here is how you would define the enums and the tool; have a look at Listing 5-5.

Listing 5-5. A pizza order tool with enums, optionals, and multiple parameter types

```
public enum PizzaSize
{
    Small, Medium, Large, ExtraLarge
}

public enum CrustType
{
    Thin, Regular, ThickCrust, Stuffed
}
```

```
[McpServerToolType]
public static class PizzaOrderTool
{
    [McpServerTool(Name = "order_pizza")]
    [Description("Places a pizza order with full customization.")]
    public static string OrderPizza(
        [Description("The size of the pizza")] PizzaSize size,
        [Description("The type of crust")] CrustType crust = CrustType.
        Regular,
        [Description("Comma-separated toppings")] string toppings =
        "cheese",
        [Description("Number of pizzas")] int quantity = 1,
        [Description("Add extra cheese")] bool extraCheese = false,
        [Description("Special delivery notes")] string?
        deliveryNotes = null)
    {
        var toppingsList = toppings
            .Split(',')
            .Select(t => t.Trim())
            .ToList();

        var order = new
        {
            OrderId = Guid.NewGuid().ToString()[..8],
            Size = size.ToString(),
            Crust = crust.ToString(),
            Toppings = toppingsList,
            Quantity = quantity,
            ExtraCheese = extraCheese,
            DeliveryNotes = deliveryNotes ?? "None",
            EstimatedDelivery = DateTime.Now.AddMinutes(30).
            ToString("HH:mm")
        };
```

```
        var json =
            JsonSerializer.Serialize(
            order,
            new JsonSerializerOptions
            {
                WriteIndented = true
            });

        return $"Order confirmed!\n{json}";
    }
}
```

There is a lot going on in this listing, so let me walk you through the highlights. The `size` parameter is required because it has no default value. The client must provide it. Meanwhile, crust, toppings, quantity, extraCheese, and deliveryNotes are all optional because they have defaults. The two enum parameters, `PizzaSize` and `CrustType`, will show up in the JSON schema with an enum array listing every valid value, so the AI model knows exactly what strings to pass.

Notice the nullable `string? deliveryNotes` parameter with a default of `null`. This is how you model a truly optional string that might not be present at all. The SDK handles the nullability correctly in the schema.

Tip When the AI model sees the JSON schema for this tool, it will know that size is required and must be one of `Small`, `Medium`, `Large`, or `ExtraLarge`. That is much more useful than a free-form string where the model might send "extra large" or "XL" or "big" and hope for the best.

Async Tools

Most real-world tools need to talk to something external: a database, a REST API, a file system, or a cloud service. In .NET, we handle that with async and await, and the MCP SDK supports this pattern out of the box.

Using Task<T> Return Types

Instead of returning a string directly, you can return `Task<string>` and mark the method as async. The SDK will await the task and then serialize the result exactly the same way it would for a synchronous method. The same goes for `Task<object>` and `Task<CallToolResult>`.

CancellationToken Support

When a client sends a cancellation request for a long-running tool, the MCP server needs a way to propagate that cancellation to your code. The SDK handles this by injecting a `CancellationToken` into your method if you include it as a parameter. You do not need to add a `Description` attribute to it; the SDK knows it is not a client-facing parameter and excludes it from the JSON schema.

In Listing 5-6 below is a practical example. Suppose you want a tool that fetches a random fact from an external API. The call might be slow depending on network conditions, so you definitely want to support cancellation.

Listing 5-6. An async tool that fetches data from an external API

```
[McpServerTool(Name = "fetch_random_fact", ReadOnly = true)]
[Description("Fetches a random fact.")]
public static async Task<string>
FetchRandomFact([Description("Category of fact")] string category =
"general",
    CancellationToken cancellationToken = default)
{
    using var httpClient = new HttpClient();
    httpClient.Timeout = TimeSpan.FromSeconds(10);
    try
    {
        var response = await httpClient.GetAsync(
            "https://uselessfacts.jsph.pl/api/v2/facts/random?language=en",
            cancellationToken);
```

```
        response.EnsureSuccessStatusCode();

        var json = await response.Content.ReadAsStringAsync(cancellat
        ionToken);

        using var doc = JsonDocument.Parse(json);
        var fact = doc.RootElement
            .GetProperty("text")
            .GetString();

        return $"Random fact ({category}): {fact}";
    }
    catch (OperationCanceledException)
    {
        return "The request was cancelled.";
    }
    catch (HttpRequestException ex)
    {
        return "Could not fetch fact: " + ex.Message;
    }
}
```

Tip You might notice we're creating an `HttpClient` directly here. For a quick demo, that's fine, but in production, you should use `IHttpClientFactory` through dependency injection. We'll cover that pattern in Chapter 9. Creating `HttpClient` instances manually can lead to socket exhaustion under load, and nobody wants to debug that on a Friday afternoon.

Notice how the `CancellationToken` is threaded through every async call: `GetAsync`, `ReadAsStringAsync`, even the `JsonDocument.Parse`. This means that if the client cancels the request at any point, the token fires and the operation unwinds cleanly. Also notice the `ReadOnly = true` on the attribute. This tool only reads data, so we tell clients that it is safe to call without user confirmation.

Tip Always pass the `CancellationToken` to every awaitable call in your tool method. Forgetting to do so means your tool will continue running even after the client has given up waiting for a response, which wastes resources and can lead to confusing behavior.

Progress Reporting

Some tools take a long time to run. Maybe you are scanning a directory tree, processing a large file, or running a complex analysis. Without progress reporting, the client and the user are left staring at a spinner wondering if anything is actually happening. The MCP protocol includes a progress notification mechanism, and the C# SDK makes it easy to use.

Using IProgress<ProgressNotificationValue>

To report progress from a tool, add an `IProgress<ProgressNotificationValue>` parameter to your method. Just like `CancellationToken`, the SDK recognizes this as a special parameter and does not include it in the JSON schema. When the tool is invoked, the SDK injects an `IProgress` implementation that sends MCP progress notifications back to the client. The `ProgressNotificationValue` type has three properties: `Progress` (the current progress value), `Total` (an optional total so the client can calculate a percentage), and `Message` (an optional human-readable description of what is happening).

Every time you call `progress.Report()` with a `ProgressNotificationValue`, the SDK sends a structured progress notification to the client. Clients that support progress display can show a progress bar, a percentage, or the message text in real time. Clients that do not support progress simply ignore the notifications, so there is no harm in always including them.

Here is something a little more creative. Listing 5-7 is a tool that scans a galaxy sector for anomalies and reports its progress along the way.

Listing 5-7. A progress-reporting tool that scans a galaxy sector

```
[McpServerTool(Name = "scan_galaxy")]
[Description("Scans a galaxy sector for anomalies.")]
public static async Task<string>
```

```
ScanGalaxy( [Description("The sector to scan")] string sector = "Alpha-7",
    [Description("Scan depth (1-10)")] int depth = 5,
    IProgress<ProgressNotificationValue>? progress = null,
    CancellationToken cancellationToken = default)
{
    var anomalies = new List<string>();
    var scanSteps = new[]
    {
         "Calibrating sensors",
         "Scanning for EM signatures",
         "Analyzing gravity anomalies",
         "Mapping stellar formations",
         "Detecting life signs",
         "Compiling scan results"
    };

    for (int i = 0; i < scanSteps.Length; i++)
    {
        cancellationToken.ThrowIfCancellationRequested();

        progress?.Report(new ProgressNotificationValue
        {
            Progress = i + 1,
            Total = scanSteps.Length,
            Message = $"{scanSteps[i]}..."
        });

        await Task.Delay(500, cancellationToken);

        if (Random.Shared.NextDouble() > 0.5)
        {
            anomalies.Add("Anomaly detected: " + scanSteps[i]);
        }
    }
```

```
    progress?.Report(new ProgressNotificationValue
    {
        Progress = scanSteps.Length,
        Total = scanSteps.Length,
        Message = "Scan complete!"
    });

    var result = anomalies.Count > 0
        ? string.Join("\n", anomalies) : "No anomalies detected.";

    return $"Sector {sector} scan complete (depth {depth})."
        + $"\nFound {anomalies.Count}"
        + $" anomalies:\n{result}";
}
```

I particularly like this example because it shows three concepts working together: async execution, cancellation support, and progress reporting. The client receives structured notifications with progress values like 2 of 6 and a message such as "Scanning for EM signatures..." while the tool is running, which is much nicer than silence. And if the user decides they do not want to wait for the full scan, the `CancellationToken` lets them abort cleanly.

Note The `IProgress<ProgressNotificationValue>` parameter is nullable and defaults to `null` because the SDK may not always provide one. Always use the `null`-conditional operator (`progress?.Report`) to avoid a `NullReferenceException`.

Error Handling

Errors are inevitable. A database connection might fail, a file might not exist, or the user might pass invalid input. How you handle errors in your tools determines whether the AI model can recover gracefully or gets stuck in a loop retrying the same broken request.

Throwing Exceptions

The simplest way to signal an error is to throw an exception. When your tool throws, the SDK catches the exception and converts it into a `CallToolResult` with `IsError` set to `true`. However, the text the client sees depends on the exception type. If your exception derives from `McpException`, its message is included verbatim in the error response. For all other exception types (such as `ArgumentException` or `InvalidOperationException`), the SDK returns a generic message like "An error occurred invoking 'tool_name'." to avoid leaking internal implementation details to the client. This is a deliberate security measure. To make sure the AI model sees a useful error message, throw an `McpException`. Have a look at an example of this in Listing 5-8 below.

Listing 5-8. Throwing an exception for invalid input

```
[McpServerTool(Name = "divide")]
[Description("Divides two numbers safely.")]
public static string Divide( [Description("The dividend")] double a,
    [Description("The divisor")] double b)
{
    if (b == 0)
    {
        throw new McpException("Cannot divide by zero. Please provide a
        non-zero divisor.");
    }

    return $"{a} / {b} = {a / b}";
}
```

Because we throw an `McpException`, the message "Cannot divide by zero." is sent verbatim to the client. The AI model sees the error message and can self-correct by asking the user for different input.

Returning Error Responses Explicitly

For more control, you can return a `CallToolResult` with `IsError` set to `true`. This lets you craft a specific error message without the overhead of exception handling, and it is useful when the "error" is really just a validation failure that you expect to happen sometimes. In Listing 5-9 underneath you can see an example of this.

Listing 5-9. Returning an error response with CallToolResult

```
[McpServerTool(Name = "validate_email")]
[Description("Validates an email address.")]
public static CallToolResult
    ValidateEmail( [Description("The email to validate")] string email)
{
    if (string.IsNullOrWhiteSpace(email))
    {
        return new CallToolResult
        {
            Content =
            [
                new TextContentBlock
                {
                    Text = "Email cannot be empty.",
                }
            ],
            IsError = true
        };
    }

    if (!email.Contains('@') || !email.Contains('.'))
    {
        return new CallToolResult
        {
            Content =
            [
                new TextContentBlock
                {
                    Text = $"'{email}' is not valid.",
                }
            ],
            IsError = true
        };
    }
```

```
    return new CallToolResult
    {
        Content =
        [
            new TextContentBlock
            {
                Text = $"'{email}' is valid.",
            }
        ],
    };
}
```

Both approaches, throwing exceptions and returning error responses, ultimately produce the same result on the wire: a CallToolResult with `IsError true`. Remember that only `McpException` messages are forwarded to the client; other exception types produce a generic error message. Exceptions are more idiomatic for unexpected failures, while explicit error responses work better for expected validation scenarios.

Best Practices for Error Messages

Remember that your error message is going to be read by an AI model, not a human. That means it should be clear, specific, and actionable. Instead of "invalid input", say, "The email address must contain an @ symbol and a dot." Instead of "something went wrong", say, "Could not connect to the database at localhost:5432. Is it running?" The more specific you are, the better chance the model has of figuring out what went wrong and either fixing the request or explaining the problem to the user.

Caution Never include sensitive information like connection strings, API keys, or internal stack traces in your error messages. Those messages are sent to the AI model and may be shown to the user.

Tool Organization

As your MCP server grows, you will inevitably end up with many tools. Keeping them all in a single class quickly becomes unwieldy. The SDK supports multiple tool classes, and there are two different registration strategies you can use.

Multiple Tool Classes

Each class decorated with McpServerToolType is discovered independently. You can spread your tools across as many classes as you like, and I recommend grouping them by domain or feature. In the ToolShowcase project, for example, I put the basic tools in BasicTools.cs, the pizza ordering in PizzaOrderTool.cs, async tools in AsyncTools.cs, and so on. Each file is focused and easy to navigate.

A natural pattern is to create a Tools folder in your project and put one class per file inside it. This keeps the root of your project clean and makes it obvious where to find tool-related code.

Assembly Scanning vs. Manual Registration

The easiest way to register tools is with the WithToolsFromAssembly() method, which we used in Chapter 4. This scans the entire assembly for classes marked with McpServerToolType and registers every tool it finds. For most projects, this is all you need.

```
builder.Services
    .AddMcpServer()
    .WithStdioServerTransport()
    .WithToolsFromAssembly();
```

But sometimes you want more control. Maybe you have a class with tools that are still in development and not ready for production. Or maybe you are building a plugin system where different tools are loaded based on configuration. In those cases, you can register tool classes manually using WithTools<T>(). Look at Listing 5-10 below and notice how each tool class is registered separately.

Listing 5-10. Manual tool registration with WithTools<T>()

```
using Microsoft.Extensions.DependencyInjection;
using Microsoft.Extensions.Hosting;
using ModelContextProtocol.Server;
using ToolShowcase.Tools;

var builder = Host.CreateEmptyApplicationBuilder(null);

builder.Services
    .AddMcpServer()
    .WithStdioServerTransport()
    .WithTools<BasicTools>()
    .WithTools<PizzaOrderTool>()
    .WithTools<AsyncTools>()
    .WithTools<GalaxyScanTool>()
    .WithTools<ErrorHandlingTools>()
    .WithTools<ComplexReturnTools>();

await builder.Build().RunAsync();
```

With manual registration, only the classes you explicitly list will have their tools exposed. This gives you fine-grained control at the cost of having to remember to update `Program.cs` every time you add a new tool class. For most projects, assembly scanning is the way to go.

There is another angle to think about here beyond developer convenience. Every tool you register ends up in the `tools/list` response that the client sends to the AI model. The model reads all those tool names, descriptions, and parameter schemas to decide which tool to call. If you register dozens of tools the model does not need, you are burning context window tokens and making it harder for the model to pick the right one. For a small server with a handful of tools this does not matter at all. But if your server grows large, being deliberate about which tools you expose can genuinely improve how well the AI selects and uses them.

Tip You can mix and match the two approaches. Call `WithToolsFromAssembly()` for the main assembly and `WithTools<T>()` for specific classes from other assemblies or plugins.

Putting It All Together

Listing 5-11 is the complete Program.cs for our ToolShowcase server. It is refreshingly short because the SDK handles all of the heavy lifting. We just tell it to use stdio transport and scan the assembly for tools.

Listing 5-11. The complete Program.cs for the ToolShowcase server

```
using Microsoft.Extensions.DependencyInjection;
using Microsoft.Extensions.Hosting;
using ModelContextProtocol.Server;

var builder = Host.CreateEmptyApplicationBuilder(null);

builder.Services
    .AddMcpServer()
    .WithStdioServerTransport()
    .WithToolsFromAssembly();

await builder.Build().RunAsync();
```

Those few lines give you a fully functional MCP server with seven tools spread across six classes. The server supports async execution, cancellation, progress reporting, and structured error handling. When a client connects, it discovers all of the tools automatically and can start calling them right away.

Here is a quick inventory of what we built in this chapter. The `BasicTools` class has greet and `add_numbers`, showing simple string returns. `ComplexReturnTools` has `get_system_info` returning a JSON-serialized object and `get_server_status` returning a `CallToolResult`. `PizzaOrderTool` demonstrates enums, optional parameters, and nullable strings. `AsyncTools` shows async/await with `CancellationToken`. `GalaxyScanTool` combines async execution with progress reporting. And `ErrorHandlingTools` illustrates both exception-based and explicit error responses.

To test the server, connect it to any MCP-compatible client the same way you did in Chapter 4. Use the `dotnet run` command path in your client configuration, and the tools will show up in the client's tool list. Try ordering a pizza, scanning a galaxy, or dividing by zero to see the different behaviors in action. Figure 5-1 shows Claude Desktop invoking one of the tools we built. If you try this yourself, you would get a prompt first that asks you if you want to allow this action. The expendable Scan galaxy session is actually an indicator of our tool being used in this prompt.

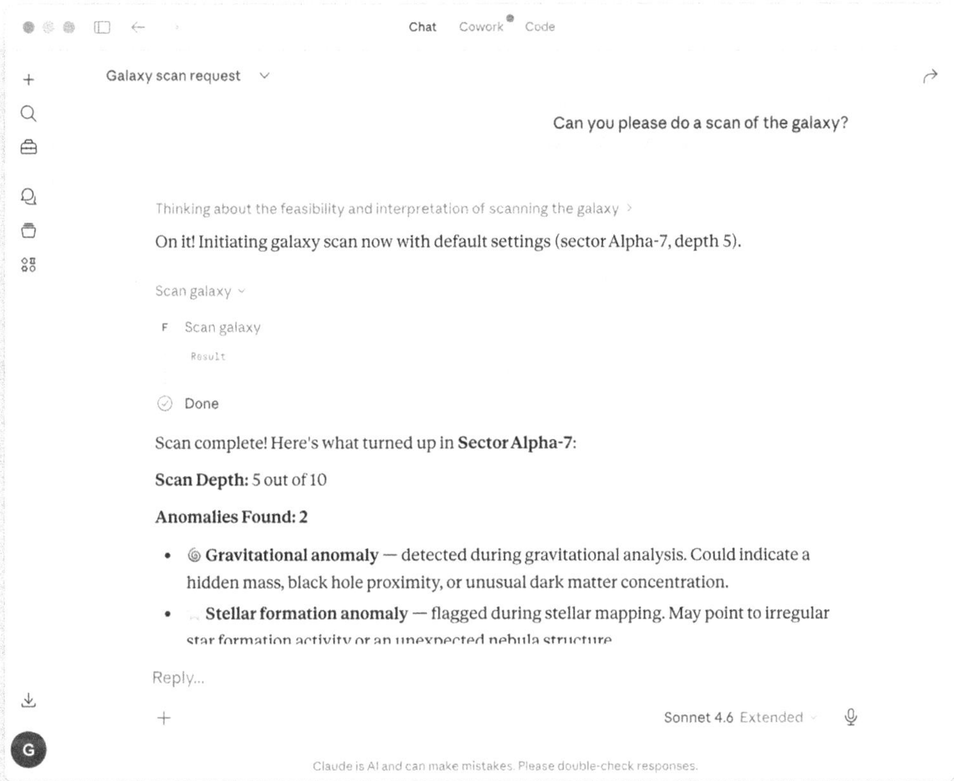

Figure 5-1. *Claude Desktop invoking a tool from the ToolShowcase server*

Note As of the 2025-11-25 specification revision, tools can declare an `outputSchema` using JSON Schema to provide typed, structured results alongside the human-readable content. This enables clients to validate tool output programmatically and makes chaining tool results more reliable. The C# SDK supports this through the `outputSchema` property on tool definitions. Check the official documentation for the latest guidance on implementing structured output in your tools.

Summary

Tools are the workhorses of an MCP server. You learned how to declare them with the `McpServerToolType` and `McpServerTool` attributes, how the SDK generates JSON schemas from your method signatures, and how to return results as strings, complex objects, or full CallToolResult instances. You explored the full range of parameter types, from simple strings and numbers to enums and nullable optionals, and you saw how a single pizza order tool can showcase all of these features together.

You also learned how to write async tools that call external APIs with proper cancellation support, how to report progress during long-running operations, and how to handle errors in a way that helps the AI model recover gracefully. Finally, you saw how to organize your tools into multiple classes and choose between assembly scanning and manual registration.

In Chapter 6, we will shift our attention to resources. While tools let the model do things, resources let it read things: files, database records, configuration values, or any other data your server wants to expose. You will learn how to define static and dynamic resources, work with resource templates, and send notifications when resources change. See you there.

CHAPTER 6

Working with Resources

In the previous chapter, you learned how to give your MCP server hands by creating tools. Tools let the AI model reach out and do things in the world, from placing pizza orders to scanning galaxies. Resources are the other side of that coin. Where a tool performs an action, a resource provides data. Think of resources as read-only documents that your server can expose so that an AI assistant has all the context it needs to give great answers.

By the end of this chapter, you will know how to declare static resources that always return the same URI, create resource templates that accept parameters, choose the right URI schemes and MIME types, and wire everything up into a complete resource server. You will also learn how clients can subscribe to resource changes so they stay up to date when the underlying data shifts.

What Are Resources?

An MCP resource is a piece of data that a server makes available for reading. It could be a text file, a JSON document, a help page, or even a base64-encoded image. The key distinction from a tool is that a resource never changes the state of the world. It only returns information. If tools are verbs, resources are nouns.

Clients discover resources in one of two ways. They can call the resources/list endpoint to get back a catalog of every direct resource the server offers. Each entry in that catalog contains a URI, a human-readable name, and an optional description and MIME type. Alternatively, clients can call resources/templates/list to discover resource templates, which are parameterized URIs that generate data on the fly. Once a client knows the URI it wants, it sends a resources/read request, and the server responds with the content.

G. Versluis, *Building MCP Servers with C#*, https://doi.org/10.1007/979-8-8688-3010-5_6

Why not just use tools for everything? You certainly could, but resources give the AI model a cleaner separation of concerns. When an AI sees a list of available resources, it understands that these are background context it can pull in at any time without side effects. That makes the model more confident about reading a resource because it knows nothing will break. Tools, on the other hand, carry the implicit promise that something might happen when you call them. Keeping data retrieval in resources and actions in tools leads to servers that are easier to reason about, both for humans and for AI models.

Getting the resource URIs right took me a few attempts. My first version had spaces in the URI paths, which is technically valid but made me feel unclean.

Creating Static Resources

A static resource has a fixed URI that never changes. Every time a client reads it, the server returns whatever data the method produces, but the URI itself contains no parameters. Think of it like a page on a website that always lives at the same address.

The C# SDK gives you two attributes to work with. The first is `McpServerResourceType`, which you place on a class to tell the SDK that this class contains resource methods. It works exactly like `McpServerToolType` from the previous chapter. The second is `McpServerResource`, which you place on each method that should be exposed as a resource. Together they follow the same pattern you already know from tools, so there is very little new ceremony to learn.

The McpServerResourceType Attribute

You place `McpServerResourceType` on any class whose methods you want the SDK to discover as resources. The class can be static or an instance class. If it is an instance class, the SDK will construct a new instance for each resource invocation, which is handy when your class implements `IDisposable` or needs per-request state. You can see an example in Listing 6-1.

Listing 6-1. A resource class for Cosmic Pizza

```
using System.ComponentModel;
using ModelContextProtocol.Server;

namespace ResourceServer.Resources;
```

```
[McpServerResourceType]
public static class CosmicPizzaResources
{
    [McpServerResource(
        UriTemplate = "cosmic-pizza://menu",
        Name = "Full Menu",
        MimeType = "text/plain")]
    [Description("The complete Cosmic Pizza menu with prices.")]
    public static string GetMenu()
    {
        return """
        Cosmic Pizza Menu
        =================
        Nebula Margherita    - $12.99
        Black Hole BBQ          - $15.99
        Asteroid Supreme     - $14.99
        Milky Way White      - $13.99
        Supernova Special    - $17.99
        Sides
        -----
        Galactic Garlic Bread  - $5.99
        Comet Cheese Sticks    - $7.99
        """;
    }

    [McpServerResource(UriTemplate = "cosmic-pizza://hours",
        Name = "Opening Hours",
        MimeType = "text/plain")]
    [Description("Cosmic Pizza opening hours for all locations.")]
    public static string GetOpeningHours()
    {
        return """
        Cosmic Pizza Opening Hours
        ==========================
        Monday - Thursday:
        11:00 AM - 10:00 PM
```

```
        Friday - Saturday:
        11:00 AM - 12:00 AM
        Sunday:
        12:00 PM -  9:00 PM
        """;
    }
}
```

There is a lot to unpack in Listing 6-1, but most of it should feel familiar since you have written some tools before in Chapter 5. The `McpServerResource` attribute carries the heavy lifting. Its `UriTemplate` property tells the SDK which URI this resource lives at. The `Name` property gives the resource a friendly label that clients can display in a resource list. And `MimeType` declares the content type, which clients can use to decide how to render the result.

The `Description` attribute works the same way it does on tools. It helps the AI model understand what the resource contains before it decides to read it. A good description saves the model from having to read every resource just to figure out which one is relevant.

Notice that both methods return a plain string. The SDK wraps that string in a `TextResourceContents` object automatically. If you need more control over the response, you can return a `ResourceContents`, a `TextResourceContents`, or even a `BlobResourceContents` for binary data. But for simple text resources, returning a string is all you need.

Resource Templates

Static resources are great when you have a handful of fixed documents to expose. But what if you have hundreds of items, or the exact set of resources is not known ahead of time? That is where resource templates come in. A template is a URI that contains one or more placeholders. The client fills in those placeholders, and the server generates the matching content on demand.

The MCP specification uses RFC 6570 URI templates. If you have seen route templates in ASP.NET, the syntax will feel natural. A placeholder is wrapped in curly braces, like `{planetName}`. When a client wants to read the resource, it replaces `{planetName}` with an actual value such as "mars" and sends the fully resolved URI to the server.

In the SDK, the only difference between a static resource and a template is whether the `UriTemplate` contains placeholders. If it does, the SDK automatically classifies the method as a resource template and lists it under resources/templates/list instead of resources/list. Your method receives the placeholder values as parameters, just like a tool receives its arguments. Have a look at Listing 6-2 where this is shown; notice the `UriTemplate` parameter on the `McpServerResource` attribute.

Listing 6-2. A resource template for planet information

```
using System.ComponentModel;
using ModelContextProtocol.Server;

namespace ResourceServer.Resources;

[McpServerResourceType]
public static class PlanetResources
{
    private static readonly Dictionary<string, PlanetInfo> Planets =
    new(StringComparer.OrdinalIgnoreCase)
    {
        ["mercury"] = new("Mercury", "Smallest planet, closest to the
        Sun.", 4879, 0.39, 0),
        ["earth"] = new("Earth", "Our home, the only world with life.",
        12756, 1.0, 1),
        ["jupiter"] = new("Jupiter", "Largest planet with a Great Red
        Spot.", 142984, 5.20, 95),
    };

    [McpServerResource(
        UriTemplate = "planets://info/{planetName}",
        Name = "Planet Information",
        MimeType = "application/json")]
    [Description("Returns detailed information about a planet.")]
    public static string GetPlanetInfo(string planetName)
    {
        if (!Planets.TryGetValue(planetName, out var planet))
```

```
        {
            return "Unknown planet: " + planetName;
        }

        return $$"""
        {
            "name": "{{planet.Name}}",
             "diameterKm": {{planet.DiameterKm}},
              "knownMoons": {{planet.Moons}}
        }
        """;
    }

    private record PlanetInfo(
        string Name,
        string Description,
        int DiameterKm,
        double DistanceAU,
        int Moons);
}
```

The key is the `UriTemplate`. The placeholder `{planetName}` tells the SDK to extract the planet name from the URI and pass it to the planetName parameter. When a client sends a read request for `planets://info/jupiter`, the SDK matches the template, pulls out "jupiter", and calls GetPlanetInfo with that value. You do not need to parse the URI yourself.

Notice that the method still returns a string. Even though the `MimeType` is set to application/json, the SDK does not validate the format of the content. It trusts you to return data that matches the declared MIME type. This is the same approach used by ASP.NET and other web frameworks, where the content type is a promise to the client rather than a runtime constraint.

Tip You can have multiple placeholders in a single `UriTemplate`. For example, a URI like `files://{project}/{path}` would map to a method with two string parameters named project and path. The SDK matches parameter names to placeholder names, so make sure they line up.

Resource URIs

Every resource in MCP is identified by a URI, and choosing the right URI scheme matters more than you might think. The MCP specification does not mandate a particular scheme. You are free to use any valid URI, but some conventions have emerged that are worth following. To give you a taste: custom schemes like cosmic-pizza://menu, standard schemes like file:///etc/config.json, or web-based ones like `https://api.example.com/data` are all valid. We will explore these patterns and their trade-offs in the next section.

Common URI Schemes

The most common scheme you will see is the custom scheme, like `cosmic-pizza://` or `planets://`. Custom schemes are great for domain-specific resources because they make the purpose of the URI obvious at a glance. When a client sees `cosmic-pizza://menu`, there is no ambiguity about what kind of data to expect.

The specification also mentions a few standard schemes. The `file://` scheme is useful when your resource maps directly to a file on disk, such as `file:///etc/config.json`. The `https://` scheme works well when you are proxying data from a web API and want the URI to reflect the original source. And the `resource://` scheme, shown in some SDK examples as `resource://mcp/...`, is a generic scheme for server-managed resources that do not map to an external location.

Naming Conventions

Good resource URIs are predictable and self-describing. A few guidelines that I have found helpful include using lowercase for consistency, using forward slashes to represent hierarchy, keeping names short but meaningful, and avoiding query strings unless they are genuinely needed. For example, prefer `cosmic-pizza://menu` over `cosmic-pizza://getMenuData?format=text`. The simpler the URI, the easier it is for both humans and AI models to reason about.

Note URI comparison in MCP is case-insensitive for the scheme and host portions, but case-sensitive for the path. The SDK handles the scheme comparison for you, but it is still a good idea to stay consistent with casing in your URI paths to avoid confusion.

Resource Metadata

When you declare a resource, you can attach several pieces of metadata through the `McpServerResource` attribute. You have already seen `Name`, `UriTemplate`, and `MimeType`. We've seen most of these in the previous chapter, but here is a rundown of each one to explain when you should use it and how to really bolster this knowledge.

The `Name` property is required and appears in the resource listing that clients receive. It should be a short, human-readable label like "Full Menu" or "Planet Information". Think of it as the title you would see in a table of contents.

The `UriTemplate` property defines the address of your resource. For static resources, it is a plain URI. For templates, it includes placeholders wrapped in curly braces. If you omit `UriTemplate` entirely, the SDK will generate a default URI based on the method name and any parameters, following the pattern `resource://mcp/MethodName`. I recommend always setting it explicitly so your URIs are meaningful and stable.

The `MimeType` property tells the client what kind of content to expect. Common values include text/plain for plain text, application/json for JSON data, text/markdown for Markdown documents, text/html for HTML, and application/octet-stream for raw binary. Setting the correct MIME type helps clients render the content appropriately. If your resource returns Markdown, for instance, a smart client might render it with formatting instead of showing raw text.

The `Description` attribute on the method is not part of `McpServerResource` itself, but it is just as important. This description travels to the client alongside the name and URI, and it is what the AI model uses to decide whether to read a particular resource. Be concise but informative. A description like "Returns the full pizza menu including prices for all items" is far more useful than "Menu data."

Finally, there is the `Title` property and the `IconSource` property. `Title` provides an additional display name that can be shown in a client's UI. `IconSource` lets you specify a URL or data URI for an icon to represent your resource visually. These are optional and not every client will use them, but they add a nice touch for clients that display resource catalogs in a graphical interface.

Return Types for Resources

Just like tools, resource methods support several return types. The simplest is a plain string. The SDK wraps it in a `TextResourceContents` object with the URI and MIME type you specified in the attribute. This is the approach I used in the Cosmic Pizza and planet examples.

If you need more control, you can return a `TextResourceContents` or `BlobResourceContents` directly. `TextResourceContents` has a `Text` property for text content, while `BlobResourceContents` has a `Blob` property that accepts a byte array for binary data. Use `BlobResourceContents` when you need to serve images, PDFs, or other non-text formats.

You can also return a list of `ResourceContents` objects by using `IEnumerable<ResourceContents>` as your return type. This is useful when a single resource read should return multiple content blocks, like a text summary followed by a binary attachment. The client receives all content blocks in a single response.

Tip Async methods work too. You can return `Task<string>` or `Task<ResourceContents>` if your resource needs to read from a database, call an API, or do any other asynchronous work. The SDK also supports `CancellationToken` parameters, so your async resources can be cancelled gracefully.

Subscribing to Resource Changes

Resources are read-only, but that does not mean they are frozen in time. The data behind a resource might change, like when a restaurant updates its menu or a server's status shifts from healthy to degraded. MCP includes a subscription mechanism that lets clients ask to be notified when a resource changes.

The subscription flow works like this. First, the client sends a resources/subscribe request with the URI of the resource it cares about. The server acknowledges the subscription. Later, when the underlying data changes, the server sends a notifications/resources/updated notification to all subscribed clients. The client can then decide to re-read the resource to get the latest data.

In the C# SDK, you wire up subscription handling through the server builder. You register a handler for subscribe requests and another for unsubscribe requests. Here is what that looks like at a high level, shown in Listing 6-3.

Listing 6-3. Registering resource subscription handlers

```
builder.Services
    .AddMcpServer()
    .WithStdioServerTransport()
    .WithResourcesFromAssembly()
    .WithSubscribeToResourcesHandler(async (ctx, ct) =>
    {
        var uri = ctx.Params?.Uri;

        if (uri is not null)
        {
            // Track this subscription
            subscriptions.TryAdd(uri, 0);
        }
        return new EmptyResult();
    })
    .WithUnsubscribeFromResourcesHandler(async (ctx, ct) =>
    {
        var uri = ctx.Params?.Uri;

        if (uri is not null)
        {
            subscriptions.TryRemove(uri, out _);
        }
        return new EmptyResult();
    });
```

The subscribe handler receives the URI the client wants to watch. You store that subscription however you like, for example, in a `ConcurrentDictionary`. When the data changes, you send a notification through the MCP server. The notification does not include the updated data itself. It only tells the client that something changed, and the client is responsible for reading the resource again if it wants the new version.

Subscriptions are an advanced feature, and many simple servers do not need them. If your resources only change when the server restarts, you can skip subscription handling entirely. But for servers that expose live data, like stock prices, monitoring dashboards, or frequently updated menus, subscriptions keep the client in sync without polling.

A Complete Resource Server

Time to bring everything together. You will build a resource server that exposes Cosmic Pizza data, solar system planet information, and server metadata. Each group of resources lives in its own class, and the `Program.cs` file ties them all together with a single line of registration.

You have already seen the `CosmicPizzaResources` class in Listing 6-1 and the `PlanetResources` class in Listing 6-2. I want to add one more resource class that demonstrates a different MIME type and a different URI scheme. You can see this in Listing 6-4 below.

Listing 6-4. Server information resources with JSON and Markdown MIME types

```
using System.ComponentModel;
using System.Text.Json;
using ModelContextProtocol.Server;

namespace ResourceServer.Resources;

[McpServerResourceType]
public static class ServerInfoResources
{
    [McpServerResource(
        UriTemplate = "info://server/status",
        Name = "Server Status",
        MimeType = "application/json")]
    [Description(
        "Returns the current server status as JSON.")]
```

```
    public static string GetServerStatus()
        {
            var status = new
            {
                ServerName = "ResourceServer",
                Version = "1.0.0",
                Status = "Running",
                StartedAt = DateTime.UtcNow.ToString("o"),
                 DotNetVersion = Environment.Version.ToString()
            };

            return JsonSerializer.Serialize(
                status,
                new JsonSerializerOptions
                {
                    WriteIndented = true
                });
        }

    [McpServerResource(
        UriTemplate = "info://server/help",
        Name = "Server Help",
        MimeType = "text/markdown")]
    [Description("Returns help documentation for the resource server.")]
    public static string GetHelpDocument()
        {
            return """
            # ResourceServer Help
            This MCP server exposes
            several resources you can
            read.
            ## Available Resources
            - **cosmic-pizza://menu**
            The full Cosmic Pizza menu.
            - **planets://info/{planet}**
            Info about a planet.
```

```
            - **info://server/status**
            Current server status.
            """;
        }
}
```

The ServerInfoResources class shows two things. First, the GetServerStatus method returns JSON by serializing an anonymous object. The MimeType is set to application/json so clients know how to interpret the content. Second, the GetHelpDocument method returns Markdown text with a MIME type of text/markdown. A capable client could render this Markdown with proper headings and bullet points.

With all three resource classes in place, the Program.cs file is delightfully simple, as seen in Listing 6-5 underneath.

Listing 6-5. Program.cs wiring up all resources

```
using Microsoft.Extensions.DependencyInjection;
using Microsoft.Extensions.Hosting;
using ModelContextProtocol.Server;

var builder = Host.CreateEmptyApplicationBuilder(null);

builder.Services
    .AddMcpServer()
    .WithStdioServerTransport()
    .WithResourcesFromAssembly();

await builder.Build().RunAsync();
```

The WithResourcesFromAssembly method works exactly like WithToolsFromAssembly did in the previous chapter. It scans the current assembly for all classes marked with McpServerResourceType, finds every method decorated with McpServerResource, and registers them all in one sweep. No need to register each class individually.

If you prefer explicit registration, you can use WithResources<T>() for each resource class. This is useful when you want to be selective about which resources to expose, or when you are working in a Native AOT scenario where reflection-based assembly scanning might not be available.

Listing 6-6. Explicit resource registration as an alternative

```
builder.Services
    .AddMcpServer()
    .WithStdioServerTransport()
    .WithResources<CosmicPizzaResources>()
    .WithResources<PlanetResources>()
    .WithResources<ServerInfoResources>();
```

Both approaches produce the same result. The assembly scanning method is more convenient, while the explicit method gives you finer control. Pick whichever feels right for your project.

Just like with tools, keep in mind that every resource you register appears in the `resources/list` response. The good news is that resources are lighter on tokens than tools: clients only fetch the actual content of a resource when the user or model explicitly asks for it. The list itself just contains URIs, names, and descriptions. Still, if your server exposes hundreds of resources, that list alone can get noisy and make it harder for the model to find the right one. Being intentional about what you expose is a habit worth building early.

Testing Your Resources

You can test your resources the same way you tested tools in the previous chapter. If you have the MCP Inspector or a compatible client, connect to your server and browse the resource list. Static resources will appear under the resources tab, and templates will appear under resource templates. Try reading the menu, checking the opening hours, and querying a few planets to make sure everything works. If you want a full walkthrough of the Inspector, we cover that in Chapter 11.

When you read a template resource like `planets://info/earth`, you should see the JSON data for Earth come back with the correct MIME type. If you request a planet that does not exist in the dictionary, you will get an error message instead. This graceful fallback is important because clients may pass unexpected values, and your resource should handle those cases without crashing.

Let me show you what this looks like in two different clients, because this is a good reminder that each client implements MCP features in its own way. In Claude Desktop, click the + button below the chat input, then select your server from the connectors list.

You will see all your static resources listed by name, as shown in Figure 6-1. Click one and its content is attached to the conversation as context for the model. However, you will notice that resource templates like the planet lookup do not appear here. At the time of writing, Claude Desktop only surfaces static resources with fixed URIs; it does not provide a way to fill in template parameters.

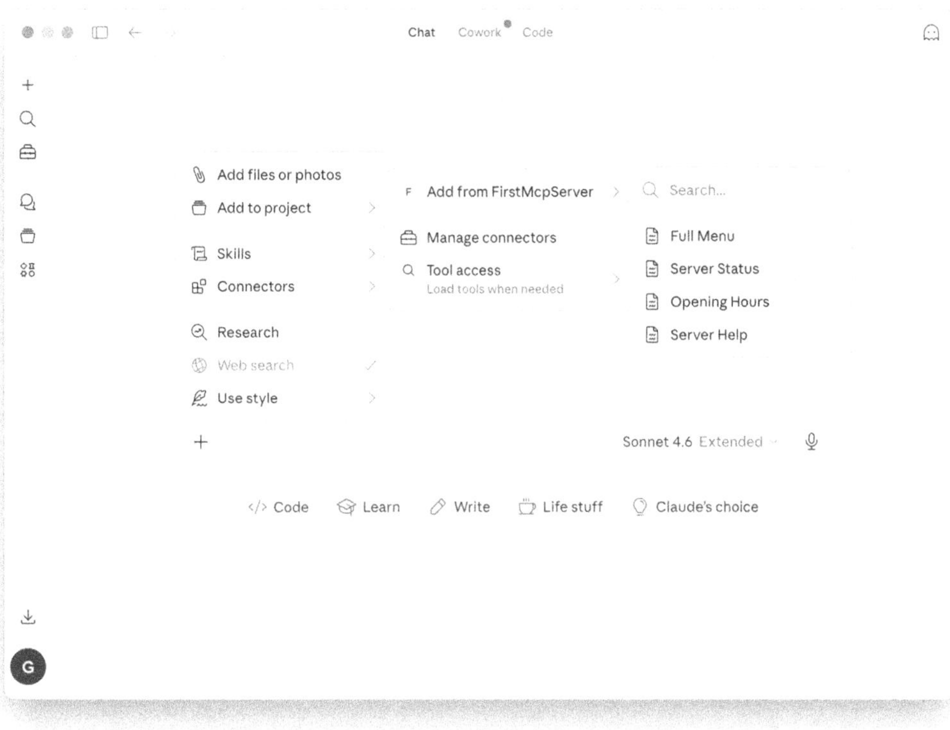

Figure 6-1. *Browsing MCP resources in Claude Desktop through the Connectors menu*

Visual Studio Code goes a step further. Open the Command Palette with `Ctrl+Shift+P` on Windows and Linux or `Cmd+Shift+P` on macOS, then search for `MCP: Browse Resources`. You can also select `Add Context` in the chat input and pick `MCP Resources` from there.

Either way, VS Code shows every resource your server exposes, including resource templates. When you pick a static resource, its content is added to the chat context right away. When you pick a template, VS Code prompts you for the template parameter values, for example, asking you to type a planet name, and then fetches the resolved resource. The result is attached to your chat as context that the model can read and reason over, as seen in Figure 6-2.

***Figure 6-2.** Browsing MCP resources in Visual Studio Code using the resource picker*

This difference between the two clients is a good example of why testing with multiple clients matters. MCP is a standard, but every client team decides which features to implement and how to surface them. Your server code stays the same either way; it is the client that determines the user experience.

When to Use Resources Instead of Tools

A question I get asked a lot is: when should I use a resource instead of a tool? The answer comes down to intent. Use a resource when you are exposing reference data that the model might want to consult. Use a tool when you want the model to perform an action that has a consequence, like placing an order, sending an email, or writing to a database.

Here are a few rules of thumb that have served me well. If the data rarely changes and has no side effects, make it a resource. If the operation modifies state or triggers something, make it a tool. If you want the AI to proactively pull in background context, a resource is usually the right choice. And if you find yourself making a read-only tool, consider whether a resource would be a better fit. There is nothing wrong with having both tools and resources in the same server. In fact, that is the most common pattern. Your Cosmic Pizza server might expose the menu as a resource and the order placement as a tool. The model reads the menu resource to learn what is available, then calls the order tool to place the customer's order.

Summary

Looking back at what we built: You learned how to expose read-only data through MCP resources. You created static resources with fixed URIs for the Cosmic Pizza menu and opening hours. You built a resource template that accepts parameters to return planet information dynamically. You explored URI schemes, naming conventions, and MIME types to make your resources easy to discover and use. And you saw how clients can subscribe to resource changes when the underlying data shifts.

The pattern is deliberately simple. Mark your class with `McpServerResourceType`, decorate your methods with `McpServerResource`, set the right `UriTemplate` and `MimeType`, and let the SDK handle the rest. Whether you register resources through assembly scanning or explicit calls, the server builder makes it straightforward to expose as many resources as your application needs.

Resources give your AI model eyes to see data without worrying about side effects. Tools give it hands to act. But there is a third primitive that rounds out the picture: prompts. In Chapter 7, you will learn how to expose prompts from your MCP server, giving clients reusable message templates that guide the AI toward specific tasks and workflows.

CHAPTER 7

Exposing Prompts

So far in this book, we have built tools that let an AI model take actions and resources that let it read data. Those two primitives cover a lot of ground, but there is a third piece of the MCP puzzle that we have not touched yet: prompts. If tools are the hands of your server and resources are its eyes, then prompts are its voice. They give your server the ability to shape how the AI model thinks about a task before it even starts working on it.

Get ready to explore what MCP prompts are, how they differ from tools and resources, and how to implement them in C# using the same attribute-driven style you are already used to. We will start simple with a single-message prompt, work our way up to parameterized and multi-message prompts, and finish with a cosmic pizza prompt server that is as entertaining to build as it is to use. By the end, you will have a solid understanding of when and how to reach for prompts in your MCP servers.

Understanding Prompts

Before we write any code, let's make sure we are on the same page about what prompts actually are in the MCP world. A prompt is a predefined message template that your server exposes to the AI client. When a user or the AI model selects one of your prompts, the server returns one or more messages that get injected into the conversation. Think of it as your server saying, "Hey, here is a great way to start this particular kind of conversation."

That might sound a lot like a system prompt that you would paste into ChatGPT, and you would not be wrong. The key difference is that MCP prompts are discoverable and parameterized. The AI client can call `prompts/list` to discover what your server offers, just like it calls `resources/list` for resources and `tools/list` for tools. The same discovery pattern you already know. The client shows the available prompts to the user and lets them pick one. The prompt can accept arguments, so the server can generate different messages depending on what the user needs. This makes prompts far more flexible than a static block of text.

G. Versluis, *Building MCP Servers with C#*, https://doi.org/10.1007/979-8-8688-3010-5_7

How Prompts Differ from Tools and Resources

I find it helpful to think about the three MCP primitives in terms of what they do and who drives them. Tools are actions that the AI model calls to get work done: send an email, query a database, calculate a value. Resources are data sources that the model reads: a file, a configuration object, a live status feed. Prompts are conversation starters that shape how the model approaches a task.

Another way to look at it: tools produce side effects, resources produce data, and prompts produce context. When you define a prompt, you are not asking the model to do anything. You are telling it how to think about the problem. That is a subtle but important distinction. A code review tool might run a linter and return warnings. A code review prompt, on the other hand, sets up the model with instructions like "You are an expert C# reviewer, focus on performance and security," and then asks it to review the code using its own reasoning.

Writing prompts for AI models to use feels a bit like writing a recipe for a chef who has never tasted food. You have to be absurdly specific about things you would normally take for granted.

In practice, prompts and tools often complement each other beautifully. You might expose a prompt that tells the model how to analyze log files and a resource that provides the actual log data. Or you might combine a prompt that sets up a code review workflow with a tool that can apply suggested fixes automatically. The MCP spec was designed so that these three primitives work together, and the best servers use all three where they make sense.

Note As we saw with resources in the previous chapter, not every MCP client implements every feature the same way. Both Claude Desktop and Visual Studio Code support prompts, but the experience differs. In Claude Desktop, you can browse and select prompts from the prompt picker. In VS Code, you type `/<server>.<prompt>` in the chat input to invoke one. Other clients may handle prompts differently or not support them at all yet. Your server code stays the same regardless; it is always worth testing with whichever clients your users are likely to use.

Creating Simple Prompts

Let's build a prompt server from scratch. The setup is the same as the earlier chapters: create a console project, add the ModelContextProtocol NuGet package, and register our prompts using the same attribute-based pattern that we used for tools and resources.

Setting Up the Project

By now, these commands should feel familiar. Open your terminal and run

```
$ dotnet new console -n PromptServer
$ cd PromptServer
$ dotnet add package ModelContextProtocol
$ dotnet add package Microsoft.Extensions.Hosting
```

The project file should look like Listing 7-1 once the packages are installed.

Listing 7-1. The PromptServer.csproj project file

```
<Project Sdk="Microsoft.NET.Sdk">
    <PropertyGroup>
        <OutputType>Exe</OutputType>
        <TargetFramework>net10.0</TargetFramework>
        <ImplicitUsings>enable</ImplicitUsings>
        <Nullable>enable</Nullable>
    </PropertyGroup>
    <ItemGroup>
        <PackageReference Include="Microsoft.Extensions.Hosting"
        Version="10.0.3" />
        <PackageReference Include="ModelContextProtocol" Version="1.3.0" />
    </ItemGroup>
</Project>
```

Now let's set up the server in Program.cs. The only difference from our tool servers is that instead of calling WithToolsFromAssembly, we call WithPromptsFromAssembly. This tells the SDK to scan the assembly for classes decorated with the prompt attributes and register them automatically. Have a look at Listing 7-2 below for an example.

Listing 7-2. Program.cs with prompt registration

```
using Microsoft.Extensions.DependencyInjection;
using Microsoft.Extensions.Hosting;
using ModelContextProtocol.Server;

var builder = Host.CreateEmptyApplicationBuilder(null);

builder.Services
    .AddMcpServer()
    .WithStdioServerTransport()
    .WithPromptsFromAssembly();

await builder.Build().RunAsync();
```

Notice how clean this is. Five lines of real code and our server is ready to go. The SDK does all the heavy lifting: registering prompt handlers, responding to discovery requests, and serializing messages. If you want to expose both tools and prompts from the same server, you can chain both calls together. Something like `WithPromptsFromAssembly().WithToolsFromAssembly()` works perfectly. For this chapter, though, we will focus on prompts alone.

Your First Prompt

With the server plumbing in place, let's write our first prompt. Just like tools use `McpServerToolType` and `McpServerTool`, prompts use `McpServerPromptType` and `McpServerPrompt`. The pattern is the same: you put the type attribute on the class and the method attribute on each prompt method. The Description attribute tells the AI client what the prompt does.

Here is a simple greeting prompt, as seen in Listing 7-3. It takes a name as input and returns a single message asking the AI model to generate a warm greeting for that person.

Listing 7-3. A simple greeting prompt in SimplePrompts.cs

```
using System.ComponentModel;
using Microsoft.Extensions.AI;
using ModelContextProtocol.Server;

namespace PromptServer.Prompts;
```

```
[McpServerPromptType]
public static class SimplePrompts
{
    [McpServerPrompt]
    [Description("Generates a friendly greeting message")]
    public static ChatMessage Greeting( [Description("Name of the person to
    greet")] string name)
    {
        return new ChatMessage(
            ChatRole.User,
            $"Please write a warm and "
            + $"friendly greeting for "
            + $"{name}. Make it enthusiastic "
            + "and welcoming.");
    }
}
```

A few things stand out here. First, the return type is `ChatMessage`, which comes from the `Microsoft.Extensions.AI` namespace. This is the same abstraction used throughout the .NET AI ecosystem; so if you have worked with `Microsoft.Extensions.AI` in other projects, you will feel right at home. The ChatRole.User indicates that this message should be treated as if the user said it, which is exactly what we want for a simple prompt.

Second, notice that the prompt method is synchronous and returns a single `ChatMessage`. For more complex scenarios, you can return an array or make the method async, but for a simple case like this, a single return value does the job nicely.

When an AI client connects to this server and lists the available prompts, it will see a prompt called "Greeting" with a description that says "Generates a friendly greeting message." The client can show this to the user, let them enter a name, and then inject the resulting message into the conversation. The AI model then takes that message and produces a creative greeting.

Parameterized Prompts

A prompt that accepts a single string is fine for introductions, but real-world prompts often need multiple parameters to be truly useful. This is where prompts start to shine over plain text templates. Because parameters are declared as method arguments with descriptions, the AI client can present a structured form to the user, and the server can generate precisely tailored messages.

Let's build something more substantial: a code review prompt. This prompt will accept three parameters: the programming language, the review style, and the actual code to review. Depending on what the user passes in, the prompt will generate completely different instructions for the AI model. Have a look at Listing 7-4 below to see an implementation of this.

Listing 7-4. A parameterized code review prompt

```
using System.ComponentModel;
using Microsoft.Extensions.AI;
using ModelContextProtocol.Server;

namespace PromptServer.Prompts;

[McpServerPromptType]
public static class CodeReviewPrompt
{
    [McpServerPrompt]
    [Description("Generates a code review prompt with configurable
    language "
        + "and style")]
    public static ChatMessage[] ReviewCode(
        [Description("The programming language e.g. csharp, python")]
        string language,
        [Description("Review style: thorough, quick, or security-focused")]
        string style,
        [Description("The code to review")] string code)
    {
        var systemMessage = new ChatMessage(
            ChatRole.System,
```

```
            $"You are an expert {language} code reviewer. Perform a "
            + $"{style} review. Focus on best practices, potential bugs,
            readability, and "
            + "maintainability.");

        var userMessage = new ChatMessage(
            ChatRole.User, "Please review the following "
            + $"{language} code:\n\n"
            + $"```{language}\n{code}\n```");

        return [systemMessage, userMessage];
    }
}
```

There is quite a bit to unpack here. The most obvious change is that the return type is now `ChatMessage[]` instead of a single `ChatMessage`. We are returning two messages: a system message that sets up the AI model's persona and a user message that contains the actual code to review. I will talk more about multi-message prompts in the next section, but even here, you can see how powerful this pattern is.

The three parameters each have their own `Description` attribute, which the AI client uses to present a form to the user. Imagine opening Claude Desktop, selecting the "ReviewCode" prompt, and seeing three input fields: Language, Style, and Code. The user fills them in, the client sends the arguments to your server, and the server generates a perfectly tailored set of review instructions.

What I find really cool about this approach is that the same prompt handles very different scenarios. Pass in "csharp" and "security-focused" and you get a security audit prompt. Pass in "python" and "quick" and you get a lightweight review prompt. The logic is simple string interpolation, but the result feels like a carefully crafted prompt for each combination.

Tip You can use any C# type as a prompt parameter, not just strings. The SDK will generate a JSON Schema for the parameter, just like it does for tool parameters. Integers, booleans, enums, and even complex objects all work. Use the type that best fits the data you need.

Multi-message Prompts

You already saw a preview of multi-message prompts in the code review example, but let's dig deeper into why this pattern matters and how to use it effectively. In the MCP protocol, a prompt can return any number of messages, each with a specific role. The three roles you will use most often are system, user, and assistant.

Understanding Message Roles

A system message sets the overall behavior and personality of the AI model. It is like giving the model a job description before it starts working. A user message is what the human would say in the conversation. An assistant message represents a previous response from the model, which is useful when you want to set up a multi-turn conversation pattern.

The beauty of returning multiple messages is that you can construct an entire conversation context in a single prompt. For example, you could return a system message that defines the model's expertise, a user message that asks a question, and an assistant message that demonstrates the expected answer format. When the model sees this sequence, it understands both what to do and how to format its response. This is essentially few-shot prompting, built right into your MCP server.

Let's look at a concrete example like the one below in Listing 7-5. Suppose you want to create a prompt that helps users write unit tests. You want the model to act as a testing expert, and you want to show it the format you expect. Here is how you might structure that with multiple messages.

Listing 7-5. A multi-message prompt with role-based context

```
[McpServerPrompt]
[Description("Sets up a unit test writing session")]
public static ChatMessage[] WriteTests([Description("The class or method
to test")]
    string targetCode,
    [Description("Testing framework: xunit, nunit, or mstest")] string
    framework)
{
    var system = new ChatMessage(
        ChatRole.System,
```

```
        "You are an expert at writing unit "
        + $"tests using {framework}. Write thorough tests that cover edge "
        + "cases, error conditions, and happy paths. Use the Arrange-Act-
        Assert pattern.");

    var user = new ChatMessage(
        ChatRole.User, "Please write unit "
        + "tests for the following code:\n\n"
        + $"```csharp\n{targetCode}\n```");

    return [system, user];
}
```

This prompt returns two messages. The system message establishes the model as a testing expert who knows the specified framework and follows the Arrange-Act-Assert pattern. The user message presents the code to test. When the model receives this sequence, it has everything it needs to generate high-quality tests without any additional coaching from the user.

You could extend this pattern further by adding an Assistant message that shows an example test in the desired format. The model would then follow that format for the rest of its response. Multi-message prompts give you fine-grained control over the conversation that is hard to achieve with a single message.

Async Prompt Methods

Just like tools, prompt methods can be async. If your prompt needs to fetch data from a database, read a file, or call an API to construct its messages, you can make the method return `Task<ChatMessage[]>` and use await inside. The SDK handles async methods transparently.

For instance, imagine a prompt that reads a project's coding standards from a file and includes them in the system message. You would mark the method as async, await the file read, and build the `ChatMessage` with the file contents. The server will wait for the Task to complete before returning the prompt to the client.

Prompt Best Practices

Now that you know how to build prompts, let's talk about when you should use them and how to make them great. I have seen a few patterns emerge from working with MCP prompts, and I think they are worth sharing before we move on to the fun stuff.

When to Use Prompts vs. Tools

The simplest rule of thumb I can offer is this: If you want the AI model to do something, use a tool. If you want the AI model to think about something in a particular way, use a prompt. Tools are for actions and side effects. Prompts are for shaping reasoning and conversation flow.

Here are some concrete examples to illustrate the difference:

- **Analyzing code for security vulnerabilities**: Use a prompt that sets up the model as a security expert and asks it to review code.
- **Running a linter on code and returning results**: Use a tool that executes the linter and returns the output.
- **Translating text with specific tone guidelines**: Use a prompt that instructs the model on tone, formality, and cultural context.
- **Sending an email**: Use a tool that calls an email API.
- **Explaining a complex concept step by step**: Use a prompt that sets up the model as a patient teacher.

Of course, the lines can blur. A sophisticated server might expose a prompt that sets up a debugging session and tools that can read log files and query databases. The prompt and tools work together, with the prompt providing the strategy and the tools providing the capabilities.

Keep Prompts Focused

A good prompt does one thing well. Resist the temptation to create a Swiss Army knife prompt that tries to cover every scenario. Instead, create multiple focused prompts, each with a clear purpose and a descriptive name. A user browsing your prompts should be able to tell at a glance what each one does.

For example, instead of a single "CodeAssistant" prompt that does everything from reviews to refactoring to documentation, create separate prompts: "ReviewCode", "RefactorCode", "DocumentCode". Each one can have parameters that fine-tune its behavior, but the core purpose stays sharp and clear.

Write Great Descriptions

The Description attribute on your prompts and parameters is not just documentation for developers. It is the primary way that AI clients communicate your prompts to users. A good description tells the user what the prompt does, what kind of results to expect, and when they might want to use it.

For parameters, the description should explain what values are valid. If a parameter accepts specific options like "thorough," "quick", or "security-focused," list them in the description. The more guidance you provide, the better the experience for the user and the AI model alike.

Tip Test your prompts with real AI clients early and often. What looks good in code might feel awkward in conversation. Run each prompt through a client like Claude Desktop and see if the model's response matches your expectations. Iterate on the wording until it feels natural.

Just like tools and resources, prompts also support the Title and IconSource properties on the `McpServerPrompt` attribute. Title gives your prompt a human-friendly display name, and IconSource points to an icon that clients can display next to the prompt in their UI. If you have a code review prompt, you might set IconSource to a magnifying glass icon, and a Title of "Code Review Assistant". Small touches like this make your server feel polished when clients list the available prompts.

A Cosmic Pizza Prompt Server

Alright, it is time for the fun part. Throughout this book, we have had a theme of space and cosmic adventures, and I see no reason to stop now. Let's build two prompts that combine the wonder of outer space with the universal love of pizza. Because if there is one thing astronauts definitely deserve, it is better pizza options.

The Pizza Recommendation Prompt

Our first cosmic prompt is a pizza recommendation engine, you can see it underneath in Listing 7-6. The user tells us what kind of crust they like and what flavor profile they are in the mood for, and our prompt sets up the AI model as a cosmic pizza chef who creates space-themed pizzas with ridiculous names and creative toppings. The kind of prompt that makes you smile while you test it.

Listing 7-6. The cosmic pizza recommendation prompt

```
using System.ComponentModel;
using Microsoft.Extensions.AI;
using ModelContextProtocol.Server;

namespace PromptServer.Prompts;

[McpServerPromptType]
public static class CosmicPizzaPrompts
{
    [McpServerPrompt]
    [Description("Recommends a space-themed pizza based on your preferences")]
    public static ChatMessage[] PizzaRecommendation(
        [Description("Preferred crust type: thin, thick, or stuffed")]
        string crust,
        [Description("Flavor preference: savory, spicy, or sweet")]
        string flavor)
    {
        var system = new ChatMessage(
            ChatRole.System,
            "You are a cosmic pizza chef on a space station orbiting "
            + "Jupiter. You specialize in creating space-themed pizzas "
            + "with creative names and out-of-this-world ingredients. "
            + "Each pizza should have a fun backstory about why it was "
            + "invented in space.");

        var user = new ChatMessage(
            ChatRole.User,
            $"I would like a {crust} crust pizza with a {flavor} flavor "
```

```
            + "profile. Please recommend a space-themed pizza with a "
            + "creative cosmic name, list the toppings, and explain why "
            + "it is perfect for eating in zero gravity.");

        return [system, user];
    }
}
```

I love this prompt because it demonstrates something important: prompts do not have to be serious. The system message puts the AI model in character as a space station pizza chef, and the user message asks for a specific recommendation. When you run this with "stuffed" and "spicy," you might get something like "The Supernova Inferno: a stuffed crust pizza loaded with ghost pepper mozzarella, sun-dried meteor tomatoes, and jalapeño stardust." The results are always creative and genuinely entertaining.

The Space Trivia Quiz Prompt

Our second cosmic prompt, below in Listing 7-7, generates space trivia quizzes. This one is particularly interesting because it uses an integer parameter for the number of questions, showing that prompts can work with non-string types just like tools can.

Listing 7-7. The space trivia quiz prompt

```
[McpServerPrompt]
[Description("Generates a space trivia quiz with configurable difficulty
and length")]
public static ChatMessage[] SpaceTriviaQuiz(
    [Description("Difficulty level: easy, medium, or hard")] string
    difficulty,
    [Description("Number of questions to generate (between 1 and 10)")]
    int count)
{
    var clampedCount = Math.Clamp(count, 1, 10);

    var system = new ChatMessage(
        ChatRole.System,
        "You are an enthusiastic and fun space trivia host. "
        + "Generate multiple-choice questions about space, "
```

```
        + "planets, stars, galaxies, and space exploration. "
        + "Include the correct answer after each question with a brief
        explanation.");

    var user = new ChatMessage(
        ChatRole.User,
        $"Generate {clampedCount} "
        + $"{difficulty} space trivia "
        + "questions. Format each as a "
        + "multiple-choice question with "
        + "four options labeled A, B, C, "
        + "and D. After each question, "
        + "reveal the correct answer.");

    return [system, user];
}
```

Notice the use of `Math.Clamp` to ensure the count stays between 1 and 10. This is a small but important detail. Even though the description tells the user to pick a number between 1 and 10, there is nothing stopping the client from sending 42 or -5. Validating your inputs in prompt methods is just as important as it is in tools. The `Description` tells the user what to do; the code ensures the server behaves correctly even when they do not listen.

Both of these prompts live in the same class, `CosmicPizzaPrompts`, which is decorated with the `McpServerPromptType` attribute. The SDK discovers both prompts automatically when the server starts. You can try them out by connecting to the server with Claude Desktop or the MCP Inspector, just like you did with tools in Chapter 4.

Testing the Cosmic Prompts

To test these prompts, build and run the server using the MCP Inspector:

```
npx @modelcontextprotocol/inspector \
dotnet run --project PromptServer
```

In the Inspector's web interface, navigate to the Prompts tab. You should see three prompts listed: `Greeting`, `PizzaRecommendation`, and `SpaceTriviaQuiz` (plus `ReviewCode` and `WriteTests` if you included those classes). Click on any prompt to see its parameters and send a test request. The Inspector will show you the exact messages that your server returns, which is invaluable for debugging. Figure 7-1 shows what this looks like. For a detailed walkthrough of every Inspector feature, see Chapter 11.

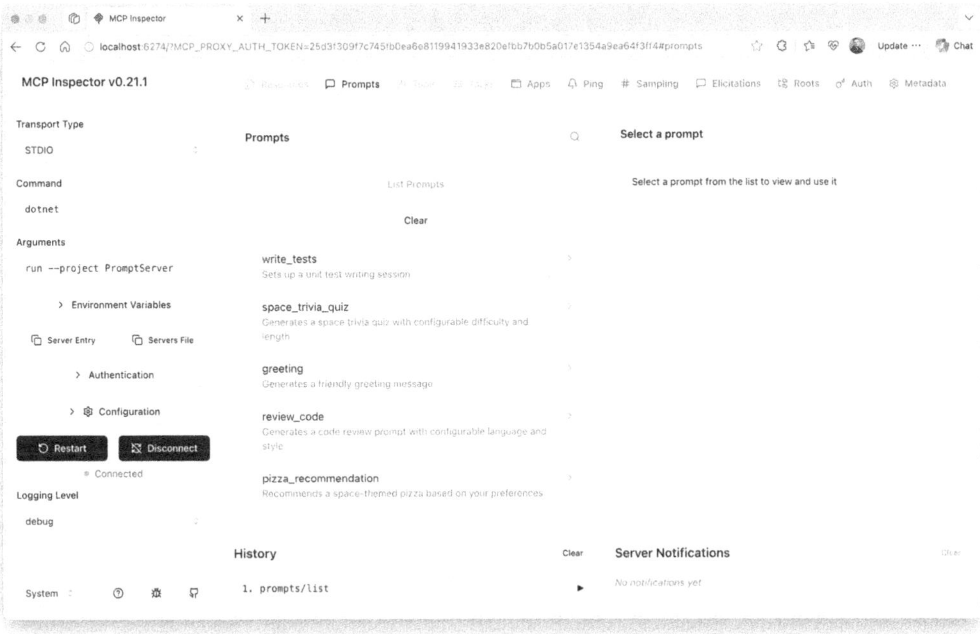

***Figure 7-1.** The MCP Inspector Prompts tab listing all prompts exposed by the Cosmic Pizza prompt server*

Select the `PizzaRecommendation` prompt and you will see input fields for each argument. Fill in a crust preference and a flavor profile, look at the expected values below the entry field, then click Get Prompt. The Inspector shows you the exact messages your server returns, including the system message and the user message with the parameters baked in. This is a great way to verify that your prompt templates produce the output you expect, as seen in Figure 7-2.

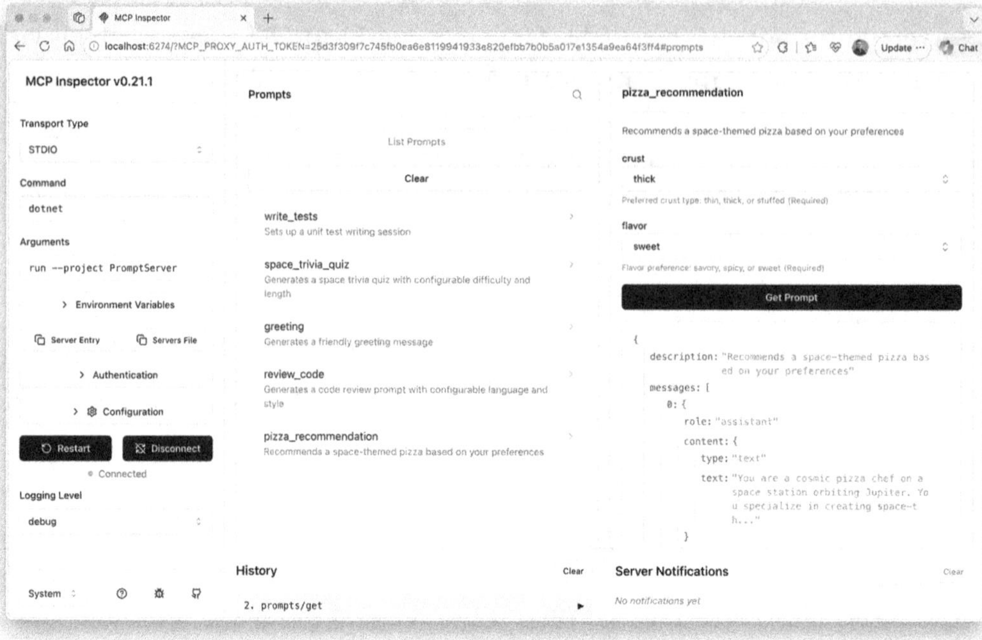

Figure 7-2. *Filling in parameters for the PizzaRecommendation prompt in the MCP Inspector*

In Claude Desktop, you will find your prompts in the prompt picker. Click the + button below the chat input and you will see your prompts listed alongside any other MCP prompts from connected servers. Select one, fill in the arguments if it has any, and Claude injects the resulting messages into your conversation. Figure 7-3 shows the prompt picker with the Cosmic Pizza prompts available.

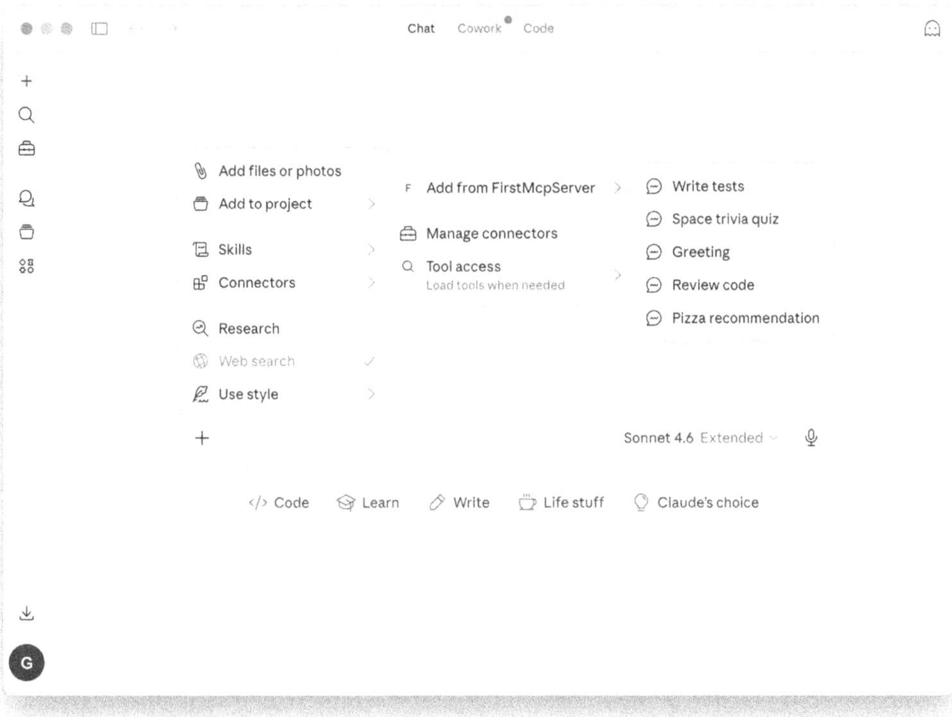

Figure 7-3. *Browsing MCP prompts in Claude Desktop through the prompt picker*

Visual Studio Code takes a different approach. Prompts are surfaced as slash commands in the chat input. Type / and you will see an autocomplete menu listing all available commands, including your MCP prompts. They appear as `/mcp.PromptServer.Greeting`, `/mcp.PromptServer.PizzaRecommendation`, and so on. Select one and VS Code inserts it into the chat. Unlike resources, which have a dedicated `MCP: Browse Resources...` command in the Command Palette, prompts live entirely inside the chat input through this slash syntax, as seen in Figure 7-4.

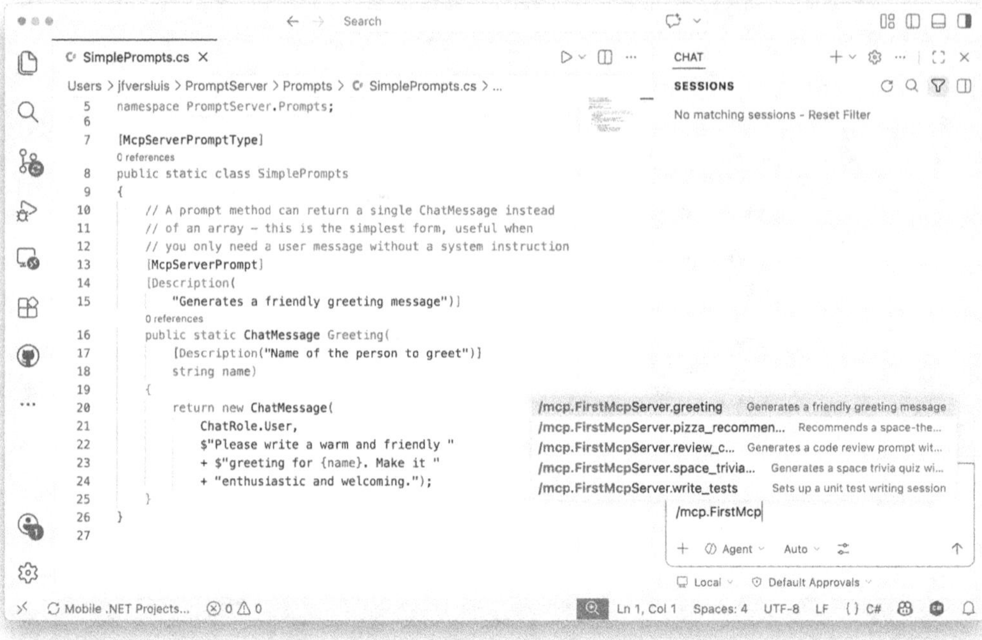

Figure 7-4. *Invoking MCP prompts in Visual Studio Code using the slash command menu*

Try the pizza prompt with different combinations of crust and flavor. Then try the trivia quiz with varying difficulty levels and question counts. You will quickly get a feel for how the parameters affect the generated messages and how the AI model responds to different setups.

Summary

We covered a lot of ground: We explored the third and final primitive that MCP servers can expose: prompts. We learned that prompts are predefined message templates that shape how an AI model approaches a task. Unlike tools, which perform actions, and resources, which provide data, prompts provide context and reasoning guidance.

We started with a simple greeting prompt that returns a single `ChatMessage`, then built a parameterized code review prompt that accepts multiple arguments and generates tailored instructions. We explored multi-message prompts that combine system and user messages to give the AI model rich context. Along the way, we discussed best practices like keeping prompts focused, writing great descriptions, and knowing when to use prompts versus tools.

We wrapped up with a cosmic pizza prompt server that proves prompts can be both practical and fun. The pizza recommendation and space trivia prompts showed how creative you can get with this feature while still demonstrating solid patterns like input validation and multi-message conversations.

Up to this point, all of our servers have communicated over standard input and output using the stdio transport. That works great for desktop AI clients that can launch your server as a process, but what about web applications, remote clients, or scenarios where you need your server to be accessible over the network? In the next chapter, we will explore MCP transport layers. You will learn about the different transport options available, how to switch between them, and when each one is the right choice for your project.

CHAPTER 8

Transport Layers

Up to this point, every server we have built communicates through standard input and output. That approach works beautifully for desktop AI clients like Claude Desktop and GitHub Copilot in VS Code, but it is not the only game in town. The MCP specification defines multiple transport layers, and in this chapter, we are going to explore all of them so you can pick the right one for your situation.

Think of a transport layer as the plumbing that carries JSON-RPC messages between client and server. The tools, resources, and prompts you write stay exactly the same regardless of which transport you choose. Only the way those messages travel changes. By the end of this chapter, you will understand the three transport options the specification offers, know when to use each one, and have a working HTTP-based MCP server that you can deploy to any web host.

Understanding Transports

Before we dive into specific transports, here is what a transport actually does. In the MCP architecture, the transport sits between your application code and the network. Your tools produce results, the SDK wraps them into JSON-RPC messages, and the transport is responsible for getting those messages to the client. On the flip side, when a client sends a request, the transport receives the raw bytes and hands them to the SDK for deserialization.

This separation is deliberate. It means you can write your tool once and run it over stdio for local development, then switch to HTTP for production deployment without touching a single line of tool code. The SDK handles the abstraction so cleanly that your tools never know or care how messages arrive.

G. Versluis, *Building MCP Servers with C#*, https://doi.org/10.1007/979-8-8688-3010-5_8

The MCP specification currently recognizes three transports:

- **Standard I/O (stdio)** communicates through `stdin` and `stdout`. We have been using this in every chapter so far.
- **Server-Sent Events (SSE)** uses HTTP with a streaming connection for server-to-client messages. This transport is deprecated in favor of Streamable HTTP.
- **Streamable HTTP** is the newest addition and uses plain HTTP requests with optional streaming. This is the transport you will use for remote and production deployments.

Each has its own strengths and ideal use cases, and we will work through them one by one.

Figure 8-1 shows the key differences at a glance. On the left, stdio keeps everything on the same machine with the host spawning the server as a child process. On the right, HTTP decouples them entirely, letting the server live anywhere on the network.

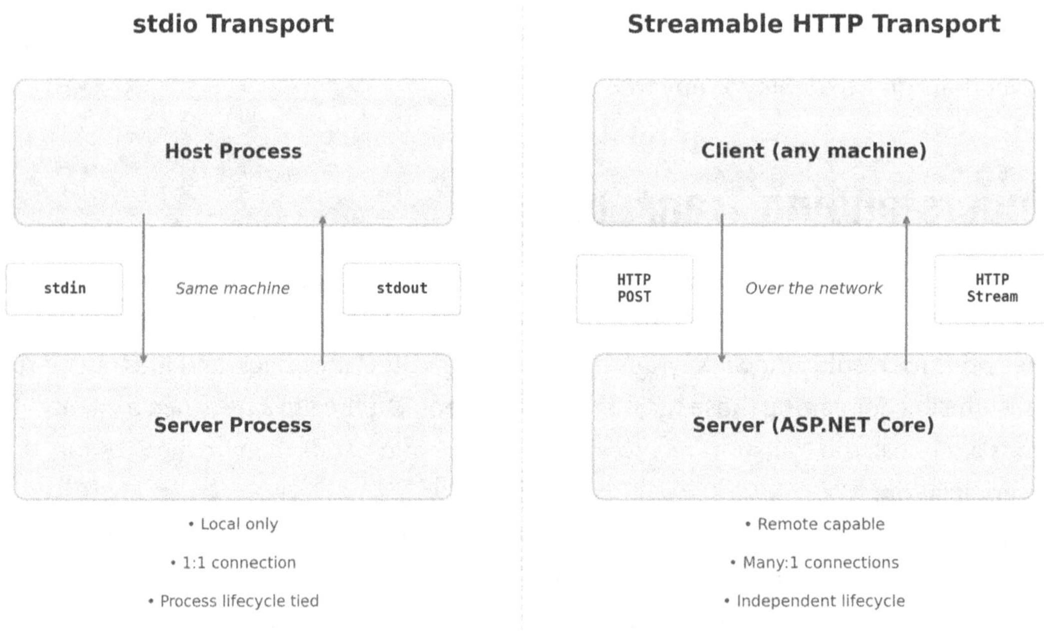

***Figure 8-1.** Comparing the stdio and HTTP transports side by side*

Standard I/O (stdio) Transport

Standard I/O is the transport we have been using in every chapter so far. It communicates by reading JSON-RPC messages from `stdin` and writing responses to `stdout`. The client launches your server as a child process and the two sides talk through the process's standard streams. No network sockets, no ports, no TLS certificates. Just pipes.

How stdio Works

When an AI client like VS Code or Claude Desktop starts your server, it spawns a new process using the command you specified in the configuration. The client takes ownership of the process's `stdin` and `stdout` handles. Every JSON-RPC request is written to your process's `stdin` as a single line of JSON, and your server writes responses to `stdout` the same way. The SDK handles all of this for you. You call `WithStdioServerTransport` during setup and never think about it again.

One critical detail is that `stdout` is exclusively reserved for protocol messages. You cannot use `Console.WriteLine` for debugging because that output would be interleaved with JSON-RPC responses and corrupt the message stream. If you need diagnostic output, write to `stderr` or use a logging framework configured to write to a file.

When to Use stdio

The stdio transport is ideal when the client and server live on the same machine. Desktop AI clients like Claude Desktop, GitHub Copilot in VS Code, and the MCP Inspector all expect stdio by default. If you are building a tool that developers run locally, such as a code analysis tool, a file system helper, or a database query assistant, stdio is the natural choice.

It is also the simplest transport to set up. There is no web server to configure, no ports to open, and no firewall rules to worry about. You just build a console application and it works. That's it! For quick prototyping and local development I almost always start with stdio and only switch to HTTP when I need remote access.

Pros and Cons of stdio

The biggest advantage of stdio is its simplicity. You need nothing beyond a console application and the `ModelContextProtocol` NuGet package. It is also inherently secure because communication never leaves the machine. There are no open ports for attackers to probe.

The downside is that stdio only works locally. The client must be able to launch the server as a child process, which means both must be on the same machine. You cannot host a stdio server in the cloud and connect to it from your laptop. You also cannot share a single server instance among multiple clients. Each client spawns its own process, which is fine for desktop tools but wasteful if you need a shared service.

Server-Sent Events (SSE) Transport

Server-Sent Events, commonly known as SSE, is the second transport the MCP specification defines. If you have ever used SSE in a web application for real-time notifications or live feeds, the concept is exactly the same. The client opens a long-lived HTTP connection to the server, and the server pushes messages down that connection whenever it needs to.

How SSE Works in MCP

In the MCP flavor of SSE, the client makes two types of HTTP requests. First, it opens a GET request to the SSE endpoint. This connection stays open and the server uses it to stream JSON-RPC responses and notifications to the client. Second, when the client wants to send a request to the server, it makes a POST request to a separate message endpoint. The server processes the request and sends the response back through the open SSE stream.

This two-channel approach means the client and server communicate over HTTP, which opens the door to remote deployments. You can host your MCP server on a cloud VM, a Kubernetes cluster, or any platform that supports HTTP, and clients can connect from anywhere.

The Status of SSE Transport

The SSE transport was part of the MCP specification from early on, but it has since been superseded by the Streamable HTTP transport. The MCP specification now marks SSE as deprecated in favor of Streamable HTTP, and the C# SDK reflects this direction. If you look at the `ModelContextProtocol.AspNetCore` package, you will find that it implements Streamable HTTP rather than SSE.

I am covering SSE here because you may encounter it in existing servers or in other language SDKs that have not yet migrated. Understanding how it works gives you useful context. But for new projects in C#, you should use Streamable HTTP instead. It offers the same remote connectivity benefits with a simpler architecture and better support for session management.

Note The SSE transport is deprecated in the MCP specification. The C# SDK's ASP.NET Core integration uses Streamable HTTP exclusively. If you are starting a new project, go straight to Streamable HTTP.

Streamable HTTP Transport

Streamable HTTP is the modern transport for MCP and the one I recommend for any server that needs to be accessible over a network. It replaces the dual-channel SSE approach with a cleaner design that uses standard HTTP POST requests. Responses can be returned as regular HTTP responses or streamed using SSE on the same connection, giving you the best of both worlds.

How Streamable HTTP Works

With Streamable HTTP, the client sends all requests as HTTP POST to a single endpoint. The server can respond in two ways. For simple request-response interactions, it returns a regular HTTP response with the JSON-RPC result. For longer-running operations that produce progress updates or multiple messages, the server switches the response to an SSE stream and pushes messages as they become available.

This design is elegant because the client does not need to maintain a persistent connection. It can fire off a POST request, get a response, and move on. But when streaming is needed, it is still available. The protocol negotiation happens transparently through HTTP content type headers.

Streamable HTTP also supports session management. The server can assign a session ID to each client and track state across multiple requests. This is essential for production deployments where you need to manage resources, enforce rate limits, or clean up idle connections.

The ASP.NET Core Integration

The C# SDK provides first-class support for Streamable HTTP through the `ModelContextProtocol.AspNetCore` NuGet package. Where the base `ModelContextProtocol` package gives you the stdio transport, this package replaces it with an HTTP-based transport built on ASP.NET Core's minimal API infrastructure. That means you get all the features you would expect from a modern .NET web application: middleware, dependency injection, authentication, logging, and more.

The setup involves two extension methods. On the service side, you call `WithHttpTransport` instead of `WithStdioServerTransport`. On the endpoint side, you call `MapMcp` to register the MCP endpoint with the ASP.NET Core routing system. That is literally all it takes to switch from stdio to HTTP.

Take a look at the minimal code to create an HTTP-based MCP server, it's shown below in Listing 8-1. We will expand on this later in the chapter, but I want you to see how little code is involved.

Listing 8-1. Minimal Streamable HTTP MCP server

```
var builder = WebApplication.CreateBuilder(args);

builder.Services
    .AddMcpServer()
    .WithHttpTransport()
    .WithToolsFromAssembly();

var app = builder.Build();
app.MapMcp();
app.Run();
```

Compare this to our stdio server from Chapter 4. The structure is almost identical. We swapped `Host.CreateEmptyApplicationBuilder` for `WebApplication.CreateBuilder`, replaced `WithStdioServerTransport` with `WithHttpTransport`, and added a call to `MapMcp`. The tools themselves stay exactly the same. That is the beauty of the transport abstraction.

Session Management

One of the key advantages of Streamable HTTP over stdio is session management. When a client connects to your server, the SDK can create a session that persists across multiple requests. Each session gets a unique identifier that the client includes in subsequent requests, allowing the server to maintain state.

The SDK provides configuration options to control session behavior, this is shown in Listing 8-2 underneath. You can set how long an idle session should stay alive before being cleaned up, and you can limit the total number of idle sessions to prevent resource exhaustion. These settings are important for production deployments where you might have many clients connecting and disconnecting throughout the day.

Listing 8-2. Configuring session management options

```
builder.Services
    .AddMcpServer()
    .WithHttpTransport(options =>
    {
        options.IdleTimeout = TimeSpan.FromMinutes(30);
        options.MaxIdleSessionCount = 100;
    })
    .WithToolsFromAssembly();
```

The `IdleTimeout` property determines how long a session can sit without any activity before the server disposes of it. The `MaxIdleSessionCount` sets an upper bound on how many inactive sessions the server will keep in memory. When the limit is reached, the oldest idle sessions are removed first. These defaults are sensible for most scenarios, but you should tune them based on your expected client behavior and available memory.

Choosing the Right Transport

Now that you know what each transport does, I want to help you decide which one to use. The decision usually comes down to two questions: where does the client run relative to the server, and do you need to support multiple simultaneous clients?

Table 8-1 summarizes the key differences between the three transports.

Table 8-1. *Comparison of MCP transport options*

Feature	stdio	SSE (Deprecated)	Streamable HTTP
Communication	`stdin/stdout`	HTTP + SSE stream	HTTP requests + optional streaming
Deployment	Local only	Remote (network)	Remote (network)
Connection model	1:1 (child process)	Many:1	Many:1
Server lifecycle	Tied to host process	Independent	Independent
SDK package	`ModelContext Protocol`	`ModelContextProtocol. AspNetCore`	`ModelContextProtocol. AspNetCore`
Best for	Local dev, desktop AI clients	Legacy deployments	Production, cloud, remote access

If your server runs locally alongside the AI client, use stdio. It is the simplest option and the one that all desktop AI clients support out of the box. If your server needs to be accessible over a network, whether that is across machines in your office or from the cloud, use Streamable HTTP. Skip SSE entirely for new projects since it is deprecated.

There is also a middle-ground scenario worth mentioning. During development, you might want to test with the MCP Inspector using stdio, then deploy with HTTP for production. Thanks to the transport abstraction you can maintain both configurations without changing your tool code. Some teams even build their server to accept a command-line argument that selects the transport at startup.

Adding MCP to an Existing ASP.NET Core Application

So far, we have built MCP servers as standalone applications. But what if you already have an ASP.NET Core web API serving REST endpoints and you want to add MCP capabilities to it? This is not only possible; in many cases, it is the recommended approach. The SDK's HTTP transport was designed to be just another endpoint in your application, sitting alongside your existing controllers and minimal APIs.

Why Integrate Instead of Running Separately?

The biggest advantage is service reuse. Your existing application already has a configured dependency injection container with database contexts, HTTP client factories, caching layers, authentication, and all the business logic you have built over time. When you add MCP to that same application, your tools can inject those exact same services. Need a tool that looks up customer data? It can use the same `DbContext` your API controllers use. Need a tool that calls a third-party API? It can use the same `IHttpClientFactory` with the same Polly retry policies you already configured.

This means no duplicated configuration, no separate connection strings to manage, and no risk of business logic drifting between your API and your MCP tools. You write the logic once and expose it through both interfaces.

The second advantage is operational simplicity. One application means one deployment pipeline, one set of health checks, one place to look at logs, and one process to monitor. For teams that already have a well-oiled deployment process for their web API, adding MCP support is just a few extra lines of code rather than a whole new service to operate.

What It Takes

The integration is remarkably lightweight. You add the `ModelContextProtocol.AspNetCore` NuGet package, register the MCP server in your existing DI container with `AddMcpServer()`, and map the endpoint with `MapMcp()`. Your tools live right next to your controllers and can inject the same services.

Because `MapMcp()` is a standard ASP.NET Core endpoint, it participates in the full middleware pipeline. That means your existing authentication, authorization, CORS policies, rate limiting, and logging all apply to the MCP endpoint automatically, no special configuration needed.

Security Considerations

This is the section you should read twice. Adding an MCP endpoint to your application means exposing a new attack surface. By default, the `MapMcp()` endpoint is open to anyone who can reach it, there is no built-in authentication. If your application is publicly accessible, an unauthenticated user could invoke your tools unless you explicitly protect the endpoint.

The good news is that protection works exactly how you would expect in ASP.NET Core. You can chain `RequireAuthorization()` directly on the endpoint:

```
app.MapMcp().RequireAuthorization();
```

This ensures that only authenticated requests reach your MCP server. Your existing JWT Bearer, cookie authentication, or any other scheme you have configured will apply. The C# SDK also provides built-in support for the MCP OAuth flow through `AddMcp()` on the authentication builder, which integrates with RFC 8707 resource metadata; we will explore this in detail in Chapter 13.

Your tools can even access the authenticated user. Register `IHttpContextAccessor` in your DI container with `AddHttpContextAccessor()`, then inject it into your tool class. From there, you can read the request headers, the authenticated user's claims, and any other HTTP context data. This is powerful because it means your tools can make authorization decisions, only showing certain data to certain users, for example.

Caution When using stateful mode (the default), the `HttpContext` reflects the current HTTP request for Streamable HTTP. However, with the legacy SSE transport, it reflects the long-lived SSE connection; not the individual tool call. User claims could become stale if tokens are refreshed after the connection was established. Stateless mode does not have this issue since every tool call is its own HTTP request.

Sharing Services: Power and Responsibility

Sharing your DI container between your API and MCP tools is the killer feature of integration, but it comes with responsibilities you need to be aware of.

Database connection pools are finite. If your API is already handling significant traffic and you add MCP tools that also hit the database, you are drawing from the same connection pool. A burst of concurrent MCP tool calls could exhaust the pool and cause your API requests to time out. The mitigation is straightforward: add rate limiting to your MCP endpoint and monitor your connection pool usage. ASP.NET Core's built-in rate limiter works perfectly here:

```
app.MapMcp().RequireRateLimiting("mcp-policy");
```

Scoped services like `DbContext` work correctly. The SDK creates a fresh DI scope for each tool invocation, so you get a new `DbContext` instance per call, just like a controller action gets one per HTTP request. Singleton services are shared across all calls, which is fine for stateless services but could be a concern if you have mutable singleton state.

Think of it this way: MCP tools are essentially additional consumers of your shared infrastructure. The same capacity planning you do for your API endpoints should include your MCP tools.

Stateless vs. Stateful Mode

When you add MCP to an existing application, you need to decide whether to run in stateless or stateful mode. The SDK defaults to stateful, which means it creates an in-memory session for each connected client using an `Mcp-Session-Id` header. But the SDK team recommends stateless mode for most servers:

```
options.Stateless = true;
```

In stateless mode, every request is independent; no session tracking, no in-memory session state, and no complications when scaling horizontally behind a load balancer. This is ideal for integration because your existing application probably already scales horizontally, and adding stateful MCP sessions would require sticky sessions or distributed session storage.

You only need stateful mode if your server sends requests back to the client (sampling, elicitation), pushes unsolicited notifications, or needs to maintain per-client state across multiple tool calls. For most "add MCP to my existing API" scenarios, stateless is the way to go.

Deployment Considerations

When your MCP endpoint and your API share the same application, they share the same port by default. This is usually what you want: one URL to expose, one SSL certificate to manage, one firewall rule to configure. You distinguish between your API and MCP through URL paths: your REST endpoints under `/api/*` and MCP at the root or a custom path like `/mcp`.

If you need isolation, Kestrel supports listening on multiple ports. You could serve your API on one port and MCP on another, then apply different network policies to each. But in practice, path-based routing with proper authentication is sufficient for most deployments.

For reverse proxies like nginx or YARP, make sure the proxy does not buffer responses. The Streamable HTTP transport can use server-sent events for streaming, and buffering would prevent those events from reaching the client in real time. In nginx, set `proxy_buffering off` for the MCP path. Also ensure your proxy timeout is long enough to accommodate your longest-running tool; a tool that queries a database and processes results might take tens of seconds.

When to Keep Them Separate

Integration is not always the right call. If your MCP tools have fundamentally different resource requirements than your API, say they are CPU-heavy or memory-intensive, running them in the same process means they compete for resources. A compute-heavy tool could starve your API of CPU time.

Similarly, if your MCP server needs a different scaling profile (you want ten API replicas but only two MCP replicas), separate deployments give you that flexibility. And if you are building an MCP server that will be used by multiple applications, a standalone server that any client can connect to is a cleaner architecture than embedding it in one specific application.

For most teams, though, starting with integration is the pragmatic choice. You can always extract the MCP server into its own service later if the need arises. The tool code itself does not change, only the hosting and configuration around it.

Converting Our Server to HTTP

Let's put theory into practice by taking the server we built in Chapter 4 and converting it from stdio to Streamable HTTP. This exercise will show you exactly what changes and, just as importantly, what stays the same. We will go through the transformation step by step.

Step 1: Create a New Web Project

Our Chapter 4 server was a console application. For HTTP transport, we need an ASP.NET Core web application. Open your terminal and create a new project using the empty web template.

```
$ dotnet new web -n HttpTransportServer
```

This gives us a minimal ASP.NET Core application with just a `Program.cs` and a project file. No controllers, no Razor pages, just the bare essentials. This is perfect for an MCP server because we do not need any of those web framework features.

Step 2: Add the NuGet Packages

Instead of the base `ModelContextProtocol` package alone, we also need the ASP.NET Core integration package. This package provides the `WithHttpTransport` and `MapMcp` extension methods.

```
$ cd HttpTransportServer
$ dotnet add package ModelContextProtocol
$ dotnet add package ModelContextProtocol.AspNetCore
```

The `ModelContextProtocol.AspNetCore` package depends on the base `ModelContextProtocol` package, so you technically only need to reference the `AspNetCore` one. But I prefer being explicit about both references so it is clear at a glance what the project depends on.

Step 3: Update the Project File

After adding the packages, your project file should look like the code shown in Listing 8-3. Notice that we are using the `Microsoft.NET.Sdk.Web` SDK instead of the plain `Microsoft.NET.Sdk`. That is what makes this an ASP.NET Core application.

Listing 8-3. The HttpTransportServer.csproj project file

```
<Project Sdk="Microsoft.NET.Sdk.Web">
    <PropertyGroup>
        <TargetFramework>net10.0</TargetFramework>
        <Nullable>enable</Nullable>
        <ImplicitUsings>enable</ImplicitUsings>
    </PropertyGroup>
    <ItemGroup>
        <PackageReference Include="ModelContextProtocol" Version="1.3.0" />
        <PackageReference Include= "ModelContextProtocol.AspNetCore"
        Version="1.3.0" />
    </ItemGroup>
</Project>
```

The SDK change from `Microsoft.NET.Sdk` to `Microsoft.NET.Sdk.Web` is the most important difference between this project file and the one from Chapter 4. This SDK brings in ASP.NET Core automatically, so we do not need a separate package reference for it.

Step 4: Rewrite Program.cs

Here is where the actual conversion happens. We need to replace the generic host setup with the ASP.NET Core web application builder, swap the transport, and add endpoint mapping. Take a look at the complete file first, then walk through the changes.

Listing 8-4. Complete Program.cs with HTTP transport

```
using ModelContextProtocol;
using ModelContextProtocol.Server;
using System.ComponentModel;
```

```
var builder = WebApplication.CreateBuilder(args);

builder.Services
    .AddMcpServer()
    .WithHttpTransport()
    .WithToolsFromAssembly();

var app = builder.Build();
app.MapMcp();
app.Run();

[McpServerToolType]
public static class EchoTool
{
    [McpServerTool, Description("Echoes the input back.")]
    public static string Echo([Description("Message to echo")] string
    message)
    {
        return $"Echo: {message}";
    }
}

[McpServerToolType]
public static class SpaceFactTool
{
    private static readonly string[] Facts =
    [
        "A day on Venus is longer than a year on Venus.",
        "Neutron stars are so dense that  a teaspoon would weigh about 6
        billion tons.",
        "There are more stars in the than grains of sand on all of Earth's
        beaches.",
        "The footprints on the Moon will be there for 100 million years.",
        "One million Earths could fit inside the Sun."
    ];
```

```
    [McpServerTool, Description("Returns a random fun fact about space.")]
    public static string GetSpaceFact()
    {
        var random = new Random();
        return Facts[random.Next(Facts.Length)];
    }
}
```

Look at how little changed. The tool classes at the bottom are identical to Chapter 4, character for character. The only differences are in the first few lines of the file. You might be thinking that the conversion would be a big deal, but it really is not. Here are the three key changes.

Before we dive into the actual code, note how I combined the `McpServerTool` and `Description` attributes this time. Before, we had these on separate lines, but you can also combine attributes. This is a C# feature and has nothing to do with MCPs; additionally, the working is the exact same, just a matter of taste which you like better.

First, we replaced `Host.CreateEmptyApplicationBuilder` with `WebApplication.CreateBuilder`. This switches us from a generic .NET host to an ASP.NET Core web host that can handle HTTP requests. Second, we swapped `WithStdioServerTransport` for `WithHttpTransport`. This tells the SDK to listen for JSON-RPC messages over HTTP instead of reading them from `stdin`. Third, we added `app.MapMcp()` to register the MCP endpoint with ASP.NET Core's routing system. Without this call, the server would start but would not accept any MCP connections.

We also dropped two using statements. `Microsoft.Extensions.DependencyInjection` and `Microsoft.Extensions.Hosting` are no longer needed because `WebApplication.CreateBuilder` brings them in automatically through the ASP.NET Core SDK.

Note We removed the `Microsoft.Extensions.Hosting` NuGet package entirely. The ASP.NET Core web SDK includes hosting support out of the box. Keeping the old package would not cause errors, but it would be a redundant dependency.

Step 5: Run and Test

Start the server the same way you would any ASP.NET Core application.

```
$ dotnet run
```

This time you *will* see output. Unlike the stdio server that sat silently, the HTTP server prints the URLs it is listening on, something like "Now listening on: `http://localhost:5000`". That is your MCP endpoint, ready to accept connections.

By default, `MapMcp()` maps the endpoint to the application root. So, if your server runs on `http://localhost:5000`, that is the URL clients will connect to. You can customize this path by passing a route pattern to `MapMcp()`. For example, `MapMcp("/mcp")`, but the default of root works well for standalone MCP servers. You can see this being configured in Listing 8-5 below.

Listing 8-5. Customizing the MCP endpoint path

```
app.MapMcp("/my-custom-mcp-endpoint");
```

To test the HTTP server, you can use any MCP client that supports the Streamable HTTP transport. You can also configure VS Code to connect to it. Instead of specifying a `command` and `args` in the MCP configuration, you provide a URL. For use with any MCP client, you can find the configuration down below in Listing 8-6.

Listing 8-6. VS Code configuration for an HTTP MCP server

```
{
    "mcp": {
        "servers": {
            "HttpTransportServer": {
                "type": "http",
                "url": "http://localhost:5000"
            }
        }
    }
}
```

Notice how the `type` changed from `stdio` to `http`, and instead of a `command` and `args`, you now just provide a `url`. There is no process to launch, no path to a project folder, the client just needs the URL. This is one of the practical advantages of HTTP transport: you can share the server URL with your team, and everyone can connect without installing anything locally. Figure 8-2 shows the MCP Inspector connected to the HTTP server. It is actually a pretty boring screenshot because it shows exactly the same as when connecting through stdio.

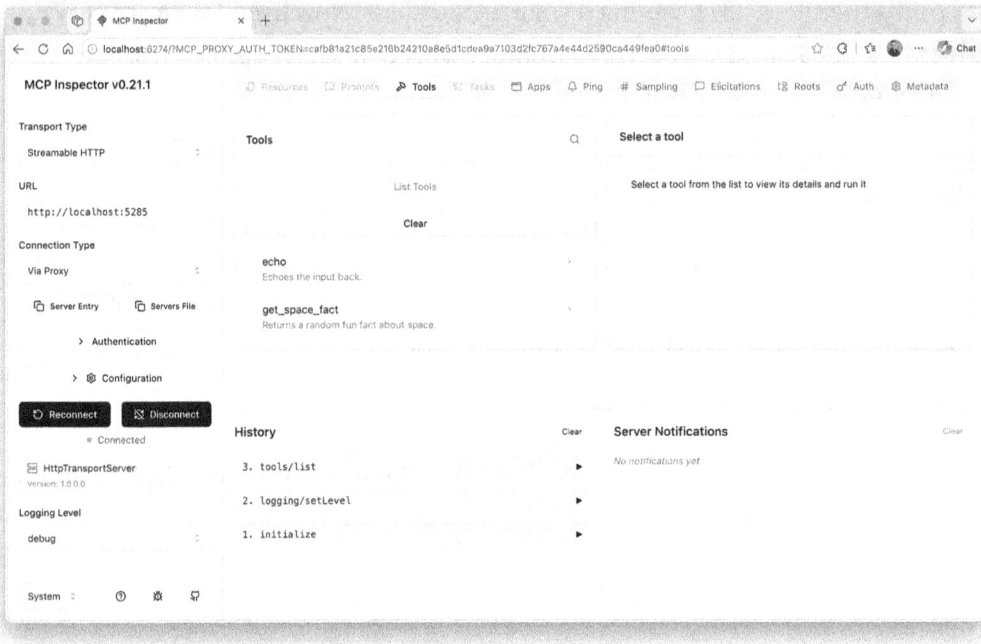

__Figure 8-2.__ The MCP Inspector connected to an HTTP-based MCP server

Configuring Transport Options

The `WithHttpTransport` method accepts an optional configuration delegate that lets you fine-tune the transport behavior. We briefly saw the session management options earlier, but there is more you can configure. Here is a rundown of the most important settings.

HttpServerTransportOptions

The `HttpServerTransportOptions` class exposes several properties that control how the transport behaves. The `IdleTimeout` and `MaxIdleSessionCount` properties manage session lifecycle as we discussed. But there are additional options worth knowing about.

The `Stateless` property controls whether the server operates in stateless mode. When set to `true`, the server does not create or track sessions. Every request is treated independently with no shared state between calls. This can be useful for simple utility servers that do not need session affinity, but most servers benefit from sessions, so the default is `false`. Have a look at Listing 8-7 below to see how to configure the stateless option.

Listing 8-7. Configuring stateless mode

```
builder.Services
    .AddMcpServer()
    .WithHttpTransport(options =>
    {
        options.Stateless = true;
    })
    .WithToolsFromAssembly();
```

Route Configuration

By default, `MapMcp()` registers the endpoint at the application root. You can change this to any route pattern that makes sense for your application by passing it as a parameter. If you are adding MCP to an existing web API, you might want to put it under a specific path prefix to keep things organized. Look at Listing 8-8 underneath to see an example of this custom configuration.

Listing 8-8. Custom route with endpoint metadata

```
app.MapMcp("/api/v1/mcp").RequireAuthorization();
```

Because `MapMcp` returns a standard ASP.NET Core endpoint builder, you can chain any endpoint metadata you want. The `RequireAuthorization` call shown above ensures that only authenticated requests can reach your MCP server. You can add CORS policies, rate limiting, or any other middleware that ASP.NET Core supports.

This is where the ASP.NET Core integration really shines. Your MCP server is not a special snowflake running on a custom HTTP stack. It is just another endpoint in your web application, which means all the patterns and practices you already know from building web APIs apply directly.

Resumability

The Streamable HTTP transport supports a feature called resumability. If the connection between client and server drops, a resumable session can pick up where it left off instead of starting over. This is particularly useful for long-running operations where losing progress would be costly.

Resumability works through event IDs. The server assigns an incrementing ID to each message it sends. If the connection drops, the client can reconnect and tell the server the last event ID it received. The server then replays any messages the client missed. The C# SDK handles the server-side bookkeeping for you, but the client must also support resumability for the feature to work end to end.

Tip Resumability is an advanced feature that most servers do not need during initial development. Start without it and add it later if you find that dropped connections are causing problems for your users.

Long-Running Requests with Polling

Some MCP tool calls just take a while. Think of a tool that kicks off a CI pipeline or crunches through a large dataset. With Streamable HTTP, you don't have to keep that SSE connection open the entire time. The server can drop the connection and let the client poll back later for the result. Pretty neat.

The SDK provides an `ISseEventStreamStore` interface for persisting SSE events while the connection is closed. There's a built-in implementation called `DistributedCacheEventStreamStore` that works with any `IDistributedCache` from ASP.NET Core. You register it in your service configuration by calling `AddDistributedMemoryCache()` and then chaining `WithDistributedCacheEventStreamStore()` on the MCP server builder. That's all the plumbing you need.

Here's the thing: in your tool handler, you can add `McpRequestContext` as a parameter. The SDK injects it automatically. From there, call `EnablePollingAsync` with a retry interval, say, five seconds, and the server drops the SSE connection on the spot. The client then polls back at that interval to check for results. This keeps your connections short-lived while still handling long-running work.

You'll also want to think about event retention. The DistributedCacheEventStreamStoreOptions class gives you fine-grained control with properties like EventSlidingExpiration, EventAbsoluteExpiration, MetadataSlidingExpiration, and MetadataAbsoluteExpiration. By default, events are cleaned up when the session terminates, but time-based expiration is a better fit for long-lived production servers. In Listing 8-9 below you can see an example of this.

Listing 8-9. Configuring long-running request support with polling

```
var builder = WebApplication.CreateBuilder(args);

// Add distributed cache for event stream persistence
builder.Services.AddDistributedMemoryCache();

builder.Services
    .AddMcpServer()
    .WithHttpTransport()
    .WithDistributedCacheEventStreamStore()
    .WithTools();

var app = builder.Build();
app.MapMcp();
app.Run();

[McpServerTool(Name = "long_running_analysis")]
public static async Task<string> LongRunningAnalysis(
    string input,
    McpRequestContext context,
    CancellationToken ct)
{
    // Drop the SSE connection; client will poll every 5 seconds
    await context.EnablePollingAsync(retryInterval: TimeSpan.
    FromSeconds(5));

    // Do the actual heavy lifting
    await Task.Delay(TimeSpan.FromMinutes(2), ct);

    return "Analysis complete!";
}
```

Progress Notifications

Polling is great for tools that run for minutes, but sometimes you want more granular feedback. The MCP specification includes a progress notification mechanism that lets your tool report exactly where it is in a multistep process. Clients that support progress, like the MCP Inspector, can display a progress indicator or status message as each step completes.

The idea is simple. Your tool injects `McpServer` and `RequestContext<CallToolRequestParams>` as parameters. The request context carries a `ProgressToken`, a token the client included to say "I want progress updates for this call." If the token is present, you send `notifications/progress` messages back through the server with the current step, total steps, and a human-readable message.

The companion source code for this chapter includes a `LongRunningServer` project that demonstrates this in practice. It exposes an `analyze_text` tool that processes text through four stages: word counting, readability scoring, sentiment analysis, and summarization, sending a progress notification after each stage. Each step takes a couple of seconds, so you can watch the progress arrive in real time when you connect with the MCP Inspector or watch the progress while invoking it in VS Code.

The core pattern looks like Listing 8-10.

Listing 8-10. Sending progress notifications from a tool

```
[McpServerTool(Name = "analyze_text")]
public static async Task<string> AnalyzeText(
    string text,
    McpServer server,
    RequestContext<CallToolRequestParams> context,
    CancellationToken cancellationToken)
{
    var progressToken = context.Params?.ProgressToken;

    for (int i = 0; i < steps.Length; i++)
    {
        if (progressToken is not null)
        {
            await server.SendNotificationAsync("notifications/progress",
                new ProgressNotificationParams
```

```
                {
                    ProgressToken = progressToken.Value,
                    Progress = new ProgressNotificationValue
                    {
                        Progress = i,
                        Total = steps.Length,
                        Message = steps[i],
                    },
                });
        }

        // Do the actual work for this step
        await Task.Delay(TimeSpan.FromSeconds(2), cancellationToken);
    }

    return string.Join("\n", results);
}
```

A few things to notice. First, the tool checks whether `ProgressToken` is present before sending notifications. Not every client sends a progress token, and your tool should work fine either way; it just skips the progress updates. Second, the `McpServer` and `RequestContext` parameters are injected by the SDK automatically, just like how `CancellationToken` gets injected. You do not register them yourself.

The `LongRunningServer` project also demonstrates stateless mode, which is the recommended configuration for HTTP servers that do not need server-to-client requests. Run it with `dotnet run`, and connect the MCP Inspector to see the progress notifications flow through in the JSON-RPC panel as the analysis progresses step by step.

Tasks (Experimental)

The 2025-11-25 MCP specification introduced tasks as a full protocol feature. Where polling lets the server drop a connection and resume later, tasks go a step further: they provide durable state tracking and deferred result retrieval for long-running operations. Think of them as a structured lifecycle for async work.

Note While tasks are fully defined in the MCP specification, the C# SDK marks its implementation as experimental (diagnostic `MCPEXP001`). This means the SDK API surface may change in future releases. That said, the SDK already includes full support so you can start building with tasks today—just be prepared for possible API adjustments as the feature matures.

On the server side, you configure an `IMcpTaskStore`. The SDK ships with `InMemoryMcpTaskStore` out of the box, which accepts a range of options: `defaultTtl`, `maxTtl`, `pollInterval`, `cleanupInterval`, `pageSize`, `maxTasks`, and `maxTasksPerSession`. For production, you'd likely implement your own store backed by a database, but the in-memory version is perfect for development and testing.

Here's a nice detail: tools automatically advertise task support based on whether they're async. You can control this explicitly with the `ToolTaskSupport` enum. Forbidden means the tool never creates tasks, that's the default for synchronous tools. Optional means the tool can create tasks if the client requests it, the default for async tools. And `Required` means the tool always creates a task. Set it right on the attribute with `[McpServerTool(TaskSupport = ToolTaskSupport.Required)]`.

The task lifecycle is straightforward. A task starts in the working state and eventually moves to one of three terminal states: completed, failed, or cancelled. The client includes a Task field in the request with `McpTaskMetadata`, and the server returns a `CreateTaskResult` containing the task ID, status, and TTL. From there, the client uses `tasks/get` to poll the status, `tasks/result` to retrieve the final result, `tasks/list` to enumerate all tasks, and `tasks/cancel` to cancel one.

On the client side, the SDK makes this easy with helper methods like `PollTaskUntilCompleteAsync` and `GetTaskResultAsync`. You set the `TimeToLive` in the task metadata to control how long the server should keep results around. Let's look at both sides, you can see it below in Listing 8-11 and 8-12.

Listing 8-11. Server-side task store configuration

```
var builder = WebApplication.CreateBuilder(args);

var taskStore = new InMemoryMcpTaskStore(
    defaultTtl: TimeSpan.FromMinutes(30),
    maxTtl: TimeSpan.FromHours(2),
```

```
    pollInterval: TimeSpan.FromSeconds(5),
    cleanupInterval: TimeSpan.FromMinutes(5),
    maxTasks: 1000,
    maxTasksPerSession: 50);

builder.Services
    .AddMcpServer(options =>
    {
        options.TaskStore = taskStore;
    })
    .WithHttpTransport()
    .WithTools();

[McpServerTool(Name = "deploy_application", TaskSupport = ToolTaskSupport.
Required)]
public static async Task<string> DeployApplication(
    string environment,
    CancellationToken ct)
{
    // Simulate a long-running deployment
    await Task.Delay(TimeSpan.FromMinutes(5), ct);
    return $"Deployed to {environment} successfully.";
}
```

Listing 8-12. Client-side task usage

```
var client = await McpClientFactory.CreateAsync(transport);

// Call the tool with task metadata
var result = await client.CallToolAsync("deploy_application",
    new Dictionary<string, object?>
    {
        ["environment"] = "production"
    },
```

```
    new CallToolRequestParams
    {
        Task = new McpTaskMetadata
        {
            TimeToLive = TimeSpan.FromHours(1)
        }
    });

// result is a CreateTaskResult with task ID and status
var taskResult = result as CreateTaskResult;

// Poll until the task completes
var finalResult = await client.PollTaskUntilCompleteAsync(taskResult.
TaskId);

// Or grab the result directly if you know it is done
var output = await client.GetTaskResultAsync(taskResult.TaskId);
```

Putting It All Together

Consider this more complete example that combines everything we have discussed. This server, below in Listing 8-13, uses HTTP transport with session management configuration and demonstrates how you might structure a real-world MCP server that is ready for deployment.

Listing 8-13. A production-ready HTTP MCP server

```
using ModelContextProtocol;
using ModelContextProtocol.Server;
using System.ComponentModel;

var builder =
    WebApplication.CreateBuilder(args);
builder.Services
    .AddMcpServer(options =>
    {
        options.ServerInfo = new()
```

```
        {
            Name = "MyProductionServer",
            Version = "1.0.0"
        };
    })
    .WithHttpTransport(options =>
    {
        options.IdleTimeout =
            TimeSpan.FromMinutes(30);
        options.MaxIdleSessionCount = 100;
    })
    .WithToolsFromAssembly();

var app = builder.Build();
app.MapMcp();
app.Run();
```

This example adds server metadata through the `AddMcpServer` options delegate. The `ServerInfo` property lets you set a name and version that clients can display. It also configures the HTTP transport with explicit session timeouts. In a real project, you would likely pull these values from your application configuration rather than hardcoding them.

The important thing to notice is that the code is still remarkably compact. A production-ready HTTP MCP server with session management fits comfortably in about 20 lines. The C# SDK and ASP.NET Core do the heavy lifting so you can focus on writing great tools.

Summary

Here's what we covered: We explored the three transport layers that MCP supports. We started with stdio, the transport we have been using since Chapter 4, and discussed its strengths as a simple, secure option for local development. We looked at SSE and learned that while it brought network support to MCP, it has been deprecated in favor of the newer Streamable HTTP transport.

We spent most of our time on Streamable HTTP, the recommended transport for any server that needs to be accessible over a network. We saw how the `ModelContextProtocol.AspNetCore` package makes it easy to create HTTP-based servers using familiar ASP.NET Core patterns. We converted our Chapter 4 server from stdio to HTTP and discovered that the transformation required changing only a handful of lines while the tool code remained untouched.

We also covered transport configuration options including session management, stateless mode, custom routing, resumability, and progress notifications for long-running operations. The LongRunningServer companion project shows these concepts working together in a multistep text analysis tool that reports its progress in real time.

A key takeaway from this chapter is that the transport layer is genuinely independent from your tool code. You can write tools once and deploy them over any transport. This separation of concerns is one of the best architectural decisions in the C# SDK.

In the next chapter, we will turn our attention to dependency injection. So far, our tools have been self-contained static methods, but real applications need to access databases, call external APIs, and share services. Chapter 9 will show you how to inject services into your MCP tools using the same dependency injection patterns you already know from ASP.NET Core.

CHAPTER 9

Dependency Injection and Service Integration

Throughout this book, we have been building MCP servers that do useful things, from returning space facts to looking up weather data. But if you have spent any time building real-world .NET applications, you know that the interesting parts rarely live inside a single static method. Real applications talk to databases, call external APIs, read configuration files, and write log entries. The glue that holds all of that together in modern .NET is dependency injection, or DI for short.

The good news is that the C# MCP SDK is built on top of the same `Microsoft.Extensions.Hosting` infrastructure that powers ASP.NET Core, worker services, and .NET MAUI apps. That means you already know most of what you need. This chapter is all about showing you how to register services, inject them into your MCP tools, work with configuration and logging, call external HTTP APIs, and even integrate a database. By the end, you will have an MCP server that feels like a proper production application instead of a quick demo.

Dependency Injection in MCP Servers

If the term dependency injection is new to you, here is the short version: instead of creating the objects your code needs by calling new everywhere, you describe what you need and let a container hand it to you. This makes your code easier to test, easier to change, and far less tangled. .NET has had a built-in DI container since the early days of ASP.NET Core, and the MCP SDK plugs straight into it.

When you call `Host.CreateEmptyApplicationBuilder`(args) in your `Program.cs`, you get back a builder that owns a `Services` collection. That collection is an `IServiceCollection`, and it is where you register every service your application needs.

G. Versluis, *Building MCP Servers with C#*, https://doi.org/10.1007/979-8-8688-3010-5_9

The MCP SDK adds itself to the same collection when you call `AddMcpServer()`. Under the hood, it registers the MCP protocol handler, the transport layer, and a tool resolver. Because everything lives in the same container, your tools can ask for any service that has been registered and the container will provide it automatically.

This is a big deal. It means you can write an MCP tool that accepts an `ILogger`, an `IHttpClientFactory`, a database context, or any custom service you dream up, and the runtime will wire it all together for you. No manual plumbing required.

Don't worry, dependency injection confuses a lot of people, especially early in career. Then one day it just clicks, and you could not imagine writing code without it. If it has not clicked for you yet, this chapter might be that moment.

Injecting Services into Tools

In earlier chapters, you saw that tool methods accept parameters that map to the arguments an AI model sends along with a tool call. A string parameter called city becomes a required input that the model fills in. But the SDK is smarter than that. When it invokes your tool method, it looks at every parameter and checks whether the type is registered in the DI container. If it is, the SDK resolves it from the container and passes it in. If it is not, the SDK treats it as a regular tool argument that the model should provide.

This means you can mix and match. A single method can have some parameters that come from the AI model and others that come from the DI container. The SDK handles the split automatically. Pretty neat. Take a look at the simplest example in Listing 9-1 below: injecting a logger. An all-time favorite example.

Listing 9-1. Injecting ILogger into an MCP tool

```
[McpServerToolType]
public class GreetingTools
{
    [McpServerTool, Description("Greets a user by name.")]
    public static string Greet(
        [Description("The user name")] string name,
        ILogger<GreetingTools> logger)
```

```
    {
        logger.LogInformation("Greeting {Name}", name);
        return $"Hello, {name}! Welcome to the MCP server.";
    }
}
```

Notice that name has a `Description` attribute, so the SDK knows it is a tool argument. The logger parameter has no `Description` attribute and its type, `ILogger`<GreetingTools>, is registered in the DI container by the hosting framework. The SDK sees that and resolves it automatically. You do not need to do anything special in `Program.cs` because `Microsoft.Extensions.Hosting` already registers `ILogger`<T> for you.

Note The SDK uses a simple rule: if a parameter type is available in the DI container, it is resolved from there. If it is not, the parameter is treated as a tool argument. Keep this in mind when naming your parameters. If you accidentally register a type called string in your container, things will get… interesting.

Registering Custom Services

Injecting `ILogger` is nice, but the real power shows up when you register your own services. The pattern is the same one you use in ASP.NET Core: define an interface, write an implementation, and register it on `builder.Services`. Allow me to walk through a practical example. We will build a pizza menu service that our MCP tools can use to look up available pizzas and their prices.

Note Before the .NET purists come for me: dependency injection does not require interfaces. At its core, DI is just about providing dependencies to the caller. You can register a concrete class like `builder.Services.AddSingleton<PizzaMenuService>()` and inject it directly, no `IPizzaMenuService` in sight. The interface-plus-implementation pattern is a .NET community convention, not a DI requirement. It shines when you genuinely need to swap implementations, say, a real database in production and an in-memory fake in tests, but for a service that will only ever have one implementation, the interface can feel like writing a permission slip to talk to your own code. Use your judgment. In this chapter, we use interfaces because they make the examples clearer and because, well, it is an Apress book and we have standards to uphold.

Defining the Interface

Start with an interface that describes what the service can do, see it below in Listing 9-2. Keeping the interface focused makes it easy to swap implementations later, for instance, when you want to replace the hardcoded menu with one that reads from a database.

Listing 9-2. The IPizzaMenuService interface

```
public interface IPizzaMenuService
{
    IReadOnlyList<string> GetAvailablePizzas();
    decimal GetPrice(string pizzaName);
    string GetDescription(string pizzaName);
}
```

Creating the Implementation

The implementation can be as simple or as complex as you like. For now, I will use an in-memory dictionary, which you can see in Listing 9-3 underneath. In a production server, you might query a database or call another API.

Listing 9-3. The PizzaMenuService implementation

```
public class PizzaMenuService : IPizzaMenuService
{
    private readonly Dictionary<string, (decimal Price, string Desc)> _
    menu = new()
    {
        ["Margherita"] = (8.99m, "Classic tomato sauce and mozzarella"),
        ["Pepperoni"] = (10.99m, "Loaded with spicy pepperoni slices"),
```

```
        ["Hawaiian"] = (11.49m, "Ham and pineapple, the debate continues"),
        ["Quattro Formaggi"] = (12.99m, "Four cheese blend of
        deliciousness"),
        ["Diavola"] = (11.99m, "Spicy salami with chili flakes")
    };

    public IReadOnlyList<string> GetAvailablePizzas() =>
        _menu.Keys.ToList().AsReadOnly();

    public decimal GetPrice(string pizzaName) =>
        _menu.TryGetValue(pizzaName, out var item)
        ? item.Price
        : throw new KeyNotFoundException($"Pizza '{pizzaName}' not found");

    public string GetDescription(string pizzaName) =>
        _menu.TryGetValue(pizzaName, out var item)
        ? item.Desc
        : throw new KeyNotFoundException($"Pizza '{pizzaName}' not found");
}
```

Registering the Service

With the interface and implementation ready, you register it in `Program.cs`. The DI container offers three lifetimes:

- **AddSingleton:** One instance for the entire lifetime of the application. Great for stateless services or in-memory caches.
- **AddScoped:** One instance per scope. In an MCP server, a scope typically maps to a single tool invocation.
- **AddTransient:** A new instance every time the service is requested. Useful for lightweight, stateless helpers.

For our pizza menu, the data does not change at runtime, so a singleton is the right choice. Have a look at the configuration in Listing 9-4 below.

Listing 9-4. Registering IPizzaMenuService as a singleton

```
var builder = Host.CreateEmptyApplicationBuilder(null);

builder.Services
    .AddSingleton<IPizzaMenuService,
    PizzaMenuService>();

builder.Services
    .AddMcpServer()
    .WithStdioServerTransport()
    .WithToolsFromAssembly();

await builder.Build().RunAsync();
```

Using the Service in a Tool

Now that the service is registered, you can inject it into any tool method just like you injected `ILogger` earlier. The SDK resolves `IPizzaMenuService` from the container and passes it to your method. Have a look at the example code for this in Listing 9-5 below. Notice how the service class is now just another parameter in the constructor.

Listing 9-5. A tool that uses IPizzaMenuService

```
[McpServerToolType]
public class PizzaTools
{
    [McpServerTool, Description("Gets the full pizza menu with prices.")]
    public static string GetMenu(
        IPizzaMenuService menuService,
        ILogger<PizzaTools> logger)
    {
        logger.LogInformation("Menu requested");

        var pizzas = menuService.GetAvailablePizzas();
        var lines = new List<string>();

        foreach (var pizza in pizzas)
        {
```

```
            var price = menuService.GetPrice(pizza);
            var desc = menuService.GetDescription(pizza);
            lines.Add($"- {pizza}: ${price}");
            lines.Add($"  {desc}");
        }

        return string.Join("\n", lines);
    }
}
```

When the AI model calls `GetMenu`, the SDK creates a scope, resolves `IPizzaMenuService` and `ILogger`<PizzaTools> from the container, and passes them in alongside any tool arguments. Your tool method is blissfully unaware of how those services were created. DI handles all of that for you.

Configuration with IOptions<T>

Hardcoding values like restaurant names or currency symbols is fine for a demo, but production servers need proper configuration. The .NET hosting stack reads from `appsettings.json`, environment variables, and command-line arguments out of the box. All you need to do is create a strongly typed options class and bind it.

Creating an Options Class

An options class is just a plain C# class with public properties, you can see it in Listing 9-6 underneath. I like to include a const string for the section name so there is a single source of truth.

Listing 9-6. The PizzaServerOptions class

```
public class PizzaServerOptions
{
    public const string SectionName = "PizzaServer";
    public string RestaurantName { get; set; } = "MCP Pizzeria";
    public string Currency { get; set; } = "USD";
    public int MaxToppingsPerPizza { get; set; } = 3;
}
```

Adding the Configuration File

Add an appsettings.json file to your project with a section that matches the class. Make sure the file is set to copy to the output directory in your .csproj. You can see mine below in Listing 9-7.

Listing 9-7. appsettings.json with the PizzaServer section

```
{
    "Logging": {
        "LogLevel": {
            "Default": "Information",
            "Microsoft": "Warning"
        }
    },
    "PizzaServer": {
        "RestaurantName":
        "Gerald's .NET Pizzeria",
        "Currency": "EUR",
        "MaxToppingsPerPizza": 5
    }
}
```

Binding and Injecting Options

In Program.cs, you bind the section to your options class with a single line. After that, you can inject IOptions<PizzaServerOptions> into any tool or service. Have a look at the registration line in Listing 9-8 below.

Listing 9-8. Binding configuration to PizzaServerOptions

```
builder.Services.Configure<PizzaServerOptions>(builder.Configuration.
GetSection(
PizzaServerOptions.SectionName));
```

Now update your tool to use the options as shown in Listing 9-9 below. Notice how the options value gives you a strongly typed object with IntelliSense support instead of raw strings and magic keys.

Listing 9-9. Using IOptions in a tool method

```
[McpServerTool, Description("Gets the full pizza menu with prices.")]
public static string GetMenu(
    IPizzaMenuService menuService,
    IOptions<PizzaServerOptions> options,
    ILogger<PizzaTools> logger)
{
    var config = options.Value;

    logger.LogInformation("Menu requested for {Restaurant}", config.
    RestaurantName);

    var pizzas = menuService.GetAvailablePizzas();
    var lines = new List<string>
    {
        $"Welcome to {config.RestaurantName}!",
            ""
    };

    foreach (var pizza in pizzas)
    {
        var price = menuService.GetPrice(pizza);
        var desc = menuService.GetDescription(pizza);
        lines.Add($"- {pizza}: {price} {config.Currency}");
        lines.Add($"  {desc}");
    }

    return string.Join("\n", lines);
}
```

If you change the values in appsettings.json and restart the server, the new values are picked up automatically. No code changes required. For scenarios where you need live reloading without a restart, look into IOptionsMonitor<T> instead of IOptions<T>.

Logging

Your MCP server uses `stdout` for JSON-RPC, so log messages need to go elsewhere: `stderr`. The MCP protocol specification requires that all protocol messages travel over `stdout` (or a similar dedicated channel). Everything else, including log output, must stay off that channel.

The .NET console logging provider writes to `stdout` by default, which would corrupt the protocol stream. To fix this, you configure the console logger to send everything to `stderr` instead. The hosting framework makes this easy with a single configuration key. Have a look at the appsettings.json configuration for this in Listing 9-10 underneath.

Listing 9-10. Redirecting console logs to stderr

```
{
    "Logging": {
        "LogLevel": {
            "Default": "Information",
                "Microsoft": "Warning",
                "DiServer": "Debug"
        },
            "Console": {
                "LogToStandardErrorThreshold": "Trace"
            }
    }
}
```

The `LogToStandardErrorThreshold` setting tells the console provider to redirect any log entry at or above the specified level to `stderr`. Setting it to Trace means every log message goes to `stderr`, which is exactly what you want for an MCP server.

Tip This is one of the most common gotchas when building MCP servers with .NET. If your server mysteriously fails to connect, check whether your logging output is leaking into `stdout`. The `LogToStandardErrorThreshold` setting is your friend.

With the configuration in place, you can use `ILogger`<T> freely throughout your tools and services, you can see some example lines of this in Listing 9-11 below. The structured logging pattern with curly brace placeholders works perfectly and gives you searchable, structured log entries.

Listing 9-11. Structured logging in a tool

```
logger.LogInformation("Price lookup for {Pizza}", pizzaName);
logger.LogWarning("Pizza not found: {Pizza}", pizzaName);
logger.LogError(ex, "Failed to fetch data from {Url}", url);
```

Notice that I am using named placeholders like `{Pizza}` instead of string interpolation. This is important. String interpolation evaluates immediately, which wastes CPU cycles if the log level is filtered out. The placeholder approach lets the logging framework decide whether to format the message at all. It also produces structured data that log aggregation tools like Seq or Application Insights can index and query.

HttpClient Integration

Many MCP tools need to call external APIs. Maybe you are fetching weather data, looking up stock prices, or in our case retrieving a random joke. The .NET way to do this is `IHttpClientFactory`, and it integrates beautifully with the DI container.

Registering the HttpClient Factory

Registration is a one-liner, you can see it in Listing 9-12 down below. Add the Microsoft. Extensions.Http NuGet package to your project and then call `AddHttpClient` on the service collection.

Listing 9-12. Registering IHttpClientFactory

```
builder.Services.AddHttpClient();
```

That single line registers `IHttpClientFactory` in the container. Under the hood, it manages a pool of HttpMessageHandler instances so you do not run into socket exhaustion, a notorious problem when you create `HttpClient` instances manually.

Calling an External API from a Tool

With the factory registered, you can inject it into any tool. Here is a fun example, seen in Listing 9-13 below, that fetches a random joke from a public API.

Listing 9-13. A tool that fetches jokes from an external API

```
[McpServerToolType]
public class JokeTools
{
    [McpServerTool, Description("Fetches a random joke from an API.")]
    public static async Task<string> GetJoke(
        IHttpClientFactory httpClientFactory,
        ILogger<JokeTools> logger)
    {
        logger.LogInformation("Fetching a joke...");

        var client = httpClientFactory.CreateClient();
        client.DefaultRequestHeaders.Add("Accept", "application/json");

        try
        {
            var response = await client.GetStringAsync(
                "https://official-joke-api.appspot.com/random_joke");

            var joke = JsonDocument.Parse(response);
            var setup = joke.RootElement
                .GetProperty("setup")
                .GetString();

            var punchline = joke.RootElement
                .GetProperty("punchline")
                .GetString();

            return $"{setup}\n\n{punchline}";
        }
```

```
        catch (Exception ex)
        {
            logger.LogError(ex, "Failed to fetch joke");

            return "Could not fetch a joke right now. Try again later!";
        }
    }
}
```

A few things to notice here. First, the method is async and returns `Task<string>`. The SDK handles async tools just fine. Second, the error handling is important. External APIs can fail for a thousand reasons, and you do not want your MCP server to crash because a joke service is having a bad day. Returning a friendly message keeps the conversation going.

Tip If you call the same API frequently, consider using a named or typed client. You can configure the base address and default headers in one place: `builder.Services.AddHttpClient("JokeApi", client => { client.BaseAddress = new Uri("https://..."); });`. Then resolve it by name in your tool.

Database Integration Patterns

For many real-world MCP servers, the data lives in a database. Entity Framework Core works perfectly with the DI setup we have been building. I will keep this section brief because EF Core is a big topic on its own, but I want you to see how naturally it fits.

Setting Up a DbContext

Suppose you want to store pizza orders. You would create a `DbContext` and register it in the container, you can see both of those things in Listing 9-14. EF Core contexts are typically registered as scoped services, which is exactly right for MCP tools because each tool invocation gets its own scope.

Listing 9-14. Registering an EF core DbContext

```
public class PizzaDbContext : DbContext
{
    public PizzaDbContext(DbContextOptions<PizzaDbContext> options)
        : base(options) { }

    public DbSet<Order> Orders => Set<Order>();
}

// In Program.cs
builder.Services.AddDbContext<PizzaDbContext>(options => options.UseSqlite(
    "Data Source=pizzas.db"));
```

Once registered, you can inject `PizzaDbContext` into your tools the same way you inject any other service like in Listing 9-15. The SDK resolves it from the scoped container and you can query or save data as you normally would.

Listing 9-15. Using DbContext in a tool

```
[McpServerTool, Description("Places a pizza order.")]
public static async Task<string> PlaceOrder(
    [Description("Pizza name")] string pizza,
    PizzaDbContext db,
    ILogger<OrderTools> logger)
{
    var order = new Order
    {
        PizzaName = pizza,
        OrderedAt = DateTime.UtcNow
    };

    db.Orders.Add(order);

    await db.SaveChangesAsync();

    logger.LogInformation("Order {Id} placed for {Pizza}", order.Id, pizza);
    return $"Order #{order.Id} confirmed!";
}
```

This pattern scales beautifully. As your MCP server grows, you can add repositories, unit-of-work abstractions, or whatever data access patterns your team prefers. The DI container ties it all together.

Putting It All Together

Time to bring everything from this chapter together into one complete `Program.cs`. The code in Listing 9-16 is the server you will find in the companion source code for this chapter. It registers a custom service, binds configuration, adds HTTP client support, and wires up the MCP server with tool discovery.

Listing 9-16. The complete Program.cs

```
using DiServer.Models;
using DiServer.Services;
using Microsoft.Extensions.DependencyInjection;
using Microsoft.Extensions.Hosting;
using ModelContextProtocol.Server;

var builder = Host.CreateEmptyApplicationBuilder(null);

// Bind configuration
builder.Services
    .Configure<PizzaServerOptions>(
    builder.Configuration.GetSection(
    PizzaServerOptions.SectionName));

// Register custom services
builder.Services
    .AddSingleton<IPizzaMenuService, PizzaMenuService>();

// Register HttpClient factory
builder.Services.AddHttpClient();

// Configure MCP server
builder.Services
    .AddMcpServer()
```

```
    .WithStdioServerTransport()
    .WithToolsFromAssembly();

await builder.Build().RunAsync();
```

Look at how clean that is. Twelve lines of real code (ignoring blanks and comments) and you have a fully configured MCP server with dependency injection, custom services, configuration binding, HTTP client support, and automatic tool discovery. The .NET hosting stack does the heavy lifting while you focus on writing the tools that make your server useful.

The project structure for this server is straightforward, see Listing 9-17. I keep things organized by creating folders for the different concerns.

Listing 9-17. Project structure for the DiServer sample

```
DiServer/
    Program.cs
    appsettings.json
    DiServer.csproj
Models/
    PizzaServerOptions.cs
Services/
    IPizzaMenuService.cs
    PizzaMenuService.cs
Tools/
    PizzaTools.cs
    JokeTools.cs
```

This is the same layout you would see in any well-structured .NET application. Models hold your data and configuration classes. Services contain your business logic behind interfaces. Tools contain the MCP tool definitions that tie everything together. As your server grows, you can add more folders like Repositories, Middleware, or whatever fits your architecture.

Testing the Server

You can test this server the same way you tested servers in earlier chapters. Add it to your MCP client configuration and try asking the AI to show you the pizza menu or tell you a joke. The AI will discover the `GetMenu`, `GetPizzaPrice`, and `GetJoke` tools through the MCP protocol and call them as needed.

What is happening behind the scenes is worth appreciating. When the AI calls `GetMenu`, the SDK creates a DI scope, resolves `IPizzaMenuService` as a singleton, resolves `IOptions<PizzaServerOptions>` from the configuration system, and resolves `ILogger`<PizzaTools> from the logging infrastructure. All of that happens in milliseconds, and your tool method never needs to know about it. When the AI calls `GetJoke`, the SDK resolves `IHttpClientFactory` and hands your tool a properly managed HTTP client. Clean, testable, and production-ready.

A Note on Service Lifetimes

Choosing the right service lifetime matters more than you might think. Here is a quick guide for MCP servers specifically:

- Use `AddSingleton` for services that are truly stateless or hold data that never changes during the server's lifetime. Our `PizzaMenuService` is a good example.
- Use `AddScoped` for services that need a fresh instance per tool invocation but can be shared within that invocation. Database contexts are the classic example.
- Use `AddTransient` for lightweight services where you do not care about instance sharing. Be careful with transient services that hold resources like file handles or network connections.

A common mistake is registering a `DbContext` as a singleton. Entity Framework contexts track changes and are not thread-safe, so sharing one across tool invocations will lead to subtle bugs and data corruption. Always keep them scoped.

Summary

That was quite a journey: you learned how to turn a simple MCP server into a properly structured .NET application with dependency injection at its core. You saw how the SDK automatically resolves services from the DI container when invoking tool methods, which means you can inject loggers, configuration, HTTP clients, database contexts, and any custom service you build. Look, once you see this pattern, you will use it everywhere. You learned the importance of redirecting console logs to `stderr` so they do not interfere with the MCP protocol on `stdout`. And you saw how `IOptions`<T> gives you strongly typed, maintainable configuration.

What makes this work is that everything you already know about .NET dependency injection applies directly. If you have built ASP.NET Core applications or .NET worker services, you are on familiar ground. The MCP SDK does not reinvent the wheel. It simply plugs into the existing ecosystem and lets you use the tools you already know and love.

Up to this point, we have focused entirely on the server side of MCP. You have been building tools, resources, and prompts that an AI model can use. But what about the other side of the conversation? In Chapter 10, we will flip the perspective and build an MCP client. You will learn how to connect to MCP servers programmatically, discover their capabilities, and invoke their tools from your own C# code. It is a fascinating change of viewpoint that will deepen your understanding of how the entire MCP ecosystem fits together.

CHAPTER 10

Building an MCP Client

So far in this book, we have spent all of our time on the server side. We have built tools, exposed resources, defined prompts, configured transports, and wired up dependency injection. Every time we wanted to test our work, we reached for an existing client like Claude Desktop or GitHub Copilot in VS Code. That is perfectly fine for many scenarios, but what happens when you need to talk to an MCP server from your own code?

Now we flip the script. Instead of building servers, we are going to build a client. The C# SDK ships with a client API that lets you connect to any MCP server, discover its capabilities, call its tools, read its resources, and retrieve its prompts. By the end of this chapter, you will have a fully working console application that connects to our Cosmic Pizza server and interacts with it programmatically.

If you have been building MCP servers and wondering how the other side of the conversation works, you are about to find out.

Building the client side after spending chapters on the server side is a bit like seeing your house from across the street for the first time. Same building, completely different perspective.

Why Build a Client?

Before we start writing code, allow me to convince you that building your own MCP client is worth the effort. You might be thinking that Claude Desktop and VS Code (and many others) already handle the client side, so why would you ever need to write one yourself? The answer is that not every use case fits neatly into an AI chat interface. Here's the thing: sometimes you need full programmatic control.

Imagine you are building an automated pipeline that needs to pull data from an MCP server as part of a larger workflow. Maybe you have a batch process that calls MCP tools to generate reports every night. Or perhaps you are building a custom dashboard that queries MCP resources to display real-time information. None of these scenarios involve a human sitting in front of a chat window typing prompts.

G. Versluis, *Building MCP Servers with C#*, https://doi.org/10.1007/979-8-8688-3010-5_10

By the time that you are reading this, there are probably already great solutions for all these scenarios as well that you can just start using without manually building something yourself. But you might still run into situations where this can be beneficial to build yourself. Or, at the very least, you know how things work under the hood.

Here are some concrete use cases where a custom MCP client might make sense:

- **Automated testing:** You can write integration tests that spin up your MCP server, call its tools, and verify the results. This is something we will explore more in the next chapter.
- **Backend integrations:** Your web API or background service can act as an MCP client, calling tools on remote MCP servers to gather data or trigger actions.
- **Custom AI agents:** If you are building your own AI agent using a library like Semantic Kernel or `Microsoft.Extensions.AI`, you can use the MCP client to dynamically discover and invoke tools from any MCP server.
- **Development utilities:** A simple console client can help you debug and explore MCP servers during development, much like Postman helps with REST APIs.

The MCP protocol is designed to be symmetric. The same JSON-RPC messages flow in both directions, and the C# SDK provides first-class support for both sides of the conversation. Building a client is not a secondary use case. It is a core capability of the SDK.

Creating a Client with McpClient

The entry point for creating an MCP client in C# is the `McpClient.CreateAsync` method. This static factory method takes a transport, connects to the server, performs the protocol handshake, and returns a fully initialized client ready for use. It handles all the low-level details of the MCP initialization sequence so you do not have to.

The simplest call is shown in Listing 10-1.

Listing 10-1. Creating a basic MCP client

```
await using var client = await McpClient.CreateAsync(
    new StdioClientTransport(new()
    {
        Command = "dotnet",
        Arguments = ["run", "--project", "./MyServer"],
        Name = "My Server",
    }));
```

That single call does quite a lot behind the scenes. It launches the server process, establishes the transport connection, sends the initialize request, and waits for the server to respond with its capabilities. When `CreateAsync` returns, you have a live connection to the server and you can start making requests immediately.

Notice the await using pattern. `McpClient` implements `IAsyncDisposable`, which means it will cleanly shut down the connection and terminate the server process when the client goes out of scope. This is important because stdio-based servers run as child processes, and you want to make sure they get properly cleaned up.

The `CreateAsync` method accepts a few optional parameters beyond the transport. You can pass `McpClientOptions` to configure client capabilities and protocol settings, and an `ILoggerFactory` for diagnostics. Here is a more complete example.

Listing 10-2. Creating a client with options

```
await using var client = await McpClient.CreateAsync(
    new StdioClientTransport(new()
    {
        Command = "dotnet",
        Arguments = ["run", "--project", serverPath],
        Name = "Pizza Server",
    }),
    clientOptions: new()
    {
        ClientInfo = new()
        {
```

```
            Name = "My Client",
            Version = "1.0.0"
        }
    });
```

The `ClientInfo` property lets you identify your client to the server. This information is sent during the initialization handshake and can be useful for server-side logging and diagnostics. If you do not provide it, the SDK will use defaults based on the current process.

Once connected, you can inspect the server's information through the `ServerInfo` and `ServerCapabilities` properties. Have a look at the code in Listing 10-3 below that queries some of these properties.

Listing 10-3. Reading server information

```
Console.WriteLine($"Server: {client.ServerInfo.Name}");
Console.WriteLine($"Version: {client.ServerInfo.Version}");

var caps = client.ServerCapabilities;

Console.WriteLine($"Tools: {caps.Tools is not null}");
Console.WriteLine($"Resources: {caps.Resources is not null}");
Console.WriteLine($"Prompts: {caps.Prompts is not null}");
```

The `ServerCapabilities` object tells you which features the server supports. If the `Tools` property is not `null`, the server has tools you can call. If `Resources` is not `null`, it exposes resources. This lets you build clients that adapt to whatever server they connect to, rather than hardcoding assumptions about what is available.

Connecting via stdio

As we've already seen, the `StdioClientTransport` is a most common way to connect to an MCP server during development. It launches the server as a subprocess and communicates through standard input and output. This is the same mechanism that Claude Desktop and VS Code use when they start your MCP servers.

When you create a `StdioClientTransport`, as seen in Listing 10-4, you need to provide at least two pieces of information: the command to run and a name for the server. The command is the executable that starts your server, and the name is a human-readable label used in logging.

Listing 10-4. StdioClientTransport configuration

```
var transport = new StdioClientTransport(
    new()
    {
        Command = "dotnet",
        Arguments = ["run", "--project", "../CosmicPizzaServer"],
        Name = "Cosmic Pizza",
    });
```

The `Command` property is the executable to launch. For .NET servers, this is typically `dotnet`, with the `run` command and project path passed as `Arguments`. But it can be any executable. If you are connecting to a Python MCP server, the command might be `python` or `uv`. For a Node.js server, it could be `npx`.

The transport handles all the process lifecycle management for you. It starts the process when the client connects and terminates it when the client is disposed. You do not need to manage child processes yourself.

Note When using `StdioClientTransport`, the server process inherits the current working directory and environment variables from the client process. If your server needs specific environment variables, make sure they are set before creating the transport.

One thing to keep in mind with stdio is that the server must be a local process. You cannot use `StdioClientTransport` to connect to a server running on another machine. For remote servers you need HTTP, which we will look at next.

Connecting via HTTP

For servers that are running remotely or deployed as web services, the SDK provides the `HttpClientTransport`. This transport uses the Streamable HTTP protocol we discussed in Chapter 8, where the client sends JSON-RPC requests over HTTP POST and receives responses back, with optional streaming via Server-Sent Events.

Creating an HTTP client is just as simple as creating a stdio one. You just swap the transport. Have a look at Listing 10-5 below for an example.

Listing 10-5. Connecting via HTTP transport

```
var transport = new HttpClientTransport(
    new()
    {
        Endpoint = new Uri("http://localhost:5000"),
    });

await using var client = await McpClient.CreateAsync(transport);
```

The `HttpClientTransport` sends all requests to the specified endpoint. The SDK handles session management, request serialization, and response parsing automatically. From your code's perspective, calling tools and reading resources works exactly the same way regardless of whether you are using stdio or HTTP.

If you need to provide custom HTTP headers, for example, for authentication, you can configure the underlying `HttpClient`. This is shown in Listing 10-6 underneath. The transport accepts an `HttpClient` instance through its options, giving you full control over the HTTP pipeline.

Listing 10-6. HTTP transport with custom headers

```
var httpClient = new HttpClient();

httpClient.DefaultRequestHeaders.Add("Authorization", "Bearer my-api-key");

var transport = new HttpClientTransport(
    new()
    {
        Endpoint = new Uri("https://api.example.com/mcp"),
    }, httpClient);

await using var client =
    await McpClient.CreateAsync(transport);
```

This pattern is especially useful when your MCP server sits behind an API gateway or requires OAuth tokens. You configure authentication on the `HttpClient` just like you would for any other HTTP API, and the MCP transport carries those headers along with every request.

Tip If you have been following along from Chapter 8 where we built an HTTP-based MCP server, you can use `HttpClientTransport` to connect your client to it. Just make sure the server is running before you start the client.

Listing Available Tools

Once you have a connected client, the first thing you will probably want to do is find out what the server can do. The `ListToolsAsync` method retrieves a list of all tools the server exposes. In Listing 10-7 you can see how I call the list method and then loop through that to query the properties of each tool.

Listing 10-7. Listing tools from a server

```
var tools = await client.ListToolsAsync();
Console.WriteLine($"Found {tools.Count} tool(s):");

foreach (var tool in tools)
{
    Console.WriteLine($"  {tool.Name}");
    Console.WriteLine($"    {tool.Description}");
}
```

The method returns an `IList` of `McpClientTool` objects. Each tool has a `Name`, a `Description`, and a `JsonSchema` property that describes its input parameters. The name is what you use to call the tool, and the description tells you what it does.

The `JsonSchema` property is particularly interesting. It is a `JsonElement` containing the JSON Schema that defines the tool's parameters. You can use this to dynamically build user interfaces, generate documentation, or validate input before sending it to the server. An example of looping through this data is seen in Listing 10-8.

Listing 10-8. Reading tool parameter schemas

```
foreach (var tool in tools)
{
    Console.WriteLine($"Tool: {tool.Name}");

    var schema = tool.JsonSchema;

    if (schema.TryGetProperty("properties", out var props))
    {
        Console.WriteLine("  Parameters:");
        foreach (var prop in props.EnumerateObject())
        {
            Console.WriteLine($"    {prop.Name}: {prop.Value}");
        }
    }
}
```

If you are building a dynamic client that needs to work with any MCP server, the schema gives you everything you need to construct valid tool calls at runtime. This is exactly how AI clients like Claude Desktop work. They read the schema, understand what parameters are needed, and generate the appropriate arguments. Figure 10-1 shows example console output from listing tools and their schemas.

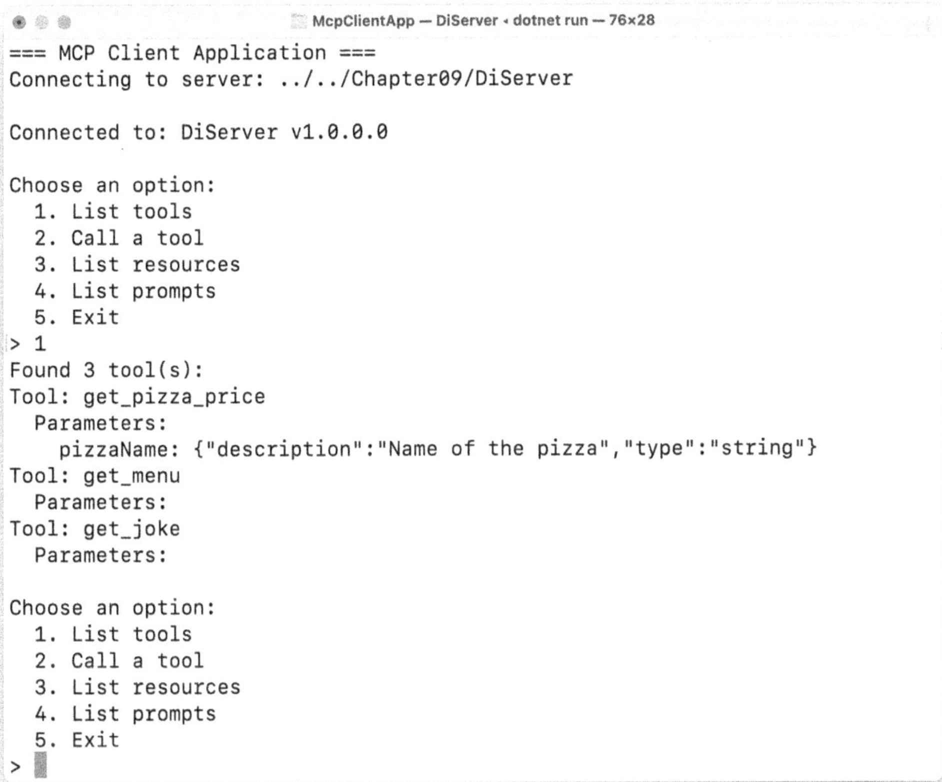

Figure 10-1. *Console output from the MCP client listing available tools and their parameter schemas*

Calling Tools

Discovering tools is useful, but the real power comes from calling them. The `CallToolAsync` method lets you invoke any tool by name and pass arguments as a dictionary. Have a look at Listing 9-10 to see how we can call a tool.

Listing 10-9. Calling a tool with arguments

```
var result = await client.CallToolAsync("get_pizza_price",
    new Dictionary<string, object?>
    {
```

```
        ["pizzaName"] = "Margherita"
    });

foreach (var content in result.Content)
{
    if (content is TextContentBlock text)
    {
        Console.WriteLine(text.Text);
    }
}
```

The method takes the tool name as a string and an optional dictionary of arguments. The keys in the dictionary must match the parameter names defined in the tool's JSON Schema. The values can be strings, numbers, booleans, or any type that serializes to JSON.

The result is a `CallToolResult` object that contains a `Content` collection. Each item in the collection is a `ContentBlock`, which is a base type that can be a `TextContentBlock`, an `ImageContentBlock`, or other content types defined by the protocol. For most tools, you will be working with `TextContentBlock`, which has a `Text` property containing the tool's response.

For tools that do not require any arguments, you can omit the dictionary entirely. Listing 10-10 shows an example of a tool call without any arguments.

Listing 10-10. Calling a tool without arguments

```
var menuResult = await client.CallToolAsync("get_menu");
foreach (var content in menuResult.Content)
{
    if (content is TextContentBlock text)
    {
        Console.WriteLine(text.Text);
    }
}
```

Handling Errors

Tool calls can fail for various reasons. The tool might not exist, the arguments might be invalid, or the server might encounter an internal error. The SDK handles these cases by throwing an `McpException`. Have a look at Listing 10-11 to see an example of how to handle that scenario.

Listing 10-11. Handling tool call errors

```
try
{
    var result = await client.CallToolAsync("non_existent_tool");
}
catch (McpException ex)
{
    Console.WriteLine($"Tool call failed: {ex.Message}");
}
```

You can also check the `IsError` property on the `CallToolResult` to determine if the tool itself reported an error without throwing an exception. Some tools choose to return error information in the result content rather than throwing. This you can see in Listing 10-12 below.

Listing 10-12. Checking for tool-reported errors

```
var result = await client.CallToolAsync("get_pizza_price",
    new Dictionary<string, object?>
    {
        ["pizzaName"] = "Unknown"
    });

if (result.IsError)
{
    Console.WriteLine("The tool reported an error.");
}
```

The distinction between exceptions and error results is important. An `McpException` means something went wrong at the protocol level, like a communication failure or a missing tool. An `IsError` result means the tool executed but reported that it could not complete the request successfully. Handle both cases in your client code.

Working with Resources

Resources are another key feature of the MCP protocol. While tools let you perform actions, resources let you read data. Think of resources as a read-only data layer that the server exposes to clients.

Listing resources works just like listing tools, but for completeness find some example code in Listing 10-13 underneath.

Listing 10-13. Listing available resources

```
var resources = await client.ListResourcesAsync();
foreach (var resource in resources)
{
    Console.WriteLine($"  {resource.Name}");
    Console.WriteLine($"    URI: {resource.Uri}");
    Console.WriteLine($"    Type: {resource.MimeType}");
}
```

Each resource has a `Name`, a `Uri` that uniquely identifies it, and an optional `MimeType` that tells you what kind of data it contains. To actually read the resource's content, you use `ReadResourceAsync` with the resource's URI. Listing 10-14 shows and example of this.

Listing 10-14. Reading a resource

```
var content = await client.ReadResourceAsync("pizza://menu/full");

foreach (var item in content.Contents)
{
    if (item is TextResourceContents text)
    {
        Console.WriteLine(text.Text);
    }
}
```

The `ReadResourceAsync` method returns a ReadResourceResult containing one or more content items. Text resources come back as `TextResourceContents` with a `Text` property, while binary resources come back as `BlobResourceContents` with Base64-encoded data.

Resource Templates

In addition to static resources, servers can expose resource templates. These are parameterized URIs that let you request specific data. For example, a server might expose a template like `pizza://menu/{category}` that lets you request pizzas from a specific category. Listing these can be seen in Listing 10-15.

Listing 10-15. Listing resource templates

```
var templates = await client.ListResourceTemplatesAsync();

foreach (var template in templates)
{
    Console.WriteLine($"  {template.Name}");
    Console.WriteLine($"    URI: {template.UriTemplate}");
}
```

Resource templates are a powerful way to expose dynamic data through MCP. The client can discover available templates, understand their parameters from the URI pattern, and construct specific resource URIs to read exactly the data it needs.

Using Prompts

Prompts are reusable templates that servers provide to help clients construct effective messages for LLMs. From the client side, you can discover what prompts are available and retrieve them with specific arguments. In Listing 10-16 you can see how to list the prompts either through a list, or retrieving a specific one.

Listing 10-16. Listing and retrieving prompts

```
var prompts = await client.ListPromptsAsync();

foreach (var prompt in prompts)
{
    Console.WriteLine($"  {prompt.Name}: {prompt.Description}");
}

// Retrieve a specific prompt
var result = await client.GetPromptAsync("order-pizza",
```

```
    new Dictionary<string, string>
    {
        ["customerName"] = "Gerald"
    });

foreach (var message in result.Messages)
{
    Console.WriteLine($"  [{message.Role}] {message.Content}");
}
```

The `ListPromptsAsync` method returns a list of `McpClientPrompt` objects, each with a `Name` and `Description`. To get the actual prompt content, you call `GetPromptAsync` with the prompt name and any required arguments.

The result contains a `Messages` collection with the prompt's content structured as chat messages. Each message has a `Role` (like user or assistant) and `Content`. This structure maps directly to how most LLM APIs expect their input, making it easy to feed MCP prompts into your AI pipeline.

Prompts are a sometimes overlooked feature of MCP, but they are incredibly useful for standardizing how your organization interacts with LLMs. A server can provide carefully crafted prompt templates, and any client can retrieve and use them without having to hardcode prompt text.

Sampling with Tool Calling

So far, we've looked at the client calling the server. But MCP also supports a pattern where the server asks the client to generate an LLM completion. This is called sampling, and it's one of the more powerful features in the protocol. With the v1.0 SDK, sampling now supports tools as well, which means the server can send a sampling request that includes tool definitions, and the client's LLM can call those tools as part of its response. Nice, right?

The key insight is this: the client is the one with access to the LLM. The server doesn't have that. So when the server needs a completion, it sends a sampling request back through the MCP connection. The client picks it up, routes it to whatever LLM it's configured with, and sends the result back. With tool support, the LLM can even invoke tools during that process, making the whole interaction much richer.

Figure 10-2 shows how sampling with tool calling works. The server sends a `CreateMessage` request with tool definitions to the client. The client forwards it to the LLM, which may request tool calls. The server executes those tools locally and sends the results back in a new `CreateMessage` request. This loop continues until the LLM produces a final response.

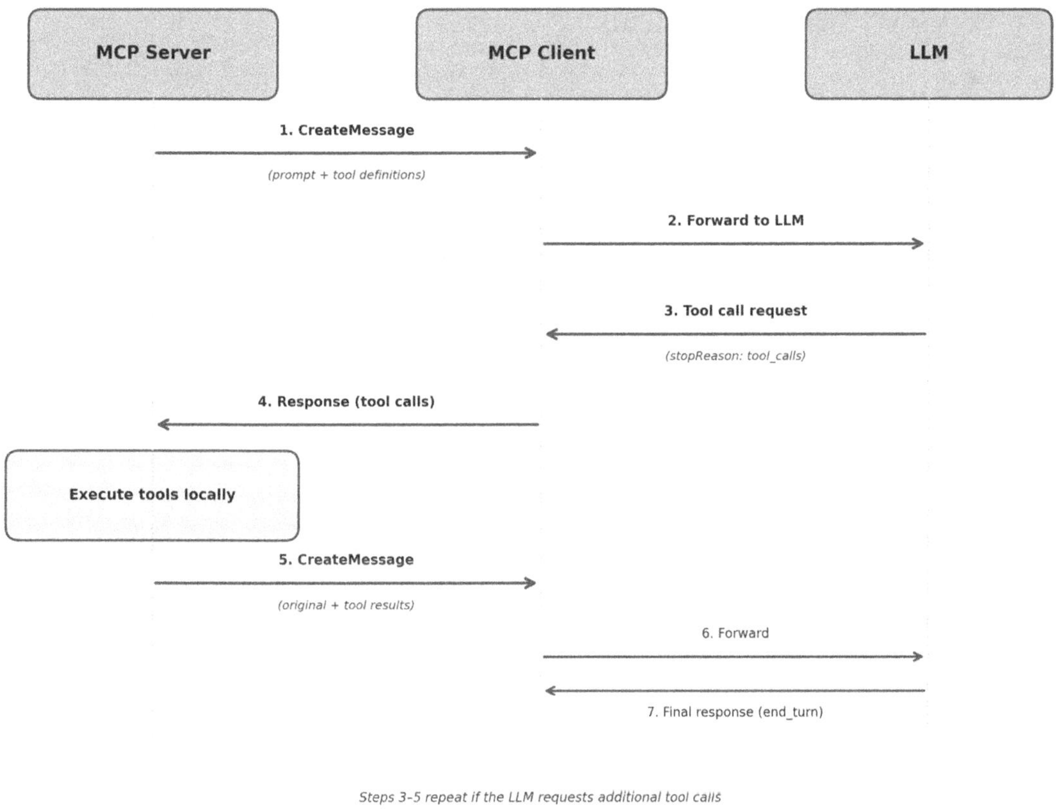

Figure 10-2. *The sampling with tool calling flow between server, client, and LLM*

On the client side, you need to opt in to sampling when you create your client. You do this by declaring the sampling capability and providing a SamplingHandler on the Handlers property of `McpClientOptions`. If you're already using an `IChatClient` from `Microsoft.Extensions.AI`, you can call `CreateSamplingHandler()` on it to get a handler that automatically wires everything up. Listing 10-17 shows how to do this.

Listing 10-17. Configuring sampling support on the client

```
var mcpClient = await McpClient.CreateAsync(
    new HttpClientTransport(new()
    {
        Endpoint = new Uri("http://localhost:6184"),
        Name = "SamplingWithTools MCP Server",
    }),
    clientOptions: new()
    {
        Capabilities = new ClientCapabilities
        {
            Sampling = new SamplingCapability
            {
                Tools = new SamplingToolsCapability {}
            }
        },
        Handlers = new()
        {
            SamplingHandler = async (c, p, t) =>
            {
                return await samplingHandler(c, p, t);
            },
        }
    });
```

The samplingHandler variable used above is created using the CreateSamplingHandler extension method on an IChatClient instance. You can create one from any chat client, such as one backed by OpenAI.

```
IChatClient chatClient = new OpenAIClient(apiKey)
    .GetChatClient(modelId)
    .AsIChatClient();

var samplingHandler =
    chatClient.CreateSamplingHandler();
```

On the server side, you can get an `IChatClient` that routes through the connected client's LLM by calling `AsSamplingChatClient()` on the `McpServer` instance. From there, you can use it like any other chat client. If you want the LLM to automatically invoke tools, compose it with `UseFunctionInvocation()`. Listing 10-18 shows how a server-side tool might use sampling.

Listing 10-18. Server-side sampling with tool calling

```
IChatClient chatClient = ChatClientBuilderChatClientExtensions
    .AsBuilder(_mcpServer.AsSamplingChatClient())
    .UseFunctionInvocation()
    .Build();
```

The flow here is straightforward: the server creates a sampling chat client, sends a message with optional tool definitions, and the client's LLM handles the rest. The result flows back to the server just like any other chat completion. This opens up scenarios where the server can use the client's LLM without needing its own.

Elicitation

Sometimes a server needs actual user input, not just an LLM completion. That's where elicitation comes in. Elicitation lets the server request structured input from the user through the client. Think of scenarios like OAuth consent screens, complex form input, or secure data entry. Instead of trying to hack around the protocol, elicitation gives you a proper mechanism for it.

The v1.0 SDK introduces elicitation support. The server sends a message and optionally a URL to the client. The client can open the URL in a browser or embedded view, the user provides input, and the data flows back to the server. This is great for things like OAuth flows where you need the user to interact with a third-party service. On the server side, you call `McpServer.ElicitAsync()` with a message, a schema describing the expected input, and an optional URL.

To enable this on the client side, you need to declare the elicitation capability and provide an `ElicitationHandler` on the `Handlers` property of `McpClientOptions`. The handler receives `ElicitRequestParams` and returns an `ElicitResult`. Listing 10-19 shows how to configure this.

Listing 10-19. Configuring elicitation on the client

```
McpClientOptions options = new()
{
    Capabilities = new ClientCapabilities
    {
        Elicitation = new ElicitationCapability
        {
            Url = new UrlElicitationCapability()
        }
    }
};
```

The handler goes on the Handlers property when creating the client. It receives ElicitRequestParams and should check the `Mode` and `Url` properties to determine what kind of elicitation the server is requesting. Listing 10-20 shows a handler that processes URL-mode elicitation requests.

Listing 10-20. Elicitation request handler

```
async ValueTask<ElicitResult> HandleElicitationAsync(
    ElicitRequestParams? requestParams,
    CancellationToken token)
{
    if (requestParams is null || requestParams.Mode != "url" ||
    requestParams.Url is null)
    {
        return new ElicitResult();
    }

    // Open the URL for the user
    Process.Start(new ProcessStartInfo
        {
            FileName = requestParams.Url,
            UseShellExecute = true
        });
```

```
    return new ElicitResult
    {
        Action = "accept",
        Content = new Dictionary<string, JsonElement>
        {
            ["confirmed"] = JsonSerializer .SerializeToElement(true)
        }
    };
}
```

Putting It All Together

Let us tie everything together by building a complete console application that connects to an MCP server and exercises all of the features we have explored in this chapter. The application will discover tools, call them with dynamically collected arguments, list resources and prompts, and present it all through a simple interactive menu. You will find the complete source code in the Chapter 10 companion project. Below in Listing 10-21 you can see the csproj file for our server. Underneath that, in Listing 10-22 you can see the first portion of the Program.cs file that starts the MCP server main loop.

Setting Up the Project

Listing 10-21. McpClientApp.csproj (excerpt)

```
<Project Sdk="Microsoft.NET.Sdk">
    <PropertyGroup>
        <OutputType>Exe</OutputType>
        <TargetFramework>net10.0</TargetFramework>
    </PropertyGroup>
    <ItemGroup>
        <PackageReference Include="ModelContextProtocol" Version="1.3.0" />
    </ItemGroup>
</Project>
```

Listing 10-22. Program.cs setup (excerpt)

```
using ModelContextProtocol;
using ModelContextProtocol.Client;
using ModelContextProtocol.Protocol;

var serverPath = args.Length > 0
    ? args[0]
    : "../../Chapter09/DiServer";

Console.WriteLine("=== MCP Client Application ===");
Console.WriteLine($"Connecting to server: {serverPath}");
Console.WriteLine();

await using var client = await McpClient.CreateAsync(
        new StdioClientTransport(new()
        {
            Command = "dotnet",
            Arguments = ["run", "--project", serverPath],
            Name = "Cosmic Pizza Server",
        }));

Console.WriteLine($"Connected to: "
    + $"{client.ServerInfo.Name} "
    + $"v{client.ServerInfo.Version}");

Console.WriteLine();
```

The setup is straightforward. We accept an optional command-line argument for the server path, defaulting to the DiServer project from Chapter 9. The client connects over stdio, just like we saw earlier in this chapter, and immediately prints the server information to confirm the connection is alive. In Listing 10-23 below you see another part of the Program.cs file. The explanation is below the code block.

Listing 10-23. The main interaction loop

```
while (true)
{
    Console.WriteLine("Choose an option:");
    Console.WriteLine("  1. List tools");
```

```
    Console.WriteLine("  2. Call a tool");
    Console.WriteLine("  3. List resources");
    Console.WriteLine("  4. List prompts");
    Console.WriteLine("  5. Exit");
    Console.Write("> ");

    var choice = Console.ReadLine()?.Trim();

    switch (choice)
    {
        case "1":
            await ListTools(client);
            break;

        case "2":
            await CallTool(client);
            break;

        case "3":
            await ListResources(client);
            break;

        case "4":
            await ListPrompts(client);
            break;

        case "5":
            Console.WriteLine("Goodbye!");
            return;
    }

    Console.WriteLine();
}
```

The loop presents a simple menu and dispatches to helper methods. Let us look at the most interesting one, the `CallTool` method, which dynamically discovers tool parameters and collects input from the user. You can see the method below in Listing 10-24.

Listing 10-24. Dynamic tool calling helper

```
static async Task CallTool(McpClient client)
{
    var tools = await client.ListToolsAsync();

    Console.WriteLine("Available tools:");

    for (var i = 0; i < tools.Count; i++)
    {
        Console.WriteLine($"  {i + 1}. {tools[i].Name}");
    }

    Console.Write("Select a tool number: ");

    if (!int.TryParse(Console.ReadLine(), out var num)
        || num < 1
        || num > tools.Count)
    {
        Console.WriteLine("Invalid selection.");
        return;
    }

    var selected = tools[num - 1];
    var arguments = new Dictionary<string, string>();
    var schema = selected.JsonSchema;

    if (schema.TryGetProperty("properties", out var props))
    {
        foreach (var prop in props.EnumerateObject())
        {
            Console.Write($"  {prop.Name}: ");
            var value = Console.ReadLine();

            if (!string.IsNullOrEmpty(value))
                arguments[prop.Name] = value;
        }
    }
```

```
    try
    {
        var result = await client.CallToolAsync(selected.Name,
            arguments.Count > 0 ? arguments : null);

        Console.WriteLine("Result:");

        foreach (var content in result.Content)
        {
            if (content is TextContentBlock txt)
            Console.WriteLine($"  {txt.Text}");
        }
    }
    catch (McpException ex)
    {
        Console.WriteLine($"Error: {ex.Message}");
    }
}
```

This helper is a great example of what makes the MCP client API so powerful. We did not hardcode any tool names or parameters. Instead, we discover everything at runtime by reading the tool list and their JSON schemas. The code works with any MCP server, not just our pizza server. Point it at a weather server, a database server, or any other MCP-compliant server and it will adapt automatically.

Running the Application

To run the client application, make sure the server project from Chapter 9 is available at the expected path, then run the client with the command as seen in Listing 10-25 underneath.

Listing 10-25. Running the client application

```
$ dotnet run --project McpClientApp
```

You will see the client connect to the server and display the server information. From there, you can list tools, call them with arguments, and explore the server's capabilities. Try selecting option 1 to list tools, then option 2 to call `GetMenu` without any arguments. You should see the full pizza menu appear right in your terminal.

If you want to connect to a different server, just pass the project path as a command-line argument as shown in Listing 10-26.

Listing 10-26. Connecting to a different server

```
dotnet run --project McpClientApp -- ../path/to/other/serverproject
```

The double dash separates the `dotnet run` arguments from the application arguments. Everything after the double dash gets passed to your application.

Note The client application in this chapter is deliberately simple. It is meant to demonstrate the MCP client API, not to be a production-grade application. In a real scenario you would add proper error handling, logging, and possibly a more sophisticated user interface. But the API calls would be exactly the same.

Summary

Looking back at what we built: We switched perspectives from server to client. We learned why building a custom MCP client is valuable and explored the full client API provided by the C# SDK.

We started with `McpClient.CreateAsync`, the factory method that creates a connected client instance. We explored two transport options: `StdioClientTransport` for launching local server processes and `HttpClientTransport` for connecting to remote servers over HTTP. Both transports present an identical API, meaning your client code works the same regardless of how it connects.

We then worked through each of the major client operations. `ListToolsAsync` discovers available tools and their parameter schemas. `CallToolAsync` invokes tools with arguments and returns structured results. `ListResourcesAsync` and `ReadResourceAsync` give you access to the server's data layer. And `ListPromptsAsync` and `GetPromptAsync` let you retrieve reusable prompt templates.

Finally, we built a complete console application that ties all of these features together into an interactive MCP explorer. This application dynamically discovers server capabilities and adapts to whatever server it connects to, demonstrating the true power of the MCP protocol.

In the next chapter, we will use everything we have learned about clients and servers to write automated tests for our MCP servers. The client API you learned in this chapter is exactly what we will use to call our servers from test code and verify they behave correctly. Testing is a critical part of building reliable MCP servers, and Chapter 11 will show you how to do it right.

CHAPTER 11

Testing Your MCP Servers

We have spent the last ten chapters building MCP servers that expose tools, resources, and prompts to AI clients. We have explored transports, wired up dependency injection, and handled configuration. Our servers do interesting things, but there is one question we have not answered yet: how do you know they actually work correctly? Time to focus on everyone's all-time favorite topic: testing!

We're going to tackle testing head on. I will show you how to unit test your tool methods, integration test the full MCP pipeline using in-memory transports, exercise HTTP-based servers with `WebApplicationFactory`, and use the MCP Inspector for manual exploratory testing. By the time we are done, you will have a testing setup that catches bugs early, covering everything from individual methods to full end-to-end scenarios.

If testing feels like the broccoli of software development, I get it. But trust me when I say that testing MCP servers is actually kind of fun. The C# SDK gives us some really nice hooks that make testing surprisingly pleasant, and the payoff in confidence is absolutely worth the effort.

And, of course, if you really don't want to do it, ask Copilot...

Why Testing Matters

I know, I know. You have heard the speech about why testing matters a hundred times before. But MCP servers have a unique angle that makes testing even more important than usual. Your server sits between an AI model and the real world. When the model calls your tool to look up a customer record, send an email, or query a database, there is no human double-checking the result before it goes back into the conversation. If your tool returns bad data, the AI model will happily use that bad data to generate its response.

G. Versluis, *Building MCP Servers with C#*, https://doi.org/10.1007/979-8-8688-3010-5_11

Think about that for a moment. In a traditional web API, a human reads the response and can spot obvious mistakes. In an MCP workflow, the consumer is an AI model that has no intuition about whether a result looks right. It trusts your server completely. That trust is only as strong as the reliability of your code.

There is also a practical consideration. MCP servers are typically consumed through AI clients like Claude Desktop or GitHub Copilot in VS Code. Debugging a misbehaving tool through an AI chat interface is, frankly, miserable. You type a prompt, wait for the model to decide to call your tool, and then try to figure out what went wrong from the model's interpretation of the error. Automated tests let you skip all of that and verify behavior directly.

Finally, MCP servers evolve quickly. As you add new tools, update schemas, or refactor shared services, you need confidence that existing functionality still works. A solid test suite gives you that confidence and lets you move fast without breaking things.

Unit Testing Tool Methods

The simplest form of testing for an MCP server is unit testing the tool methods themselves. Remember that MCP tools are just regular C# methods decorated with attributes. Strip away the MCP ceremony and you are left with a method that takes some parameters and returns a result. That is exactly the kind of thing that unit tests are built for.

Let's start by creating a test project. I will use MSTest because it is the testing framework built into .NET and maintained by Microsoft. Everything we cover works just as well with xUnit or NUnit. We also need the Moq library for mocking dependencies. Open your terminal and create the project by using the commands as shown in Listing 11-1.

Listing 11-1. Creating an MSTest test project

```
$ dotnet new mstest -n McpServerTests
$ cd McpServerTests
$ dotnet add package Moq
$ dotnet add package ModelContextProtocol
$ dotnet add package Microsoft.AspNetCore.Mvc.Testing
```

Now let's imagine we have a tool class from one of our earlier chapters. It has a simple tool that converts temperatures between Celsius and Fahrenheit. This is representative of the kind of tool you will find in a real MCP server: it takes some input, applies logic, and returns a result. My implementation is shown in Listing 11-2 below.

Listing 11-2. A simple tool class to test

```
using System.Globalization;
using ModelContextProtocol.Server;
using System.ComponentModel;

[McpServerToolType]
public static class TemperatureTools
{
    [McpServerTool]
    [Description("Converts Celsius to Fahrenheit")]
    public static string CelsiusToFahrenheit(double celsius)
    {
        var f = celsius * 9.0 / 5.0 + 32;

        return string.Format(CultureInfo.InvariantCulture, "{0}C = {1:F1}
        F", celsius, f);
    }

    [McpServerTool]
    [Description("Converts Fahrenheit to Celsius")]
    public static string FahrenheitToCelsius(double fahrenheit)
    {
        var c = (fahrenheit - 32) * 5.0 / 9.0;

        return string.Format(CultureInfo.InvariantCulture,"{0}F = {1:F1}C",
        fahrenheit, c);
    }
}
```

Notice that I used `CultureInfo.InvariantCulture` for the number formatting. This is important because your MCP server might run on machines with different locale settings. You do not want your tests to fail just because someone in a different country uses a comma instead of a period for decimal separators. Now let's write the tests as shown in Listing 11-3.

Listing 11-3. Unit tests for TemperatureTools

```
using Microsoft.VisualStudio.TestTools.UnitTesting;

[TestClass]
public class TemperatureToolsTests
{
    [TestMethod]
    public void CelsiusToFahrenheit_BoilingPoint_Returns212()
    {
        var result = TemperatureTools.CelsiusToFahrenheit(100);

        Assert.AreEqual("100C = 212.0F", result);
    }

    [TestMethod]
    public void CelsiusToFahrenheit_FreezingPoint_Returns32()
    {
        var result = TemperatureTools.CelsiusToFahrenheit(0);

        Assert.AreEqual("0C = 32.0F", result);
    }

    [DataTestMethod]
    [DataRow(32, "32F = 0.0C")]
    [DataRow(212, "212F = 100.0C")]
    [DataRow(-40, "-40F = -40.0C")]
    public void FahrenheitToCelsius_ReturnsExpected(double input, string
    expected)
    {
        var result = TemperatureTools.FahrenheitToCelsius(input);

        Assert.AreEqual(expected, result);
    }
}
```

Notice how I used both `[TestMethod]` and `[DataTestMethod]` attributes. TestMethod marks a single test case, while DataTestMethod lets you run the same test logic with multiple inputs. The `[DataTestMethod]` approach with `[DataRow]` is perfect for conversion tools where you want to verify several known values.

Testing Tools with Dependencies

Static methods without dependencies are the easy case. In real applications, your tools will depend on services like databases, HTTP clients, or configuration objects. In Chapter 9, we saw how to inject services into MCP tools. Let's look at how to test a tool that has dependencies.

Consider a tool that looks up product information from a repository. In production, this repository talks to a database, but in our tests, we want to control exactly what data it returns. In Listing 11-4 below, notice how the interface for the product repository is declared and then injected in the ProductTools class constructor.

Listing 11-4. A tool with an injected dependency

```
public interface IProductRepository
{
    Task<Product?> GetByIdAsync(int id);
}

public record Product(int Id, string Name, decimal Price);

[McpServerToolType]
public class ProductTools(IProductRepository repo)
{
    [McpServerTool]
    [Description("Looks up a product by ID")]
    public async Task<string> GetProduct(int productId)
    {
        var product = await repo.GetByIdAsync(productId);

        if (product is null)
            return "Product not found.";

        return string.Format(CultureInfo.InvariantCulture, "{0}: ${1:F2}",
            product.Name, product.Price);
    }
}
```

Now we can use Moq to create a fake repository and test the tool in isolation. This is shown in Listing 11-5 below.

Listing 11-5. Testing a tool with mocked dependencies

```
using Moq;
using Microsoft.VisualStudio.TestTools.UnitTesting;

[TestClass]
public class ProductToolsTests
{
    private readonly Mock<IProductRepository> _mockRepo = new();
    private readonly ProductTools _tools;

    public ProductToolsTests()
    {
        _tools = new ProductTools(_mockRepo.Object);
    }

    [TestMethod]
    public async Task GetProduct_Exists_ReturnsFormatted()
    {
        _mockRepo.Setup(r => r
            .GetByIdAsync(42))
            .ReturnsAsync(new Product(42, "Widget", 9.99m));

        var result = await _tools.GetProduct(42);

        Assert.AreEqual("Widget: $9.99", result);
    }

    [TestMethod]
    public async Task GetProduct_NotFound_ReturnsMessage()
    {
        _mockRepo.Setup(r => r
            .GetByIdAsync(99)).ReturnsAsync((Product?)null);

        var result = await _tools.GetProduct(99);

        Assert.AreEqual("Product not found.", result);
        }
}
```

This pattern scales to any dependency. Need to test a tool that calls an external API? Mock the `HttpClient`. Need to test a tool that reads from configuration? Mock `IConfiguration`. The key insight is that MCP tools are just regular C# classes, and you test them the same way you test any other C# class.

Integration Testing with In-Memory Transport

Unit tests verify that your tool logic is correct, but they don't tell you whether the full MCP pipeline works. Does the SDK correctly discover your tools? Does it serialize the request, route it to the right method, and serialize the response back? To answer those questions, we need integration tests that exercise the complete server stack.

The C# MCP SDK does not ship a dedicated in-memory transport class, but it gives us something just as good: stream-based transports. The `WithStreamServerTransport` method on the server side and the `StreamClientTransport` class on the client side let us wire up a server and client through in-process pipes. No network, no child processes, no ports to manage. It is fast, deterministic, and perfect for automated tests.

The way it works is straightforward. You create two `System.IO.Pipelines`.Pipe instances, one for each direction of communication. The server reads from one pipe and writes to the other. The client does the reverse. You start the server in the background, create a client connected to the opposite ends of the pipes, and then use the client to call tools exactly the way a real AI client would. Have a look at the code for this in Listing 11-6 underneath.

Listing 11-6. Integration test with stream-based transport

```
using System.IO.Pipelines;
using ModelContextProtocol.Client;
using ModelContextProtocol.Protocol;
using ModelContextProtocol.Server;
using Microsoft.Extensions.DependencyInjection;
using Microsoft.Extensions.Hosting;
using Microsoft.VisualStudio.TestTools.UnitTesting;

[TestClass]
public class ServerIntegrationTests
{
    [TestMethod]
```

```
    public async Task CanCallToolViaProtocol()
        {
            var clientToServer = new Pipe();
            var serverToClient = new Pipe();
            var builder = Host.CreateApplicationBuilder();

            builder.Services.AddMcpServer()
                .WithStreamServerTransport(
                    clientToServer.Reader.AsStream(), serverToClient.
                    Writer.AsStream())
                .WithToolsFromAssembly();

            var host = builder.Build();
            await host.StartAsync();

          var clientTransport = new StreamClientTransport(
                clientToServer.Writer.AsStream(), serverToClient.Reader.
                AsStream());

            await using var client = await McpClient.
            CreateAsync(clientTransport);

            var result = await client.CallToolAsync(
                "celsius_to_fahrenheit",
                new Dictionary<string, object?>{ ["celsius"] = 100.0 });

            var text = result.Content.OfType<TextContentBlock>().
            First().Text;

            Assert.AreEqual("100C = 212.0F", text);

            await host.StopAsync();
        }
}
```

Here is what is happening. First, we create two `Pipe` instances from `System.IO.Pipelines`. These give us pairs of readers and writers. The server reads from one pipe's reader and writes to the other pipe's writer. The client does the reverse: it writes to the first pipe's writer and reads from the second pipe's reader.

We use `WithToolsFromAssembly` to register all tools found in the test assembly, then start the host with `StartAsync`. On the client side, `McpClient.CreateAsync` takes a `StreamClientTransport` and handles the MCP initialization handshake. After that, `CallToolAsync` sends a real JSON-RPC request through the pipes. The server receives it, finds the matching tool, invokes it, and sends the response back. This exercises the entire pipeline from end to end.

Testing Tool Discovery

One particularly useful integration test is to verify that all your tools are properly discovered by the server. This catches issues like forgetting to add the `[McpServerTool]` attribute or not registering a tool class with the server. Note that the SDK automatically converts your C# method names to snake_case when exposing them as MCP tools.

Snake_case is a naming convention where words are separated by underscores and everything is lowercase. Think celsius_to_fahrenheit instead of CelsiusToFahrenheit. The MCP specification requires tool names to follow this format. The C# SDK handles that conversion automatically for you, so your PascalCase method names like CelsiusToFahrenheit become celsius_to_fahrenheit in the protocol. That is why in the following test in Listing 11-7, we assert against the snake_case versions of the tool names.

Listing 11-7. Testing tool discovery

```
[TestMethod]
public async Task AllToolsAreDiscovered()
    {
        var clientToServer = new Pipe();
        var serverToClient = new Pipe();

        var builder = Host.CreateApplicationBuilder();

        builder.Services.AddMcpServer()
            .WithStreamServerTransport(
                clientToServer.Reader.AsStream(), serverToClient.Writer.
                AsStream())
            .WithToolsFromAssembly();
```

```
        var host = builder.Build();
        await host.StartAsync();

        var clientTransport =
            new StreamClientTransport(
                clientToServer.Writer.AsStream(), serverToClient.Reader.
                AsStream());

        await using var client = await McpClient.CreateAsync
        (clientTransport);
        var tools = await client.ListToolsAsync();

        // Tool names are auto-converted
        // to snake_case by the SDK
        Assert.IsTrue(tools.Any(t => t.Name == "celsius_to_fahrenheit"));
        Assert.IsTrue(tools.Any(t => t.Name == "fahrenheit_to_celsius"));

        await host.StopAsync();
    }
```

This test is a great safety net. If someone accidentally removes a tool attribute or changes a method signature in a way that breaks tool registration, this test will catch it immediately.

Testing with the MCP Inspector

Automated tests are essential, but sometimes you just need to poke at your server interactively. Maybe you are developing a new tool and want to see exactly what JSON it returns. Maybe you need to test edge cases that are easier to explore by hand than to codify in a test. This is where the MCP Inspector comes in.

The MCP Inspector is an official tool from the MCP project that gives you a web-based interface to connect to any MCP server and interact with it. You can list tools, call them with custom arguments, list resources, read resource contents, and see the raw JSON-RPC messages flowing back and forth. It is invaluable for development and debugging.

We have already used the Inspector a couple of times in earlier chapters, so the setup should be familiar by now. As a quick reminder, you launch it with npx as shown in Listing 11-8.

Listing 11-8. Launching the MCP Inspector

```
npx @modelcontextprotocol/inspector dotnet run --project \
    ./MyMcpServer/MyMcpServer.csproj
```

This command starts the MCP Inspector and opens a web interface in your browser. If you pass a `dotnet run` command as shown above, the Inspector pre-fills the connection fields for you, but you still need to click Connect to actually start your server and establish the connection.

This book obviously targets .NET, but just for completeness; the `dotnet run` command can be any command, on any stack, to start your MCP server.

Once the Inspector is running, it should typically open your default browser by itself. If not, open your browser to the URL it displays, usually `http://localhost:6274`. Let me walk you through the interface step by step, because this tool will save you hours of debugging throughout this book and beyond.

When the page loads, you will see a left sidebar with the connection settings. The Transport Type dropdown is set to STDIO by default, and the Command and Arguments fields are pre-filled if you passed them on the command line. Below those fields, you will find collapsible sections for Environment Variables, Authentication, and Configuration. Click the Connect button at the bottom of the sidebar to launch your server and establish the connection. The status indicator below the button changes from Disconnected to Connected when everything is working. If it stays disconnected, double-check that your server project path is correct and that it builds without errors. Because `dotnet run` might first have to build the project, the MCP Inspector interface might take a little while to show you some feedback if something isn't quite right while connecting, but some error message should pop up. That is your queue to look a bit closer at your MCP server build command.

Note The MCP Inspector is under active development, so the interface may look slightly different by the time you read this. The core workflow stays the same though: connect, pick a tab, and poke your server.

Once connected, the center area comes alive with tabs for Tools, Resources, Prompts, and more. Start with the Tools tab, as shown in Figure 11-1 underneath. You will see every tool your server exposes listed by name with its description. Click on a tool and the right side of the screen shows a detail panel with the tool's description, annotation badges such as read-only, destructive, and idempotent, and a labeled input field for each parameter. Required parameters are marked with an asterisk. This is all derived from the JSON schema your server advertises during tool discovery, but the Inspector renders it as a friendly form instead of raw JSON.

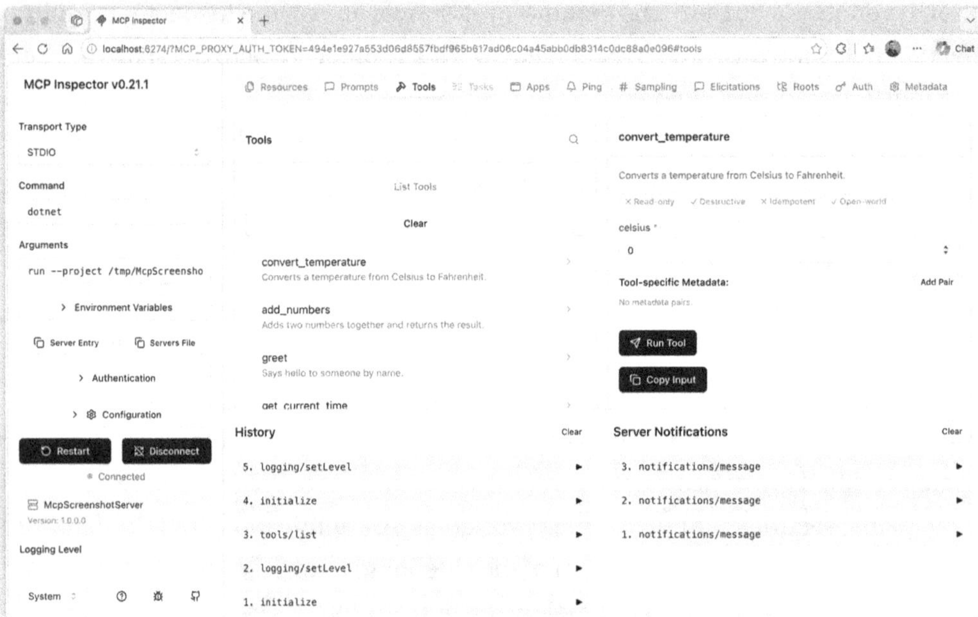

Figure 11-1. *The MCP Inspector Tools tab showing the tool list*

Fill in the input fields and click the Run Tool button. The Inspector sends a real `tools/call` request to your server and displays the response. You see the full `CallToolResult`, including the content blocks, any error flags, and metadata. This is the fastest way to verify that a tool returns what you expect without wiring up a full AI client.

Switch to the Resources tab to see every static resource and resource template your server exposes. You can see this being shown in Figure 11-2 below. Click a static resource to read its content immediately. For resource templates, the Inspector shows input fields for the template parameters. Fill them in and it resolves the template and fetches the resource, just like a real client would.

The Prompts tab works the same way. You see all registered prompts, and clicking one shows its arguments. Fill in the parameters and the Inspector calls `prompts/get` to retrieve the messages your server would inject into a conversation. This is especially useful for multi-message prompts where you want to verify the system and user messages are structured correctly.

At the bottom of the screen, you will find two panels: History and Server Notifications. The History panel logs every interaction you trigger, whether it is listing tools, calling a tool, or reading a resource. You can see the raw JSON-RPC requests and responses flowing between the Inspector and your server. The Server Notifications panel captures any notifications your server sends, such as progress updates or resource change events. Together, these panels give you full visibility into the protocol-level conversation.

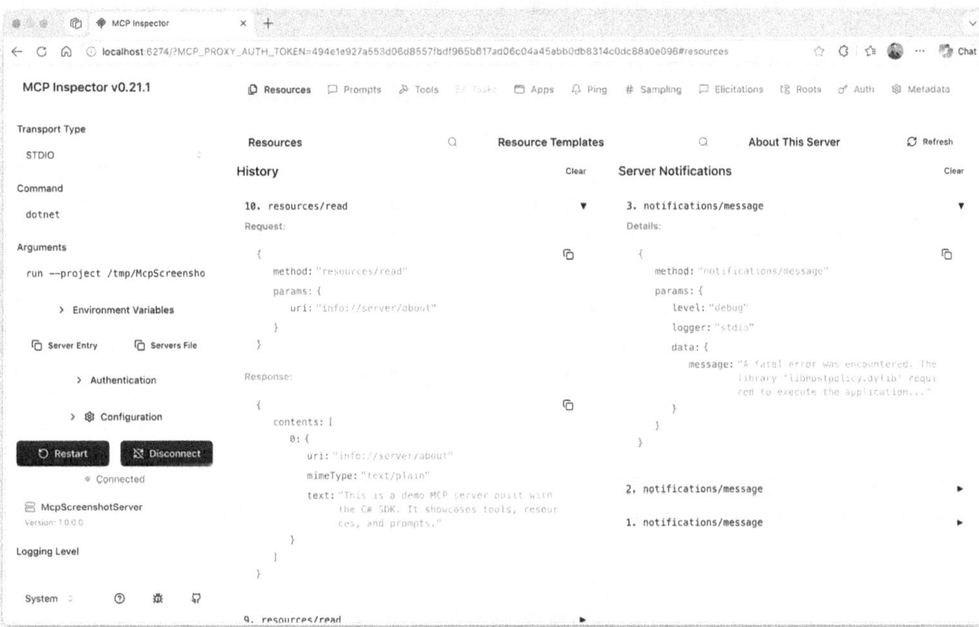

Figure 11-2. *The JSON-RPC message panel in the MCP Inspector showing the raw protocol messages*

For HTTP-based servers using Streamable HTTP transport, you can also point the inspector at your server's URL instead of launching it as a subprocess. Notice in Listing 11-9 below how we specify the transport type and URL explicitly.

Listing 11-9. Inspecting an HTTP-based MCP server

```
npx @modelcontextprotocol/inspector \
--transport http \
--url http://localhost:5000
```

The MCP Inspector is not a replacement for automated tests. Think of it as a complement. The Postman for MCP servers. Use the inspector during development to explore and experiment, then codify the behavior you discover into automated tests that run in your CI pipeline.

Testing HTTP Servers

If your MCP server uses the Streamable HTTP transport from Chapter 8, you have an additional testing tool at your disposal: ASP.NET Core's `WebApplicationFactory`. This class, part of the `Microsoft.AspNetCore.Mvc.Testing` package, creates an in-memory test server that you can send HTTP requests to without actually opening a network port. It is the standard way to integration test ASP.NET Core applications, and it works beautifully with MCP servers.

The idea is straightforward. `WebApplicationFactory` spins up your entire ASP.NET Core application in memory, including all your middleware, routing, and dependency injection. It gives you an `HttpClient` that sends requests directly to this in-memory server. You can then use the MCP client to connect over HTTP and call tools just as a real client would. An example test class demonstrating this can be seen in Listing 11-10 below.

Listing 11-10. Testing an HTTP MCP server with WebApplicationFactory

```
using Microsoft.AspNetCore.Mvc.Testing;
using ModelContextProtocol.Client;
using Microsoft.VisualStudio.TestTools.UnitTesting;

[TestClass]
public class HttpServerTests
{
    private readonly WebApplicationFactory<Program> _factory = new();

    [TestMethod]
    public async Task CanCallToolOverHttp()
```

```
    {
        var httpClient = _factory.CreateClient();
        var client = await McpClient.CreateAsync(
            new HttpClientTransport(new HttpClientTransportOptions
            {
                Endpoint = new Uri(httpClient.BaseAddress!, "/mcp")
            },
            httpClient));

            var tools = await client.ListToolsAsync();

            Assert.IsTrue(tools.Count > 0);
        }
}
```

There are a few things to note about this approach. First, you need to make your `Program` class accessible to the test project. The easiest way is to add a partial class declaration at the bottom of your `Program.cs` file, or use an `InternalsVisibleTo` attribute in your server project. Second, `WebApplicationFactory` handles all the lifecycle management for you: it creates the server on demand and tears it down after.

Note HttpClientTransportOptions points to the /mcp endpoint because that is where `MapMcp` registers the handler. The `WebApplicationFactory`'s `CreateClient` method returns an `HttpClient` that already knows the server's base address, so only the path segment is needed.

`WebApplicationFactory` also lets you override services for testing. If your MCP server depends on a database, you can swap in an in-memory database for tests. If it calls external APIs, you can register mock implementations. This is the same pattern used throughout the ASP.NET Core ecosystem, so if you have experience testing web APIs, you will feel right at home.

Testing Error Scenarios

So far, we have tested the happy path, where everything works as expected. But AI clients can send your server all kinds of unexpected input. The model might pass the wrong type for a parameter, send a negative number where you expect a positive one, or call a tool with missing required arguments. Your server needs to handle these cases gracefully, and your tests should verify that it does.

Let's look at some common error scenarios and how to test them.

Testing Invalid Inputs

When an AI model sends invalid input to your tool, the SDK will often catch type mismatches before your code even runs. But your tools should also validate their own inputs and return helpful error messages. Listing 11-11 shows a tool with input validation and the corresponding test.

Listing 11-11. Testing a tool with input validation

```
[McpServerToolType]
public static class ValidationTools
{
    [McpServerTool]
    [Description("Gets info about a page")]
    public static string GetPageInfo(int pageNumber)
    {
        if (pageNumber < 1)
            return "Error: Page number must be positive.";

        return $"Page {pageNumber} info.";
    }
}

[TestClass]
public class ValidationTests
{
    [TestMethod]
    public void GetPageInfo_NegativeInput_ReturnsError()
```

```
    {
            var result = ValidationTools.GetPageInfo(-1);

            StringAssert.Contains(result, "must be positive");
    }

    [TestMethod]
    public void GetPageInfo_ValidInput_ReturnsInfo()
        {
            var result = ValidationTools.GetPageInfo(5);

            StringAssert.Contains(result, "Page 5");
        }
}
```

Testing Exception Handling

Your tools should never throw unhandled exceptions at the client. The MCP SDK will catch unhandled exceptions and return a JSON-RPC error, but the error message will be generic and unhelpful to the AI model. It is much better to catch exceptions in your tool and return a meaningful error message. In Listing 11-12 you can see a possible implementation of this pattern.

Listing 11-12. Testing exception handling in tools

```
[TestMethod]
public async Task GetProduct_RepositoryThrows_ReturnsError()
{
    var mockRepo = new Mock<IProductRepository>();
    mockRepo.Setup(r => r
        .GetByIdAsync(It.IsAny<int>()))
        .ThrowsAsync(new InvalidOperationException("DB connection lost"));

        var tools = new ProductTools(mockRepo.Object);

        // If the tool handles exceptions:
        var result = await tools.GetProduct(1);

        StringAssert.Contains(result.ToLower(), "error");
}
```

Testing error scenarios is not the most glamorous work, but it pays off enormously. AI models are creative with their inputs, and the edge cases they discover will surprise you. Better to discover those edge cases in a test than in production.

Debugging Tips

Even with good tests, you will occasionally need to debug your MCP server. Debugging an MCP server is slightly different from debugging a typical application because the server communicates through `stdin/stdout`, which makes attaching a debugger tricky. Here are some techniques that I have found helpful.

Use stderr for Diagnostic Output

When your server runs over the stdio transport, `stdout` is reserved for JSON-RPC messages. If you write anything else to `stdout`, you will corrupt the protocol and crash the connection. Instead, write diagnostic output to `stderr` using `Console.Error.WriteLine`. The AI client will typically show `stderr` output in its logs. Below, in Listing 11-13, you can see how to write things to the error stream.

Listing 11-13. Using stderr for diagnostic output

```
[McpServerTool]
public static string MyTool(string input)
{
    Console.Error.WriteLine($"MyTool called: {input}");

    // ... tool logic ...
    Console.Error.WriteLine("MyTool completed");

    return "result";
}
```

Structured Logging

For more sophisticated logging, use the built-in `ILogger` infrastructure. When you register your MCP server with the host builder, you can configure logging providers that write to files or other destinations that don't interfere with the stdio transport. Listing 11-14 shows you the code to do that in your Program.cs.

Listing 11-14. Configuring logging for an MCP server

```
var builder = Host.CreateEmptyApplicationBuilder(null);
builder.Logging.ClearProviders();
builder.Logging.AddDebug();
builder.Logging.SetMinimumLevel(LogLevel.Debug);

builder.Services
    .AddMcpServer()
    .WithTools<TemperatureTools>();
```

The Debug logging provider writes to the diagnostic output that Visual Studio and other debuggers capture. This way you get full logging without interfering with the stdio transport.

Step-Through Debugging

If you need to set breakpoints and step through your tool code, the easiest approach is to use the stream-based transport in a test. Write a test that calls the tool you want to debug, set a breakpoint in your tool method, and run the test in debug mode. Visual Studio, VS Code, and Rider all support debugging MSTest tests natively.

If you need to debug the server while it is connected to a real AI client, you can add a `Debugger.Launch()` call at the start of your `Program.cs`. This will prompt you to attach a debugger when the server starts. Just remember to remove it before shipping. Listing 11-15 shows you a little trick using the #if compiler directives to only trigger this code for debug builds.

Listing 11-15. Attaching a debugger on startup

```
#if DEBUG
System.Diagnostics.Debugger.Launch();
#endif
var builder = Host
    .CreateEmptyApplicationBuilder(null);

// ... rest of setup ...
```

Tip When debugging stdio-based servers, remember that the AI client has a timeout for server startup. If you spend too long at a breakpoint during initialization, the client may give up and report the server as unresponsive. Increase the client's timeout or focus your debugging on tool invocation rather than startup.

Continuous Integration

Tests are only valuable if they actually run. And let's be honest, most developers are terrible at remembering to run tests manually before every commit. That is why continuous integration exists. By running your tests automatically on every push or pull request, you catch regressions before they reach your main branch.

The good news is that MCP server tests are just regular .NET tests. Any CI system that can run `dotnet test` will work. That's it! Take a look at a GitHub Actions workflow, below in Listing 11-16, that builds and tests your MCP server project.

Listing 11-16. GitHub Actions workflow for MCP server tests

```
name: MCP Server Tests
on:
  push:
    branches: [ main ]
  pull_request:
    branches: [ main ]
jobs:
  test:
    runs-on: ubuntu-latest
    steps:
      - uses: actions/checkout@v4
      - name: Setup .NET
        uses: actions/setup-dotnet@v4
        with:
          dotnet-version: '10.0.x'
      - name: Restore dependencies
        run: dotnet restore
      - name: Build
```

```
      run: dotnet build --no-restore
    - name: Test
      run: dotnet test \
        --no-build \
        --verbosity normal \
        --logger \
        "trx;LogFileName=results.trx"
    - name: Publish results
      uses: actions/upload-artifact@v4
      if: always()
      with:
        name: test-results
        path: "**/*.trx"
```

This workflow is intentionally simple. It checks out your code, sets up .NET 10, restores packages, builds the solution, and runs all tests. The test results are saved as a TRX file and uploaded as a build artifact so you can download and inspect them if anything fails.

There are a few CI-specific considerations for MCP server tests worth keeping in mind:

- Stream-based transport tests run perfectly in CI because they don't need any external processes or network ports.
- If your tests depend on external services like databases, use Docker containers in your CI pipeline or mock those dependencies.
- Integration tests that spawn actual MCP server processes need the correct runtime installed on the CI agent.
- Set reasonable timeouts for integration tests. A test that hangs waiting for a server response can block your entire pipeline.

For teams that use other CI systems like Azure DevOps, Jenkins, or GitLab CI, the workflow translates directly. The commands are the same, only the YAML syntax changes.

Putting It All Together

Here is a practical testing strategy that I recommend for MCP server projects. This is not a rigid prescription, just a starting point that you can adapt to your situation.

Start with unit tests for every tool method. These are fast, easy to write, and catch the most common bugs. Cover both the happy path and error cases. If your tool has dependencies, mock them and test the tool in isolation.

Add integration tests using the stream-based transport. At minimum, have one test that verifies tool discovery, meaning all your expected tools show up in the tools/list response. Then add tests that call each tool through the protocol and verify the response. These tests catch serialization bugs, routing issues, and configuration mistakes that unit tests miss.

If your server uses HTTP transport, add `WebApplicationFactory` tests to verify the HTTP layer works. These tests exercise your middleware, authentication, and routing in addition to the MCP protocol.

Use the MCP Inspector during development for exploratory testing and debugging. It is not a substitute for automated tests, but it is invaluable for understanding what your server actually does.

Finally, run everything in CI. Tests that don't run automatically are tests that eventually stop running. Set up a GitHub Actions workflow, or whatever CI system your team uses, and make sure tests run on every pull request.

Summary

Here's what we covered: We built tests that actually mean something for MCP servers. We started with unit tests for individual tool methods, using MSTest and Moq to test both simple static tools and tools with injected dependencies. We moved up to integration tests using the C# SDK's stream-based transport, which let us exercise the full MCP pipeline without starting any external processes.

We explored the MCP Inspector as a tool for manual testing and debugging, and we saw how to use ASP.NET Core's `WebApplicationFactory` to test HTTP-based MCP servers. We covered error scenario testing to make sure our servers handle bad input gracefully, and we looked at debugging techniques including `stderr` output, structured logging, and step-through debugging.

We wrapped up with continuous integration, showing how a simple GitHub Actions workflow can run your tests automatically on every push. The key takeaway is that MCP servers are just regular C# applications, and you can test them with the same tools and patterns you already know.

In the next chapter, we are going to put everything we have learned together and build something fun. Chapter 12 is all about building the Cosmic Pizza Server, a complete, real-world MCP server that manages a pizza ordering system from start to finish. We will combine tools, resources, prompts, dependency injection, and yes, testing, into one delicious project. Get hungry, because it is going to be a good one.

CHAPTER 12

Building the Cosmic Pizza Server

Welcome to the most fun chapter in this entire book. If you have been following along from Chapter 1, you have learned about tools, resources, prompts, dependency injection, transports, testing, and clients. Now it is time to put it all together into something truly spectacular. We are going to build the Cosmic Pizza Server, an MCP server for a fictional intergalactic pizza delivery service.

Why pizza? Why space? Because learning should be fun, and nothing says fun quite like delivering Saturn's Ring-ion Burger Pizza to a colony on Neptune. This chapter is your showcase project, the grand finale of the building section of this book. We will combine every concept you have learned into a single, polished, complete MCP server that you can actually run and interact with.

By the end of this chapter, you will have a working MCP server that serves up a planetary pizza menu, takes orders with delivery times measured in light-years, tells space-themed dad jokes, dishes out fascinating space facts, recommends pizzas based on your zodiac sign, and even helps plan cosmic pizza parties. Buckle up, astronaut. It is going to be a delicious ride.

Designing the Cosmic Pizza Server

Before we write a single line of code, let us take a step back and think about what we want our server to do. Good software starts with good design, and even a fun project like this deserves a thoughtful architecture. Allow me to walk you through the requirements I came up with while daydreaming about interplanetary pizza delivery.

G. Versluis, *Building MCP Servers with C#*, https://doi.org/10.1007/979-8-8688-3010-5_12

Our Cosmic Pizza Server needs to fulfill several roles. It needs to be an information source (resources), a set of actions an AI can take (tools), and a provider of structured conversation starters (prompts). Sound familiar? These are the three core MCP primitives we covered in Chapters 5, 6, and 7. Here is what I planned out:

- A full pizza menu as a static resource, featuring five planetary pizzas that would make any astronaut's mouth water
- A daily specials resource that rotates the deals based on what day it is
- An order placement tool that handles pizza ordering with sizes, toppings, and delivery destinations across the solar system
- A space facts tool for those moments when you want to learn something amazing while waiting for your pizza
- A dad jokes tool, because what is a pizza party without some groan-worthy humor?
- A pizza recommender tool that matches pizzas to zodiac signs, because why not?
- A party planner prompt to help organize the ultimate space pizza party

For the architecture, we will use the patterns from Chapter 9. That means proper dependency injection, configuration through `appsettings.json`, service interfaces, and clean separation of concerns. Listing 12-1 shows what our project structure will look like.

Listing 12-1. Cosmic Pizza Server project structure

```
CosmicPizzaServer/
    CosmicPizzaServer.csproj
    Program.cs
    appsettings.json
Models/
    Pizza.cs
    Order.cs
    CosmicPizzaOptions.cs
Services/
    IPizzaMenuService.cs
```

```
    PizzaMenuService.cs
    IOrderService.cs
    OrderService.cs
Tools/
    OrderTool.cs
    SpaceFactsTool.cs
    DadJokesTool.cs
    PizzaRecommenderTool.cs
Resources/
    MenuResource.cs
    DailySpecialsResource.cs
Prompts/
    PartyPlannerPrompt.cs
```

That is a lot of files, but each one has a clear, focused responsibility. Let us start building this thing from the ground up, beginning with our models and the menu that makes it all possible.

The Pizza Menu

Every great pizza place starts with a great menu, and ours is out of this world. Literally. I spent an embarrassing amount of time coming up with these pizza names, and I regret nothing. Let us start with the models that define our cosmic cuisine.

The Models

We need two core data models: Pizza for our menu items and Order for tracking what customers buy. We use C# records instead of classes here because records give you immutability, value-based equality, and a concise syntax all in one line. They are ideal for data that is created once and never modified, which is exactly how menu items and orders behave. Plus, you get a nice `ToString()` for free, which never hurts during debugging. Have a look at our definition of the pizza object below in Listing 12-2.

Listing 12-2. The Pizza record (Models/Pizza.cs)

```
namespace CosmicPizzaServer.Models;

public record Pizza(
    string Name,
    string Description,
    decimal Price,
    string Planet,
    string[] DefaultToppings);
```

Simple and clean. Each pizza has a name, a description, a price in GalactiCoins (our fictional currency), the planet it originates from, and its default toppings. Now for the `Order` record, find it in Listing 12-3 underneath.

Listing 12-3. The Order record (Models/Order.cs)

```
namespace CosmicPizzaServer.Models;

public record Order(
    string OrderId,
    string PizzaName,
    string Size,
    string[] ExtraToppings,
    string DeliveryPlanet,
    decimal TotalPrice,
    string EstimatedDelivery,
    DateTime OrderedAt);
```

Notice the `EstimatedDelivery` is a string, not a `TimeSpan`. That is because our delivery times are measured in light-years and galactic minutes, which do not exactly fit into standard .NET time types. We also need a configuration options class to make our server configurable:

With our data shapes locked down, we need one more model: the configuration class. The `CosmicPizzaOptions` holds the constants that give our server its personality: the restaurant name, the currency we charge in, and the all-important delivery speed, You can see it in Listing 12-4 below.

Listing 12-4. Configuration options (Models/CosmicPizzaOptions.cs)

```
namespace CosmicPizzaServer.Models;

public class CosmicPizzaOptions
{
    public const string SectionName = "CosmicPizza";
    public string RestaurantName { get; set; } = "Cosmic Pizza -
    Intergalactic Pizzeria";
    public string Currency { get; set; } = "GalactiCoins";
    public int MaxToppingsPerPizza { get; set; } = 6;
    public int DeliverySpeedLightYearsPerHour { get; set; } = 42;
}
```

The delivery speed is 42 light-years per hour, which is of course a reference to The Hitchhiker's Guide to the Galaxy. If you got that reference, we should be friends.

The Menu Service

With our models in place, let us build the service that manages our cosmic menu. Following the patterns from Chapter 9, we start with an interface as seen in Listing 12-5:

Listing 12-5. Menu service interface (Services/IPizzaMenuService.cs)

```
using CosmicPizzaServer.Models;

namespace CosmicPizzaServer.Services;

public interface IPizzaMenuService
{
    IReadOnlyList<Pizza> GetFullMenu();
    Pizza? GetPizza(string name);
    IReadOnlyList<Pizza> GetDailySpecials();
}
```

Three methods: get the full menu, look up a specific pizza, and get today's specials. Now for the implementation. This is where the real fun begins, because we get to define our five planetary pizzas. It's a bit hard to parse maybe in print form, but have a look at our delicious menu below in Listing 12-6.

Listing 12-6. The PizzaMenuService with planetary pizzas (Services/PizzaMenuService.cs)

```
using CosmicPizzaServer.Models;

namespace CosmicPizzaServer.Services;

public class PizzaMenuService : IPizzaMenuService
{
    private readonly List<Pizza> _menu =
    [
        new Pizza("The Mars Margherita",
            "A classic margherita with Martian red sauce, space-aged
            mozzarella"
            + ", and fresh basil grown in zero gravity.", 12.99m, "Mars",
            ["Martian Red Sauce", "Space Mozzarella", "Zero-G Basil"]),

        new Pizza("Saturn's Ring-ion Burger Pizza", "A ring-shaped pizza
        loaded with"
            + " cosmic ground beef, caramelized onion rings, and a tangy"
            + " asteroid ketchup drizzle.", 15.99m, "Saturn",
            ["Cosmic Beef", "Onion Rings", "Asteroid Ketchup", "Cheddar
            Nebula"]),

        new Pizza("Neptune's Deep Sea Supreme", "Topped with space
        shrimp from"
            + " Neptune's methane oceans, tentacle-style calamari, and"
            + " blue cheese from the outer rim.", 18.49m, "Neptune",
            ["Space Shrimp", "Cosmic Calamari", "Blue Cheese Nebula",
            "Seaweed Stardust"]),

        new Pizza("Jupiter's Gas Giant Garlic Bread Pizza", "An oversized
        garlic bread pizza"
            + " so big it has its own gravitational pull. Loaded with
            roasted garlic butter"
            + " and three types of cheese.", 14.49m, "Jupiter",
            ["Roasted Garlic Butter", "Triple Cheese", "Herb
            Constellation"]),
```

```
        new Pizza("Pluto's Dwarf Delight","Small but mighty! A personal"
            + " pizza packed with bold flavors. Spicy pepperoni from
            the Kuiper"
            + " Belt and jalapenos hotter than a supernova.", 9.99m,
            "Pluto",
        ["Kuiper Belt Pepperoni", "Supernova Jalapenos", "Dwarf Cheese"])
    ];

    public IReadOnlyList<Pizza> GetFullMenu() => _menu.AsReadOnly();

    public Pizza? GetPizza(string name) =>_menu.FirstOrDefault(p =>
        p.Name.Contains(name, StringComparison.OrdinalIgnoreCase));

    public IReadOnlyList<Pizza> GetDailySpecials()
    {
        var dayIndex =  (int)DateTime.UtcNow.DayOfWeek;

        return _menu
            .Skip(dayIndex % _menu.Count)
            .Take(2)
            .ToList()
            .AsReadOnly();
    }
}
```

I want to walk you through the pizza menu because I am quite proud of it. The Mars Margherita is your classic choice with a cosmic twist. Saturn's Ring-ion Burger Pizza is a pun that I refuse to apologize for. It is ring-shaped, get it? Neptune's Deep Sea Supreme plays on Neptune being the ocean planet. Jupiter's Gas Giant Garlic Bread Pizza is so massive it has its own gravitational pull. And Pluto's Dwarf Delight is the personal-sized pizza, because Pluto may be a dwarf planet but it is still mighty.

The `GetPizza` method uses a case-insensitive `Contains` search, so users do not have to type the exact pizza name. Asking for "Mars" or "Margherita" will both find The Mars Margherita. The daily specials rotate based on the day of the week, ensuring variety for our customers across the cosmos.

The Order Tool

Now let us build the part that makes the money. The order tool lets an AI assistant place pizza orders on behalf of users, complete with size selection, extra toppings, and delivery to any planet in the solar system. First, we need the order service that handles the business logic.

The Order Service

The order service manages order creation and tracking. You can see the interface definition for it in Listing 12-7. It calculates delivery times based on actual planetary distances (well, approximately actual) and supports four pizza sizes including the coveted "cosmic" size.

Listing 12-7. Order service interface (Services/IOrderService.cs)

```
using CosmicPizzaServer.Models;

namespace CosmicPizzaServer.Services;

public interface IOrderService
{
    Order PlaceOrder(
        string pizzaName,
        string size,
        string[] extraToppings,
        string deliveryPlanet);

    Order? GetOrder(string orderId);
    IReadOnlyList<Order> GetRecentOrders();
}
```

That is our contract, lean and to the point. Now let us look at the implementation in Listing 12-8, which is where the real fun happens. The `OrderService` calculates delivery times based on planetary distances, generates cosmic order IDs, and keeps track of everything in a thread-safe dictionary.

Listing 12-8. Order service implementation (Services/OrderService.cs)

```
using System.Collections.Concurrent;
using CosmicPizzaServer.Models;

namespace CosmicPizzaServer.Services;

public class OrderService : IOrderService
{
    private readonly IPizzaMenuService _menuService;

    private readonly ConcurrentDictionary<string, Order> _orders = new();

    private static readonly Dictionary<string, double>
    PlanetDistances = new()
    {
        ["Mercury"] = 0.39,
        ["Venus"] = 0.72,
        ["Earth"] = 1.0,
        ["Mars"] = 1.52,
        ["Jupiter"] = 5.20,
        ["Saturn"] = 9.58,
        ["Uranus"] = 19.22,
        ["Neptune"] = 30.05,
        ["Pluto"] = 39.48
    };

    public OrderService(IPizzaMenuService menuService)
    {
        _menuService = menuService;
    }

    public Order PlaceOrder(
        string pizzaName, string size,
        string[] extraToppings,
        string deliveryPlanet)
    {
        var pizza = _menuService.GetPizza(pizzaName)
            ?? throw new ArgumentException($"Pizza '{pizzaName}' not found
            on menu");
```

```
        var sizeMultiplier = size.ToLower()
        switch
        {
            "small" or "dwarf" => 0.8m,
            "medium" or "standard" => 1.0m,
            "large" or "giant" => 1.3m,
            "cosmic" => 1.8m,
            _ => 1.0m
        };

        var toppingCost = extraToppings.Length * 1.50m;
        var totalPrice = (pizza.Price * sizeMultiplier) + toppingCost;
        var distance = PlanetDistances.GetValueOrDefault(deliveryPlanet, 10.0);

        var deliveryTime = $"{distance:F2} light-years $"({distance *
        15:F0} galactic " + "minutes)";

        var order = new Order(
            OrderId: GenerateOrderId(),
            PizzaName: pizza.Name,
            Size: size,
            ExtraToppings: extraToppings,
            DeliveryPlanet: deliveryPlanet,
            TotalPrice: totalPrice,
            EstimatedDelivery: deliveryTime,
            OrderedAt: DateTime.UtcNow);

        _orders[order.OrderId] = order;
        return order;
    }

    public Order? GetOrder(string orderId) => _orders.
    GetValueOrDefault(orderId);

    public IReadOnlyList<Order> GetRecentOrders() => _orders.Values
        .OrderByDescending(o => o.OrderedAt)
        .Take(10).ToList().AsReadOnly();
```

```
    private static string GenerateOrderId() =>
        $"COSMIC-{Guid.NewGuid().ToString()[..8]
        .ToUpper()}";
}
```

There is a lot going on here, so here are the interesting parts. The planet distances are based on their average distance from the Sun in astronomical units. The delivery time calculation is pure fantasy, of course, but it gives the server a delightful personality. I also added some fun size names: you can order a "dwarf" size (an alias for small, perfect for Pluto's Dwarf Delight) or go all out with "cosmic" size at 1.8 times the base price.

The ConcurrentDictionary for order storage makes our service thread-safe, which is important because MCP tools can be called concurrently. Each order gets a unique ID prefixed with "COSMIC-" followed by a short GUID segment, making it easy to reference in conversations.

The Order Tool Class

With the service ready, let us build the tool that exposes ordering capabilities to AI assistants, have a look at the code for that in Listing 12-9:

Listing 12-9. The OrderTool with place and status methods (Tools/OrderTool.cs)

```
using System.ComponentModel;
using CosmicPizzaServer.Models;
using CosmicPizzaServer.Services;
using Microsoft.Extensions.Logging;
using Microsoft.Extensions.Options;
using ModelContextProtocol.Server;

namespace CosmicPizzaServer.Tools;

[McpServerToolType]
public class OrderTool
{
    [McpServerTool(Name = "place_pizza_order")]
    [Description("Places a cosmic pizza order for delivery to any planet.")]
    public static string PlaceOrder(
        [Description("Name of the pizza")] string pizzaName,
```

```
        [Description("Size: small, medium, large, or cosmic")] string size,
        [Description("Planet for delivery")] string deliveryPlanet,
        [Description("Extra toppings, comma-separated")] string
        extraToppings,
        IOrderService orderService,
        IOptions<CosmicPizzaOptions> options,
        ILogger<OrderTool> logger)
    {
        var config = options.Value;

        logger.LogInformation("New order: {Pizza} to {Planet}",
            pizzaName, deliveryPlanet);

        var toppings =
            string.IsNullOrWhiteSpace(extraToppings)
            ? Array.Empty<string>()
            : extraToppings.Split(',', StringSplitOptions.TrimEntries);

        if (toppings.Length > config.MaxToppingsPerPizza)
        {
            return "Whoa there, space cowboy! Maximum "
                + $"{config.MaxToppingsPerPizza} extra toppings allowed.";
        }

        try
        {
            var order =
                orderService.PlaceOrder(pizzaName, size, toppings,
                deliveryPlanet);

            return FormatOrderConfirmation(
                order, config);
        }
        catch (ArgumentException ex)
        {
            return $"Order failed: $"{ex.Message}";
        }
    }
```

```
    private static string
        FormatOrderConfirmation(
        Order order,
        CosmicPizzaOptions config)
    {
        return
        "--- ORDER CONFIRMED ---\n" +
            $"Order ID: {order.OrderId}\n" +
            $"Pizza: {order.PizzaName}\n" +
            $"Size: {order.Size}\n" +
            $"Delivery: {order.DeliveryPlanet}\n" +
            $"Total: {order.TotalPrice:F2} {config.Currency}\n" +
            $"ETA: order.EstimatedDelivery}";
    }
}
```

There are two key design decisions here. First, the extra toppings parameter is a comma-separated string rather than an array. This is because MCP tool parameters work best with simple types that an AI can easily provide. The tool handles the parsing internally. Second, notice how we inject both the `IOrderService` for business logic and `IOptions<CosmicPizzaOptions>` for configuration. The maximum toppings limit is configurable, so you can adjust it in `appsettings.json` without touching the code.

The error handling is user-friendly and stays in character. If someone tries to add too many toppings, they get a playful "Whoa there, space cowboy!" message instead of a dry error. When the pizza is not found, we suggest using the menu tool. This kind of personality in your error messages makes the AI interactions much more engaging.

The Space Facts Tool

Not everything has to be about pizza. Sometimes you just want to learn something amazing about the universe while waiting for your order. The space facts tool serves up random fascinating facts about space. I researched these myself, and I have to say, some of them genuinely blew my mind. Read through the code yourself in Listing 12-10.

Listing 12-10. The SpaceFactsTool with curated facts (Tools/SpaceFactsTool.cs)

```
using System.ComponentModel;
using ModelContextProtocol.Server;

namespace CosmicPizzaServer.Tools;

[McpServerToolType]
public static class SpaceFactsTool
{
    private static readonly string[]
    SpaceFacts =
    [
        "A day on Venus is longer than a year on Venus. Talk about a long
        Monday!",
        "Neutron stars are so dense that a teaspoon would weigh about 6
        billion tons.",
        "There are more stars in the universe than grains of sand on all of
        Earth's beaches.",
        "The footprints on the Moon will last for 100 million years since
        there is no wind.",
        "Saturn's density is low enough that it would float in water, if "
            + "you had a big enough bathtub.",
        "One million Earths could fit inside the Sun. That is a lot of
        pizza deliveries.",
        "There is a planet made of diamonds called 55 Cancri e. Our "
            + "delivery team refuses to go there due to parking fees."
    ];

    [McpServerTool(Name = "get_space_fact")]
    [Description("Returns a random fascinating space fact.")]
    public static string GetSpaceFact()
    {
        var index = Random.Shared.Next(SpaceFacts.Length);

        return $"Space Fact: {SpaceFacts[index]}";
    }
```

```
    [McpServerTool(Name = "get_space_facts")]
    [Description("Returns multiple random space facts.")]
    public static stringGetMultipleSpaceFacts(
        [Description("Number of facts (1-5)")] int count = 3)
    {
        count = Math.Clamp(count, 1, 5);

        var facts = SpaceFacts
            .OrderBy(_ => Random.Shared.Next())
            .Take(count)
            .Select((f, i) => $"{i + 1}. {f}");

        return "Random Space Facts:\n" +
            string.Join("\n\n", facts);
    }
}
```

This tool is intentionally simple. It is a static class with no dependencies because it does not need any. The facts are hardcoded, and the randomization uses `Random.Shared`, which is thread-safe in modern .NET. I included two variants: `get_space_fact` for a single random fact, and `get_space_facts` for when you want a mini astronomy lesson. The `count` parameter defaults to 3 and is clamped between 1 and 5 to prevent abuse.

Notice how some of the facts tie back to our pizza theme. The one about a million Earths fitting in the Sun ends with "That is a lot of pizza deliveries." These little touches create a cohesive experience and remind users that this is still a pizza server at heart.

The Dad Jokes Tool

I am not going to lie; this was my favorite tool to build. There is something deeply satisfying about writing code that is specifically designed to make people groan. Every good pizza place has that one person who tells terrible jokes, and in our cosmic pizzeria, that is the AI assistant. Try not to roll your eyes while looking at the code below in Listing 12-11.

Listing 12-11. The DadJokesTool (Tools/DadJokesTool.cs)

```
using System.ComponentModel;
using ModelContextProtocol.Server;

namespace CosmicPizzaServer.Tools;

[McpServerToolType]
public static class DadJokesTool
{
    private static readonly string[] SpaceDadJokes =
    [
        "Why did the sun go to school? " +
        "To get a little brighter!",

        "How do you organize a space " +
        "party? You planet!",

        "Why did the cow go to outer " +
        "space? To see the Milky Way!",

        "What is an astronaut's favorite key on the keyboard? " +
        "The space bar!",

        "How does the solar system hold up its pants? " +
        "With an asteroid belt!",

        "Why was the restaurant on the moon so bad? " +
        "No atmosphere!",
    ];

    [McpServerTool(Name = "get_space_dad_joke")]
    [Description("Returns a random space-themed dad joke. Guaranteed to
    make you "
        + "groan!")]
    public static string GetDadJoke()
    {
        var index = Random.Shared.Next(SpaceDadJokes.Length);

        return SpaceDadJokes[index];
    }
```

```
    [McpServerTool(Name = "get_space_dad_jokes")]
    [Description("Returns multiple space-themed dad jokes.")]
    public static string GetMultipleDadJokes(
        [Description("Number of jokes (1-5)")] int count = 3)
    {
        count = Math.Clamp(count, 1, 5);

        var jokes = SpaceDadJokes
            .OrderBy(
            _ => Random.Shared.Next())
            .Take(count)
            .Select((j, i) => $"{i + 1}. {j}");

        return "Space Dad Jokes:\n" +
            string.Join("\n\n", jokes);
    }
}
```

The structure mirrors the SpaceFactsTool, which is intentional. When you have similar tools, keeping a consistent pattern makes the codebase easier to navigate. Both have a single-item variant and a multi-item variant. Both use the same randomization technique. The only difference is the content.

My personal favorite is the moon restaurant one: "Why was the restaurant on the moon so bad? No atmosphere!"... I'll see myself out.

The Pizza Recommender Tool

This tool adds a fun, personality-based element to our server. Instead of just listing the menu and letting users choose, this tool, shown in Listing 12-12, recommends a pizza based on your zodiac sign. It is completely unscientific, obviously, but it creates a delightful interaction pattern where the AI can ask users their zodiac sign and give them a personalized recommendation.

Listing 12-12. The PizzaRecommenderTool (Tools/PizzaRecommenderTool.cs)

```
using System.ComponentModel;
using CosmicPizzaServer.Services;
using CosmicPizzaServer.Models;
using Microsoft.Extensions.Options;
using Microsoft.Extensions.Logging;
using ModelContextProtocol.Server;

namespace CosmicPizzaServer.Tools;

[McpServerToolType]
public class PizzaRecommenderTool
{
    private static readonly Dictionary<string, string> ZodiacPizzas = new(
        StringComparer.OrdinalIgnoreCase)
    {
        ["Aries"] = "Pluto's Dwarf Delight",
        ["Taurus"] = "Jupiter's Gas Giant Garlic Bread Pizza",
        ["Gemini"] = "Saturn's Ring-ion Burger Pizza",
        ["Cancer"] = "Neptune's Deep Sea Supreme",
        ["Leo"] = "The Mars Margherita",
        ["Virgo"] = "Pluto's Dwarf Delight",
        ["Libra"] = "Saturn's Ring-ion Burger Pizza",
        ["Scorpio"] = "Pluto's Dwarf Delight",
        ["Sagittarius"] = "Jupiter's Gas Giant Garlic Bread Pizza",
        ["Capricorn"] = "The Mars Margherita",
        ["Aquarius"] = "Neptune's Deep Sea Supreme",
        ["Pisces"] = "Neptune's Deep Sea Supreme"
    };

    [McpServerTool(Name = "recommend_pizza")]
    [Description("Recommends a cosmic pizza based on your zodiac sign.")]
    public static string RecommendPizza(
        [Description("Your zodiac sign, e.g. Aries")] string zodiacSign,
        IPizzaMenuService menuService,
        IOptions<CosmicPizzaOptions> options,
        ILogger<PizzaRecommenderTool> logger)
```

```
    {
        logger.LogInformation("Recommendation for {Sign}", zodiacSign);
        var config = options.Value;

        if (!ZodiacPizzas.TryGetValue(zodiacSign, out var pizzaName))
        {
            return $"'{zodiacSign}' is not a recognized zodiac sign.";
        }

        var pizza = menuService.GetPizza(pizzaName);

        if (pizza is null)
            return "Pizza not found!";

        return $"Based on your sign " +
            $"({zodiacSign}):\n\n" +
            $"  {pizza.Name}\n" +
            $"  {pizza.Description}\n" +
            $"  Price: {pizza.Price} {config.Currency}";
    }
}
```

The zodiac-to-pizza mappings are carefully chosen to match the personality traits of each sign. Aries gets the spicy Pluto's Dwarf Delight because they are bold and fiery. Taurus gets the indulgent garlic bread pizza because they appreciate the finer things. Pisces gets Neptune's Deep Sea Supreme because, well, fish and ocean, the connection writes itself.

This tool also demonstrates an important pattern: it injects the `IPizzaMenuService` to look up the recommended pizza's full details. Rather than duplicating the pizza data in the recommender, it delegates to the existing service. This is good practice. If you ever update the menu, the recommender automatically reflects those changes.

Resources and Prompts

With our tools complete, let us add the resources and prompts that round out our server. Resources provide static data that AI assistants can read, and prompts give them structured ways to start conversations.

The Menu Resource

The menu resource exposes our full pizza menu as a readable resource, you can see the code for it in Listing 12-13 underneath. This is different from the order tool's menu access because resources are designed for reading, not acting. An AI assistant can read this resource to learn about our menu before recommending a pizza or placing an order.

Listing 12-13. The MenuResource (Resources/MenuResource.cs)

```
using System.ComponentModel;
using System.Text;
using CosmicPizzaServer.Services;
using CosmicPizzaServer.Models;
using Microsoft.Extensions.Options;
using ModelContextProtocol.Server;

namespace CosmicPizzaServer.Resources;

[McpServerResourceType]
public class MenuResource
{
    [McpServerResource(
        UriTemplate = "cosmic-pizza://menu",
        Name = "Cosmic Pizza Full Menu",
        MimeType = "text/plain")]
    [Description("The complete Cosmic Pizza menu.")]
    public static string GetFullMenu(
        IPizzaMenuService menuService,
        IOptions<CosmicPizzaOptions> options)
    {
        var config = options.Value;
        var sb = new StringBuilder();
        sb.AppendLine("===========================");
        sb.AppendLine("   COSMIC PIZZA MENU");
        sb.AppendLine("===========================");
        sb.AppendLine();
```

```
        foreach (var pizza in menuService.GetFullMenu())
        {
            sb.AppendLine($"  {pizza.Name}");
            sb.AppendLine($"  {pizza.Description}");
            sb.AppendLine($"  Price: {pizza.Price} {config.Currency}");
            sb.AppendLine($"  Origin: {pizza.Planet}");
            sb.AppendLine($"  Toppings: " +
                string.Join(", ", pizza.DefaultToppings));
            sb.AppendLine();
        }

        return sb.ToString();
    }
}
```

The Daily Specials Resource

Our daily specials resource rotates deals based on the day of the week, offering 20% off on two featured pizzas. This is a great example of a resource that returns dynamic content even though the data source is static. See the implementation in Listing 12-14 below.

Listing 12-14. The DailySpecialsResource (Resources/DailySpecialsResource.cs)

```
using System.ComponentModel;
using System.Text;
using CosmicPizzaServer.Services;
using CosmicPizzaServer.Models;
using Microsoft.Extensions.Options;
using ModelContextProtocol.Server;

namespace CosmicPizzaServer.Resources;
[McpServerResourceType]
public class DailySpecialsResource
{
    [McpServerResource(
        UriTemplate =
        "cosmic-pizza://daily-specials",
```

```
        Name = "Daily Specials",
        MimeType = "text/plain")]
    [Description("Today's special cosmic pizza deals.")]
    public static string GetDailySpecials(
        IPizzaMenuService menuService,
        IOptions<CosmicPizzaOptions> options)
    {
        var config = options.Value;
        var specials = menuService.GetDailySpecials();
        var dayName = DateTime.UtcNow.DayOfWeek.ToString();

        var sb = new StringBuilder();
        sb.AppendLine($"{dayName} Specials!");
        sb.AppendLine("========================");

        foreach (var pizza in specials)
        {
            var discountPrice = pizza.Price * 0.8m;

            sb.AppendLine($"  {pizza.Name}");
            sb.AppendLine($"  Was: {pizza.Price} {config.Currency}");
            sb.AppendLine($"  NOW: {discountPrice:F2} {config.Currency} "
                + "(20% off!)");

            sb.AppendLine();
        }

        return sb.ToString();
    }
}
```

Both resources inject `IPizzaMenuService` through their method parameters. This is the same dependency injection pattern that tools use, but applied to resources. The MCP SDK resolves these dependencies automatically when the resource is requested.

The Party Planner Prompt

Finally, let us add the crown jewel of our prompts: the party planner. This prompt helps users plan a cosmic pizza party by generating a structured conversation with the AI assistant. It uses the multi-message pattern from Chapter 7 to set up both a system instruction and a user request. Listing 12-15 shows you the code for this.

Listing 12-15. The PartyPlannerPrompt (Prompts/PartyPlannerPrompt.cs)

```
using System.ComponentModel;
using Microsoft.Extensions.AI;
using ModelContextProtocol.Server;

namespace CosmicPizzaServer.Prompts;

[McpServerPromptType]
public static class PartyPlannerPrompt
{
    [McpServerPrompt]
    [Description("Helps plan an epic space pizza party.")]
    public static ChatMessage[] PlanParty(
        [Description("Number of guests attending")] string guestCount,
        [Description("Planet where the party will be held")] string planet,
        [Description("Type of occasion: birthday, graduation, or just-
        because")] string occasion)
    {
        var systemMessage = new ChatMessage(
            ChatRole.System,
            "You are the official Cosmic Pizza Party Planner. You know " +
            "everything about the Cosmic Pizza menu. Use space puns and " +
            "cosmic humor. Include pizza quantities, drink suggestions, " +
            "decoration ideas, and fun activities.");

        var userMessage = new ChatMessage(
            ChatRole.User,
            $"I am planning a {occasion} party on {planet} for " +
            $"{guestCount} guests. Help me plan the perfect cosmic pizza
            party!");
```

```
        return [systemMessage, userMessage];
    }
}
```

The system message establishes the AI's persona as the "official Cosmic Pizza Party Planner" and instructs it to use space puns, suggest specific menu items, and be enthusiastic. The user message incorporates the three parameters (guest count, planet, and occasion) into a natural request. When an AI assistant uses this prompt, it will generate a complete party plan with pizza quantities, drinks, decorations, and activities.

This is one of those features that really showcases what MCP prompts can do. Instead of the user having to explain what they want from scratch, the prompt provides a structured starting point that the AI can build upon.

Wiring It All Together

We have built all the pieces. Now it is time to wire them together in `Program.cs`. This is where the magic of the host builder and dependency injection comes together. If you have been following the patterns from Chapter 9, this will feel very familiar.

Configuration

First, let us look at the `appsettings.json` file that configures our cosmic pizzeria (Listing 12-16).

Listing 12-16. Configuration (appsettings.json)

```
{
    "Logging": {
        "LogLevel": {
            "Default": "Information",
            "Microsoft": "Warning",
            "CosmicPizzaServer": "Debug"
        },
        "Console": {
            "LogToStandardErrorThreshold":
            "Trace"
```

```
            }
        },
        "CosmicPizza": {
            "RestaurantName": "Cosmic Pizza - Intergalactic Pizzeria",
            "Currency": "GalactiCoins",
            "MaxToppingsPerPizza": 6,
            "DeliverySpeedLightYearsPerHour": 42
        }
}
```

The logging configuration sends console logs to `stderr`, which is critical for MCP servers using the stdio transport. Remember, `stdout` is reserved for MCP protocol messages. If your logs go to `stdout`, they will interfere with the protocol communication and things will break in confusing ways. The `CosmicPizza` section contains our custom configuration that maps to the `CosmicPizzaOptions` class.

The Program.cs File

With all our services, tools, resources, and prompts defined, the `Program.cs` is refreshingly short. The host builder pattern and the SDK's assembly scanning do most of the heavy lifting, we just need to register our services and point the SDK at our code.

Listing 12-17 shows the file that ties everything together.

Listing 12-17. Complete Program.cs for the Cosmic Pizza Server

```
using CosmicPizzaServer.Models;
using CosmicPizzaServer.Services;
using Microsoft.Extensions.DependencyInjection;
using Microsoft.Extensions.Hosting;
using ModelContextProtocol.Server;

var builder = Host.CreateEmptyApplicationBuilder(null);

builder.Services
    .Configure<CosmicPizzaOptions>(
    builder.Configuration.GetSection(CosmicPizzaOptions.SectionName));

builder.Services.AddSingleton<IPizzaMenuService, PizzaMenuService>();
builder.Services.AddSingleton<IOrderService, OrderService>();
```

```
builder.Services
    .AddMcpServer()
    .WithStdioServerTransport()
    .WithToolsFromAssembly()
    .WithResourcesFromAssembly()
    .WithPromptsFromAssembly();

await builder.Build().RunAsync();
```

Look at how clean that is. In just a few lines, we configure our custom options, register our two business services as singletons, and set up the MCP server with all three primitives: tools, resources, and prompts. The `WithToolsFromAssembly`, `WithResourcesFromAssembly`, and `WithPromptsFromAssembly` methods use reflection to discover all the decorated classes we created. No manual registration needed.

Both services are registered as singletons because they maintain in-memory state. The `PizzaMenuService` holds the menu data, and the `OrderService` tracks active orders in a `ConcurrentDictionary`. If you were to use a real database backend, you might switch to scoped lifetime instead, but for our cosmic demo, singletons work great.

The Project File

Let us also look at the .csproj file to make sure we have all the right dependencies, shown in Listing 12-18.

Listing 12-18. The CosmicPizzaServer.csproj file

```
<Project Sdk="Microsoft.NET.Sdk">
    <PropertyGroup>
        <OutputType>Exe</OutputType>
        <TargetFramework>net10.0</TargetFramework>
        <ImplicitUsings>enable</ImplicitUsings>
        <Nullable>enable</Nullable>
    </PropertyGroup>
    <ItemGroup>
        <PackageReference Include="Microsoft.Extensions.Hosting"
        Version="10.0.3" />
        <PackageReference Include="ModelContextProtocol" Version="1.3.0" />
    </ItemGroup>
```

```
    <ItemGroup>
        <Content Include="appsettings.json">
            <CopyToOutputDirectory>
                PreserveNewest
            </CopyToOutputDirectory>
        </Content>
    </ItemGroup>
</Project>
```

Just two NuGet packages. `Microsoft.Extensions.Hosting` gives us the host builder, dependency injection, configuration, and logging. `ModelContextProtocol` gives us everything MCP-related including the server attributes, transport, and assembly scanning. The `appsettings.json` file is configured to copy to the output directory so it is available at runtime.

Testing the Server

With everything in place, let us make sure our cosmic creation actually works. We have two great options for testing: the MCP Inspector and Claude Desktop.

Using the MCP Inspector

The MCP Inspector is the fastest way to test, but you should know how to set up the server in VS Code or Claude Desktop so feel free to try and do that. If you have been following along since Chapter 4, you already know the drill. First, build the project, as shown in Listing 12-19.

Listing 12-19. Building the Cosmic Pizza Server

```
dotnet build
```

Then fire up the MCP Inspector and point it at your server. In the Inspector, you will see all six tools listed: `place_pizza_order`, `get_space_fact`, `get_space_facts`, `get_space_dad_joke`, `get_space_dad_jokes`, and `recommend_pizza`. You will also see the two resources (`cosmic-pizza://menu` and `cosmic-pizza://daily-specials`) and the `PlanParty` prompt.

Try placing an order for a Mars Margherita, cosmic size, delivered to Jupiter. You should get back a confirmation with an order ID starting with "COSMIC-" and a delivery estimate of 5.20 light-years. Then try asking for a pizza recommendation for Leo (you will get The Mars Margherita) or request a few dad jokes to brighten your day. Figure 12-1 shows the tools available in Visual Studio Code.

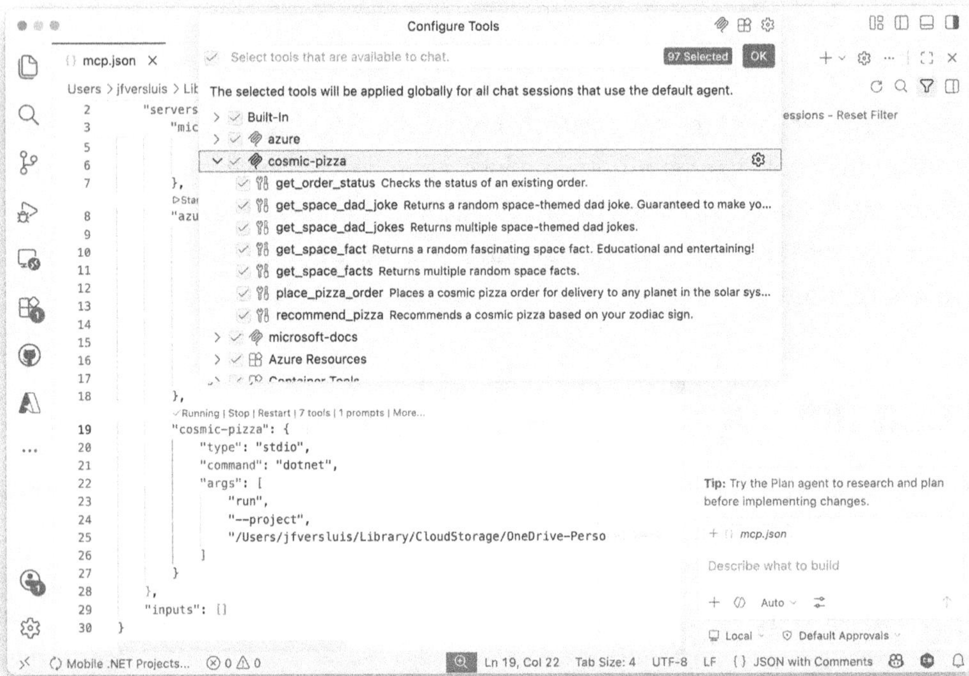

Figure 12-1. *The Cosmic Pizza tools available in Visual Studio Code*

Using Claude Desktop

For a more natural testing experience, configure Claude Desktop to use our server. Add the code shown in Listing 12-20 to your Claude Desktop configuration file.

Listing 12-20. Claude Desktop configuration for Cosmic Pizza Server

```
{
    "mcpServers": {
        "cosmic-pizza": {
            "command": "dotnet",
            "args": [
                "run",
                "--project",
                "/path/to/CosmicPizzaServer"
            ]
        }
    }
}
```

Once configured, you can have natural conversations like "What is on the Cosmic Pizza menu?" or "I am a Scorpio, what pizza should I get?" or even "Help me plan a birthday party on Mars for 20 people." Claude will use the appropriate tools, resources, and prompts to provide engaging, themed responses.

One of my favorite things to test is the party planner prompt. Ask Claude to plan a graduation party on Saturn for 50 guests, and watch as it generates a complete party plan with pizza quantities, Milky Way Milkshakes, ring-themed decorations, and space-themed activities. It is genuinely delightful. Figure 12-2 shows Claude Desktop in action with the Cosmic Pizza server.

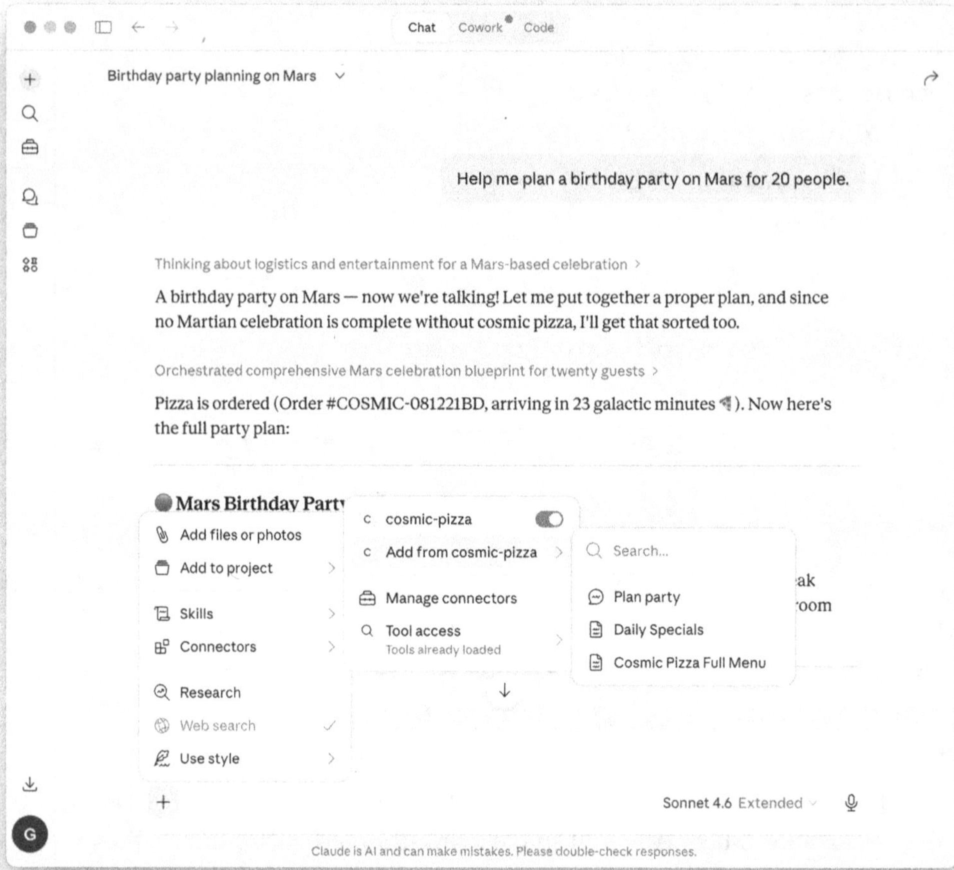

Figure 12-2. *A conversation in Claude Desktop powered by the Cosmic Pizza MCP server*

What We Learned

This chapter was about bringing everything together. We took the individual concepts from previous chapters and combined them into a complete, polished, and genuinely fun MCP server. Let us recap what we demonstrated:

- Project architecture with clean separation into Models, Services, Tools, Resources, and Prompts directories

- Multiple tool classes with different patterns: tools with dependency injection (`OrderTool`, `PizzaRecommenderTool`) and simple static tools (`SpaceFactsTool`, `DadJokesTool`)
- Service interfaces and implementations with `IPizzaMenuService` and `IOrderService`, demonstrating proper abstraction
- Resources that inject services to generate dynamic content from static data sources
- Multi-message prompts that set up both a system instruction and a user request for structured AI interactions
- Configuration through `appsettings.json` with strongly typed options classes
- The complete `Program.cs` that wires everything together with minimal boilerplate

More importantly, I hope this chapter showed you that building MCP servers can be fun. The best way to learn a technology is to build something you enjoy, and I genuinely enjoyed building the Cosmic Pizza Server. Feel free to extend it with your own ideas. Maybe add a constellation-based delivery tracking system, or a tool that generates custom pizza names based on user preferences, or even a multiplayer pizza ordering game.

Looking Ahead

In Chapter 13, we will shift gears from fun to serious as we explore enterprise integration patterns. We will look at how to connect MCP servers to real databases, authenticate users, handle production logging, and build servers that are ready for deployment in professional environments. The cosmic pizza party was a blast, but now it is time to suit up for the enterprise.

CHAPTER 13

Enterprise Integration Patterns

From Fun to Production

So far we have been building fun pizza servers, but at some point, your boss walks in and asks: "Can this thing actually talk to our database? And, you know, not let the entire internet in?" Fair questions. I was recently putting the finishing touches on a proof-of-concept MCP server for a side project when it hit me: everything I had built worked great on my laptop, but it would last about five minutes in a real production environment. No auth, no error handling, no observability. Not great for maintainability.

Here is the good news. The patterns you need to take an MCP server from demo to production are the exact same patterns you already know from ASP.NET Core development. Database access with Entity Framework Core? Same as always. HTTP calls to external APIs? `IHttpClientFactory`, just like any other project. Authentication middleware? Yep, that too. If you have built a web API in .NET before, you are going to feel right at home.

What we are going to do in this chapter is build a single project that grows section by section. We will start with a database, layer on REST API integration, add security, handle failures gracefully, and finish with monitoring and rate limiting. By the end, you will have something you could genuinely hand off to your ops team without cringing. Think of it as our Cosmic Pizza server growing up, getting a real job, and moving out of the garage.

G. Versluis, *Building MCP Servers with C#*, https://doi.org/10.1007/979-8-8688-3010-5_13

Database Integration with EF Core

I was genuinely surprised at how well EF Core and MCP play together. The secret is dependency injection. Back in Chapter 9, we explored how DI works in the MCP C# SDK. The same mechanism that let us inject services into our Cosmic Pizza tools works perfectly with `DbContext`. You register it in the container, and your tool methods can ask for it as a parameter. That is it. No ceremony, no adapters, no magic.

For our enterprise example, picture a customer management scenario. We have customers and orders stored in a SQLite database, and an AI assistant that can search and report on that data through MCP tools. Take a look at the project file in Listing 13-1 below first.

Listing 13-1. Project file with EF Core and MCP Dependencies

```xml
<Project Sdk="Microsoft.NET.Sdk.Web">
    <PropertyGroup>
        <TargetFramework>net10.0</TargetFramework>
        <Nullable>enable</Nullable>
        <ImplicitUsings>enable</ImplicitUsings>
    </PropertyGroup>
    <ItemGroup>
        <PackageReference
            Include="ModelContextProtocol.AspNetCore" Version="1.3.0" />
        <PackageReference
            Include="Microsoft.EntityFrameworkCore.Sqlite"
            Version="10.0.5" />
        <PackageReference
            Include="Microsoft.EntityFrameworkCore.Design"
            Version="10.0.5" />
        <PackageReference
            Include="Microsoft.Extensions.Http.Polly" Version="10.0.5" />
        <PackageReference Include="Microsoft.AspNetCore .Authentication.
        JwtBearer"
            Version="10.0.5" />
    </ItemGroup>
</Project>
```

Nothing surprising here if you have worked with ASP.NET Core before. We pull in the MCP SDK, EF Core with the SQLite provider, and the Polly integration package that we will use later for resilience. What we need next is a couple of domain models. Find these below in Listing 13-2.

Listing 13-2. Customer and order models

```
namespace EnterpriseServer.Models;

public class Customer
{
    public int Id { get; set; }
    public required string Name { get; set; }
    public required string Email { get; set; }
    public string? Phone { get; set; }
    public DateTime CreatedAt { get; set; } = DateTime.UtcNow;
}

public class Order
{
    public int Id { get; set; }
    public int CustomerId { get; set; }
    public Customer Customer { get; set; } = null!;
    public required string Product { get; set; }
    public decimal Amount { get; set; }
    public string Status { get; set; } = "Pending";
    public DateTime OrderDate { get; set; } = DateTime.UtcNow;
}
```

I am keeping these intentionally simple. In a real project, you would have validation attributes, value objects, maybe a full domain model. But these capture the shape of a typical enterprise entity, and that is what matters for our purposes.

Below, in Listing 13-3, is the `DbContext`. Notice the `HasData` calls at the bottom. Seed data is incredibly useful when you are developing MCP tools because it means you can test your tools the moment the server starts. No manual `INSERT` statements, no Postman calls. Just run the server and start chatting. A nice touch.

Listing 13-3. AppDbContext with seed data

```
using EnterpriseServer.Models;
using Microsoft.EntityFrameworkCore;

namespace EnterpriseServer.Data;

public class AppDbContext : DbContext
{
    public AppDbContext(DbContextOptions<AppDbContext> options)
        : base(options)
    {
    }

    public DbSet<Customer> Customers => Set<Customer>();
    public DbSet<Order> Orders => Set<Order>();

    protected override void OnModelCreating(ModelBuilder modelBuilder)
    {
        modelBuilder.Entity<Customer>().HasData(
            new Customer
            {
                Id = 1,
                Name = "Alice Johnson",
                Email = "alice@example.com",
                Phone = "555-0101"
            },
            new Customer
            {
                Id = 2,
                Name = "Bob Smith",
                Email = "bob@example.com",
                Phone = "555-0102"
            }
        );
    }
}
```

Now for the fun part. Here is where MCP and EF Core actually meet. Because we registered AppDbContext in the DI container, our tool methods can declare it as a parameter, and the framework hands it over automatically. Same story for ILogger. You have seen this pattern with our pizza tools, and it works exactly the same way here. Have a look at Listing 13-4 for the code in this case.

Listing 13-4. Customer lookup and order history tools

```
using System.ComponentModel;
using EnterpriseServer.Data;
using Microsoft.EntityFrameworkCore;
using Microsoft.Extensions.Logging;
using ModelContextProtocol.Server;

namespace EnterpriseServer.Tools;

[McpServerToolType]
public static class CustomerTools
{
    [McpServerTool, Description("Look up a customer by name or email.")]
    public static async Task<string>
    CustomerLookup(
        AppDbContext db,
        ILogger<AppDbContext> logger,
        [Description("Search term: partial name or email")] string
        searchTerm)
    {
        logger.LogInformation("Looking up customer: {Search}", searchTerm);

        var customers = await db.Customers
            .Where(c => c.Name.Contains(searchTerm)
                || c.Email.Contains(searchTerm)).ToListAsync();

        if (customers.Count == 0)
            return $"No customers found matching '{searchTerm}'." ;

        var results = customers.Select(c =>
            $"ID: {c.Id}, Name: {c.Name}, Email: {c.Email}");
```

```
        return string.Join("\n", results);
    }

    [McpServerTool, Description("Get order history for a customer.")]
    public static async Task<string>
    OrderHistory(
        AppDbContext db,
        ILogger<AppDbContext> logger,
        [Description("The customer ID to look up")] int customerId)
    {
        var customer = await db.Customers
            .FindAsync(customerId);

        if (customer is null)
            return $"Customer {customerId} not found.";

        var orders = await db.Orders
            .Where(o => o.CustomerId == customerId)
            .OrderByDescending(o => o.OrderDate)
            .ToListAsync();

        if (orders.Count == 0)
            return $"No orders found for {customer.Name}.";

        var lines = orders.Select(o =>
            $"  #{o.Id}: {o.Product} "
            + $"- ${o.Amount} "
            + $"({o.Status})");

        return $"Orders for {customer.Name}:\n"
            + string.Join("\n", lines);
    }
}
```

A couple of things worth calling out here. First, the tools return plain strings, not complex objects. As mentioned before, this is deliberate. The AI model consuming these results works best with human-readable text. Second, the `Description` attributes on each tool and parameter are detailed and clear. Remember, these descriptions are what the AI uses to decide when and how to call your tools, so investing time in writing good descriptions pays off enormously. Think of them as the API documentation that your AI colleague reads before deciding which tool to use.

Note A few things about `DbContext` in MCP tools worth knowing. The SDK creates a new DI scope for each tool invocation, which means each call gets a fresh `DbContext`. This is exactly what you want: no stale data, no cross-request change tracking leaks. For read-only queries like `CustomerLookup`, consider adding `AsNoTracking()` to skip change tracking and improve performance. Also, while SQLite works great for development and this example, it has a single-writer limitation that will bottleneck under concurrent AI clients. For production, use SQL Server or PostgreSQL with `EnableRetryOnFailure()` for connection resiliency.

Finally, here is how everything wires together in `Program.cs`. You can see it in Listing 13-5 underneath The `DbContext` registration looks exactly like it would in any ASP.NET Core app. We apply any pending EF Core migrations on startup to make sure the schema and seed data are there when we need them. In a real project, you would generate migrations with `dotnet ef migrations add` and keep them in source control. Never use EnsureCreated in production because it silently ignores schema changes after the first run.

Listing 13-5. Program.cs with EF Core Registration

```
using EnterpriseServer.Data;
using Microsoft.EntityFrameworkCore;

var builder = WebApplication.CreateBuilder(args);

builder.Services
    .AddDbContext<AppDbContext>(options =>
        options.UseSqlite(builder.Configuration.GetConnectionString
        ("Default")));

builder.Services.AddHttpContextAccessor();

builder.Services
    .AddMcpServer()
    .WithHttpTransport()
```

```
    .WithToolsFromAssembly();

var app = builder.Build();

// Ensure DB is created with seed data
using (var scope = app.Services.CreateScope())
{
    var db = scope.ServiceProvider
        .GetRequiredService<AppDbContext>();

    db.Database.Migrate();
}

app.MapMcp();
app.Run();
```

REST API Wrapping

Here is where it gets really practical. Almost every company I have worked with has a pile of REST APIs that were built long before anyone was thinking about AI assistants. Inventory services, CRM endpoints, payment gateways, you name it. These APIs work great for app-to-app communication, but they were never designed for an AI to consume directly. By wrapping them in MCP tools, you give AI models a clean, well-described interface to your existing infrastructure without rewriting a single line of backend code.

The idea is simple: use `HttpClient` through `IHttpClientFactory` (as you should in any production .NET app) to call the external API, then format the response so it is meaningful to the AI model. If you think about our Cosmic Pizza server, imagine the pizza kitchen has its own REST API for inventory. Rather than duplicating that logic, you just wrap it. Listing 13-6 shows a weather API example to show the pattern.

Listing 13-6. REST API Wrapper Tool

```
[McpServerToolType]
public static class ApiTools
{
    [McpServerTool, Description("Look up the current weather for a city.")]
    public static async Task<string>
    GetWeather(
```

```
        IHttpClientFactory
        httpClientFactory,
        ILogger<Program> logger,
        [Description("City name")] string city)
    {
        var client = httpClientFactory.CreateClient("WeatherApi");

        try
        {
            var response = await client
                .GetAsync($"/weather?city=" + Uri.EscapeDataString(city));

            response.EnsureSuccessStatusCode();

            var json = await response.Content.ReadAsStringAsync();

            return $"Weather data for {city}: {json}";
        }
        catch (HttpRequestException ex)
        {
            logger.LogError(ex, "Weather API failed");

            return "Unable to fetch weather. The service "
                + "may be temporarily unavailable.";
        }
    }
}
```

You might be thinking: this looks like a normal `HttpClient` call with a try-catch around it. And you would be right! That is exactly the point. MCP does not force you into some exotic framework. Your existing .NET knowledge transfers directly. The only difference is that instead of returning an IActionResult to a browser, you are returning a string that an AI model can understand.

The `HttpClient` itself gets configured through the named client pattern in `Program.cs`. This is the recommended approach because it centralizes your base addresses, default headers, and retry policies in one place instead of scattering them through your tool code. And example of this can be seen in Listing 13-7 below.

Listing 13-7. Registering a named HttpClient with retry policy

```
builder.Services.AddHttpClient(
    "WeatherApi", client =>
    {
        client.BaseAddress = new Uri(builder.Configuration["WeatherApi:
        BaseUrl"]
            ?? "https://api.example.com");

        client.Timeout = TimeSpan.FromSeconds(30);
    })
    .AddPolicyHandler(HttpPolicyExtensions
    .HandleTransientHttpError()
    .WaitAndRetryAsync(3, attempt => TimeSpan.FromSeconds(Math.Pow
    (2, attempt))));
```

See that retry policy at the end? I am using the `Microsoft.Extensions.Http.Polly` package to add automatic retries with exponential backoff. If the API returns a transient error like a 503 Service Unavailable, the client will automatically retry up to three times, waiting two, four, and eight seconds between attempts. This kind of resilience is something you absolutely want in production. We will explore it further in the error handling section later in this chapter.

Authentication and Authorization

Now, here is the thing about running MCP servers in production: you probably do not want just anyone calling your tools. When your server can query a customer database or call internal APIs, security stops being optional real fast. The good news is that since our MCP server is a standard ASP.NET Core application, every authentication pattern you already know works here too.

The simplest approach, and honestly often perfectly fine for internal tools, is API key authentication. Each client connecting to your MCP server must present a valid key in a custom HTTP header. Listing 13-8 shows a middleware implementation that enforces exactly that.

Listing 13-8. API key authentication middleware

```
public class ApiKeyMiddleware
{
    private readonly RequestDelegate _next;
    private readonly IConfiguration _config;

    public ApiKeyMiddleware(RequestDelegate next, IConfiguration config)
    {
        _next = next;
        _config = config;
    }

    public async Task InvokeAsync(HttpContext context)
    {
        var path = context.Request .Path.Value ?? "";

        if (path == "/health")
        {
            await _next(context);
            return;
        }

        if (!context.Request.Headers.TryGetValue("X-API-Key", out var
        providedKey))
        {
            context.Response.StatusCode = 401;
            await context.Response.WriteAsync("API key required.");

            return;
        }

        var expectedKey = _config["ApiKey"] ?? "";
        var providedBytes =Encoding.UTF8.GetBytes(providedKey.ToString());
        var expectedBytes = Encoding.UTF8.GetBytes(expectedKey);
```

```
        if (!CryptographicOperations.FixedTimeEquals(providedBytes,
        expectedBytes))
        {
            context.Response.StatusCode = 403;
            await context.Response.WriteAsync("Invalid API key.");

            return;
        }

        await _next(context);
    }
}
```

A few things to notice. The middleware skips health check endpoints so they stay open without authentication. We use `CryptographicOperations.FixedTimeEquals` for the key comparison instead of a simple `string.Equals`. This is important: a regular string comparison short-circuits on the first mismatched character, which leaks timing information an attacker could exploit to brute-force the key one character at a time. `FixedTimeEquals` always takes the same amount of time regardless of how many characters match. You register the middleware in the pipeline before `MapMcp()`, and you are done. Setting HTTP status codes is fine in middleware because it runs before the JSON-RPC connection is established. The simple lines of configuration for this can be seen in Listing 13-9 underneath.

Listing 13-9. Registering the API key middleware

```
app.UseMiddleware<ApiKeyMiddleware>();
app.MapMcp();
```

Tip Never store API keys or connection strings in `appsettings.json` and commit them to source control. For local development, use `dotnet user-secrets`. For production, use environment variables, Azure Key Vault, AWS Secrets Manager, or your platform's equivalent. The `IConfiguration` abstraction reads from all these sources transparently, so your code does not need to change. For a full walkthrough, see the official documentation at `https://learn.microsoft.com/aspnet/core/security/app-secrets`.

For more sophisticated scenarios, you might want per-tool authorization. Maybe most tools are fine for any authenticated user, but deleting a customer record? That should probably require admin privileges. You can handle this right inside the tool method, have a look at Listing 13-10.

Listing 13-10. Per-tool authorization check

```
[McpServerTool, Description("Delete a customer record. Requires admin
privileges.")]
public static async Task<string>
DeleteCustomer(
    AppDbContext db,
    IHttpContextAccessor httpContext,
    [Description("Customer ID to delete")] int customerId)
{
    var user = httpContext.HttpContext?.User;

    if (user?.IsInRole("Admin") != true)
        return "Access denied. This tool requires admin privileges.";

    var customer = await db.Customers.FindAsync(customerId);

    if (customer is null)
        return $"Customer {customerId} not found.";

    db.Customers.Remove(customer);
    await db.SaveChangesAsync();

    return $"Customer {customer.Name} has been deleted.";
}
```

For OAuth-based authentication, you would integrate ASP.NET Core's built-in authentication middleware. The MCP server does not need any special configuration because it is a standard ASP.NET Core application. You configure your authentication scheme in `Program.cs` exactly like you would for any web API, and the MCP endpoints benefit from the same security pipeline. And seriously, if you are exposing tools that touch production data, please add auth. I cannot stress that enough.

To be clear about when to use each pattern: per-tool authorization checks like the one above work well for role-based access control where returning an error message to the AI is sufficient. However, when you need to trigger OAuth re-consent flows with specific scopes, you must use middleware. The Streamable HTTP transport flushes response headers before tool execution, so by the time your tool code runs, it is too late to return a proper 401 or 403 HTTP status with a WWW-Authenticate header. Middleware runs before the headers are sent, making it the right place for scope enforcement.

OAuth and JWT Bearer Authentication

The API key approach works great for internal tools, but what about production systems that need proper identity? The official .NET MCP SDK provides dedicated authentication support through `McpAuthenticationDefaults` and the `AddMcp()` extension method. You configure JWT Bearer authentication for token validation, call `AddMcp()` to set up your Protected Resource Metadata and protect your MCP endpoint with `RequireAuthorization()`. This integrates with ASP.NET Core's standard authentication pipeline while adding MCP-specific discovery metadata.

You set the default authentication scheme to `McpAuthenticationDefaults.AuthenticationScheme`, then chain `AddJwtBearer()` for token validation and `AddMcp()` to configure your Protected Resource Metadata. The `AddMcp()` call tells the SDK to automatically host a discovery document, so clients know which authorization server to use and what scopes are supported. Finally, you call `RequireAuthorization()` on the MCP endpoint to enforce authentication on every request. Figure 13-1 illustrates this authentication flow.

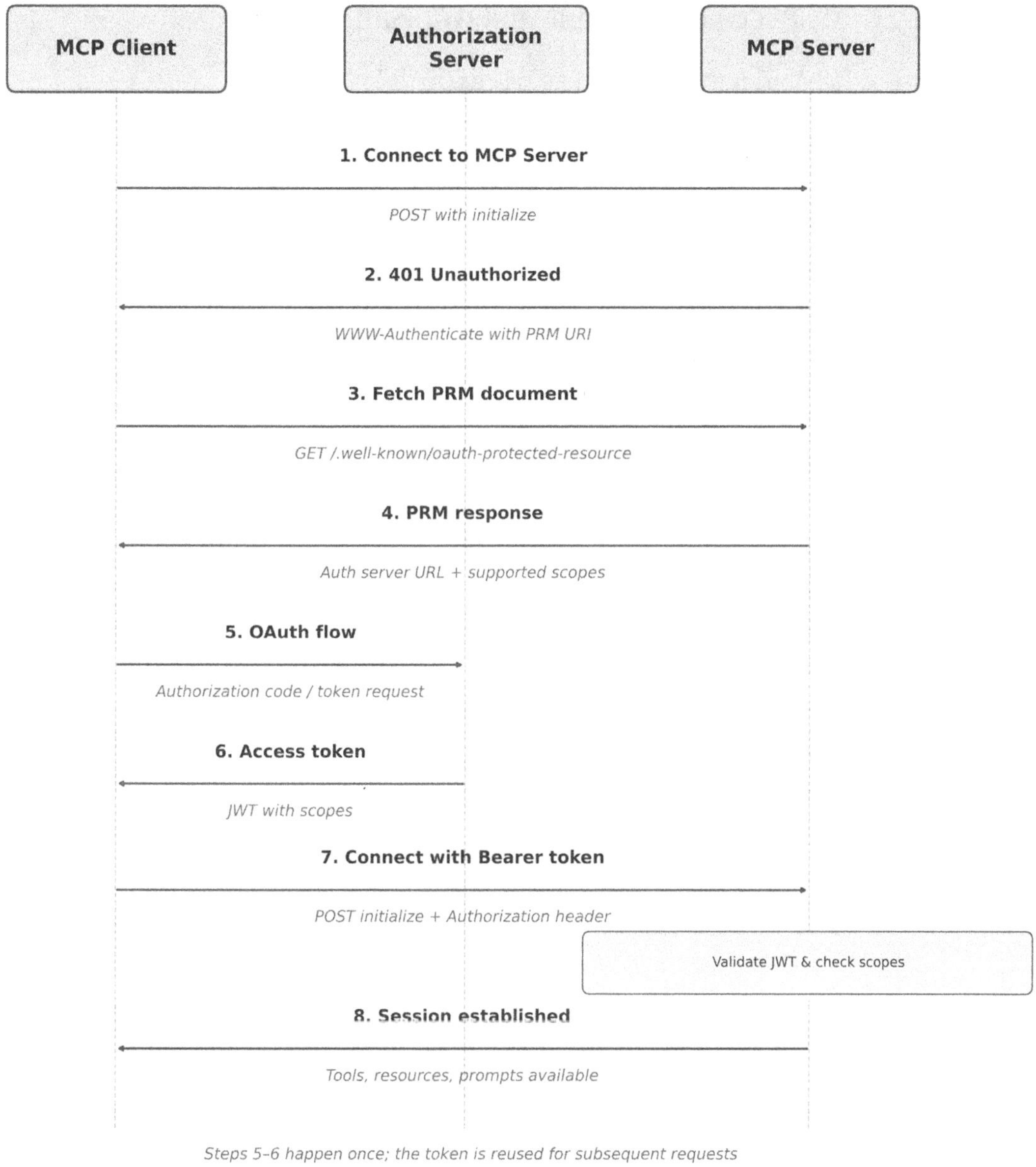

Figure 13-1. *The OAuth and JWT authentication flow for a production MCP server*

Let me show you a complete server setup that uses JWT authentication. Listing 13-11 shows what a production MCP server configuration looks like when you want proper OAuth security.

Listing 13-11. MCP server with OAuth and JWT authentication

```
var builder = WebApplication.CreateBuilder(args);

builder.Services.AddAuthentication(
    options =>
{
    options.DefaultAuthenticateScheme =
        McpAuthenticationDefaults
        .AuthenticationScheme;

    options.DefaultChallengeScheme =
        McpAuthenticationDefaults
        .AuthenticationScheme;
})
.AddJwtBearer(options =>
{
    options.Authority = "https://auth.cosmicpizza.dev";
    options.Audience = "api://cosmic-pizza-mcp";
    options.TokenValidationParameters = new()
    {
        ValidateIssuer = true,
        ValidateAudience = true,
        ValidateLifetime = true,
        ValidateIssuerSigningKey = true
    };
})
.AddMcp(options =>
{
    options.ResourceMetadata = new()
    {
        ResourceDocumentation = "https://docs.cosmicpizza.dev/api",
        AuthorizationServers = { "https://auth.cosmicpizza.dev" },
        ScopesSupported = ["mcp:tools", "mcp:resources"],
    };
});
```

```
builder.Services.AddAuthorization();

builder.Services
    .AddMcpServer()
    .WithHttpTransport()
    .WithToolsFromAssembly();

var app = builder.Build();

app.UseAuthentication();
app.UseAuthorization();
app.MapMcp().RequireAuthorization();

app.Run();
```

Notice how we set the default authentication scheme to McpAuthenticationDefaults.AuthenticationScheme instead of JwtBearerDefaults. This tells the SDK to use the MCP-aware authentication handler. The AddJwtBearer() call configures the actual token validation, pointing at your identity provider. Then AddMcp() configures the Protected Resource Metadata, which tells clients where to find the authorization server and what scopes are supported. The key addition is RequireAuthorization() on the MapMcp() call, which ensures every MCP request must carry a valid token.

Protected Resource Metadata

The MCP specification follows RFC 9728 for Protected Resource Metadata. The idea is that a protected MCP server can expose a /.well-known/oauth-protected-resource endpoint so clients can discover how to authenticate: which authorization servers to use, what scopes are supported, and what bearer methods are available. When you configure AddMcp() with ResourceMetadata as shown in Listing 13-11, the SDK automatically hosts the PRM document at this well-known location. You do not need to create a separate endpoint or manually serialize anything.

The ResourceMetadata record has properties like ScopesSupported, AuthorizationServers, and ResourceDocumentation. You saw these in Listing 13-11 where we configured them through the AddMcp() options. Because the SDK automatically hosts the PRM document, clients connecting for the first time can simply fetch it and discover everything they need to start the OAuth flow. This is a significant improvement over having to manually configure each client with server-specific auth details.

This matters because it makes your MCP server self-describing. A client connecting for the first time does not need out-of-band configuration to figure out how to authenticate. It can fetch the metadata, discover the auth server URL, and kick off the OAuth flow. That is a big deal for tooling ecosystems where you want things to just work.

Incremental Scope Consent

MCP supports a really clean pattern for permissions called incremental scope consent. The idea is simple: don't ask for all permissions up front. Instead, start with minimal access and request additional scopes only when a specific tool actually needs them.

Authorization checks should be implemented in ASP.NET Core middleware instead of inside the tool method itself. This is because the Streamable HTTP transport flushes response headers (including the 200 status code) before invoking the tool. By the time a tool executes, it is too late to return a proper 401 or 403 HTTP status code. Instead, you write middleware that inspects the incoming request, checks the required scopes, and returns a 403 with a WWW-Authenticate header if the scopes are missing.

Let me show you what this looks like in practice, have a look at Listing 13-12 below. Here is middleware that inspects the MCP request body, determines whether the operation requires elevated permissions and returns a 403 Forbidden with a WWW-Authenticate header if the required scope is missing.

Listing 13-12. Scope enforcement middleware

```
app.Use(async (context, next) =>
{
    var path = context.Request.Path.Value;

    if (context.Request.Method == "POST")
    {
            context.Request.EnableBuffering();

            var body =
                await ReadRequestBodyAsync(
                context.Request);
```

```
            if (RequiresDeleteScope(body))
            {
                var user = context.User;
                var scopes = user?.Claims
                    .Where(c => c.Type == "scope" || c.Type == "scp")
                    .SelectMany(c =>c.Value.Split(' '))
                    .Distinct()
                    .ToList() ?? [];

            if (!scopes.Contains("projects.delete"))
            {
                context.Response.StatusCode = 403;
                context.Response.Headers.WWWAuthenticate =
                    "Bearer error="\"insufficient_scope\",
                    scope=\"projects.delete\"";

                return;
            }
        }
    }

    await next();
});
```

The middleware intercepts MCP requests before they reach the tool. Notice the `EnableBuffering` call at the top. This is critical because ASP.NET Core request bodies are forward-only streams by default. Without `EnableBuffering`, reading the body in middleware would leave an empty stream for the downstream JSON-RPC handler, breaking everything. The `ReadRequestBodyAsync` and `RequiresDeleteScope` methods are helper methods you would write yourself. `ReadRequestBodyAsync` reads the request body as a string and resets the stream position back to zero so the MCP handler can read it again. `RequiresDeleteScope` parses the JSON-RPC request to check if the tool being called is a destructive operation. If the token does not carry the required scope, the middleware returns a 403 with a WWW-Authenticate header indicating the missing scope. The AI client can then prompt the user to reauthenticate with the additional scope, get a new token, and retry.

Client OAuth Configuration

From the client side, you configure OAuth through the `ClientOAuthOptions` class. You set your `ClientId`, `RedirectUri`, and the `Scopes` you want to request. This is standard OAuth stuff, nothing surprising. The SDK provides the OAuth plumbing: `ClientOAuthOptions`, token cache abstractions, and redirect handling hooks, but you still wire up the redirect delegate and choose your token storage strategy. It handles the protocol dance; you handle the infrastructure.

One option worth mentioning is client metadata configuration. Some OAuth setups use Dynamic Client Registration (DCR), where the client registers itself with the authorization server at runtime. An alternative approach is to publish a metadata document at a URL that describes your client's redirect URIs, grant types, and other configuration. The auth server fetches that document to learn about your client. Check the SDK's `ClientOAuthOptions` for the available configuration properties, as they may evolve across releases.

Multi-tool Orchestration

Remember our Cosmic Pizza server from earlier chapters? Imagine a customer wants to place an order and check delivery status in one conversation. The AI model does not need a single monolithic "do everything" tool for that. Instead, it calls multiple smaller tools in sequence, using the output of one as input to the next. This is one of the most powerful aspects of MCP, and it happens naturally when you design your tools well.

Here is how it works in our enterprise scenario. A user asks, "What are the recent orders for Alice?" The AI model calls `CustomerLookup` with "Alice" to get her customer ID, then calls `OrderHistory` with that ID to fetch her orders. It works because `CustomerLookup` returns the ID as part of its output, and `OrderHistory` accepts an ID as input. The tools were not explicitly designed to chain, they just do, because each one produces output that is useful on its own.

That said, you can make orchestration even smoother by adding convenience tools that handle common multistep workflows in a single call. Think of it like our pizza server having both a `GetMenu` tool and a `PlaceOrder` tool, but also offering a `QuickReorder` tool that looks up someone's last order and places it again. Listing 13-13 shows the customer equivalent.

Listing 13-13. Combined Lookup Tool for Common Workflows

```
[McpServerTool, Description("Find a customer by name and "
    + "return their recent orders.")]
public static async Task<string> CustomerOrderSummary(
    AppDbContext db,
    [Description("Customer name to search")] string customerName)
{
    var customer = await db.Customers
        .FirstOrDefaultAsync(c => c.Name.Contains(customerName));

    if (customer is null)
        return $"No customer found matching '{customerName}'.";

    var orders = await db.Orders
        .Where(o => o.CustomerId == customer.Id)
        .OrderByDescending(o => o.OrderDate)
        .Take(5)
        .ToListAsync();

    var summary =
        $"Customer: {customer.Name}"
        + $" ({customer.Email})\n"
        + $"Recent orders ({orders.Count}):\n";

    foreach (var order in orders)
    {
        summary += $"  #{order.Id}: "
            + $"{order.Product} "
            + $"- ${order.Amount} "
            + $"({order.Status})\n";
    }

    return summary;
}
```

There is an important design tension here, and I want to be upfront about it. Fine-grained tools give the AI maximum flexibility. Coarse-grained tools reduce roundtrips and the chance of errors in multi-step workflows. My recommendation? Provide both. Keep your atomic tools for flexibility, but add convenience tools for the workflows you see happening most often. The AI model will naturally pick the most efficient option.

When tools need to participate in transaction-like patterns, you can lean on EF Core's built-in transaction support. If a workflow requires multiple database changes that should either all succeed or all fail, wrap them in an explicit transaction. Think of it like our pizza server transferring an order from one customer to another: you would not want the order to vanish from one account without appearing in the other. This example is shown underneath in Listing 13-14.

Listing 13-14. Transaction-like pattern in MCP tools

```
[McpServerTool, Description("Transfer an order from one customer to
another.")]
public static async Task<string>
TransferOrder(
    AppDbContext db,
    [Description("Order ID to transfer")] int orderId,
    [Description("New customer ID")] int newCustomerId,
    ILogger<CustomerTools> logger)
{
    using var transaction = await db.Database.BeginTransactionAsync();

    try
    {
        var order = await db.Orders.FindAsync(orderId);
        var newCustomer = await db.Customers
            .FindAsync(newCustomerId);

        if (order is null || newCustomer is null)
            return "Order or customer not found.";

        order.CustomerId = newCustomerId;

        await db.SaveChangesAsync();
        await transaction.CommitAsync();
```

```
        return $"Order #{orderId} transferred to {newCustomer.Name}.";
    }
    catch (Exception ex)
    {
        await transaction.RollbackAsync();

        logger.LogError(ex, "Order transfer failed");

        return "Transfer failed. No changes were made.";
    }
}
```

The try-catch with explicit rollback is key. If anything goes wrong mid-transaction, the database stays consistent and the AI gets a clear message about what happened. No partial updates, no corrupted state. Your future self will thank you.

Error Handling and Resilience

If you have shipped anything to production, you know that things will go wrong. Not if, when. Databases go down for maintenance. External APIs time out during traffic spikes. Users pass in data that nobody anticipated. The question is not whether your MCP server will encounter errors, but how gracefully it handles them when it does.

The golden rule for MCP error handling is this: never let an unhandled exception bubble up to the AI model. Instead, always return a meaningful error message that helps the AI communicate what happened to the user. A stack trace is useless to an AI assistant. A message like "The database is temporarily unavailable, please try again in a moment" is exactly what it needs.

We already saw retry policies when configuring `HttpClient`. Listing 13-15 shows you how you layer on a circuit breaker using Polly. A circuit breaker is particularly useful for MCP servers because it prevents your server from hammering a downstream service that is already struggling. If you have ever watched a failing API drag down everything connected to it, you know why this matters.

Listing 13-15. Circuit breaker policy with Polly

```
using Polly;
using Polly.Extensions.Http;

builder.Services.AddHttpClient("WeatherApi", client =>
    {
        client.BaseAddress = new Uri(builder.Configuration["WeatherApi:
        BaseUrl"]
            ?? "https://api.example.com");
    })
    .AddPolicyHandler(HttpPolicyExtensions.HandleTransientHttpError()
        .WaitAndRetryAsync(3, attempt =>
           TimeSpan.FromSeconds(Math.Pow(2, attempt))))
    .AddPolicyHandler(HttpPolicyExtensions
        .HandleTransientHttpError().CircuitBreakerAsync(5,
            TimeSpan.FromSeconds(30)));
```

Sorry about the somewhat confusing code formatting shown in Listing 13-15; this one was hard to make readable in print. Here is what that configuration does: retry transient errors up to three times with exponential backoff. If five consecutive requests fail, open the circuit breaker for 30 seconds. During those 30 seconds, all requests fail immediately rather than waiting for a timeout. This protects both your MCP server and the downstream service. Pretty cool, and you get it practically for free with `Polly`.

Note The `Microsoft.Extensions.Http.Polly` package used here wraps Polly v7, which works perfectly but is in maintenance mode. For new projects, consider `Microsoft.Extensions.Http.Resilience`, which builds on Polly v8 and offers a more streamlined API with resilience pipelines. The concepts are the same; only the syntax differs.

For database operations, wrap your EF Core calls in try-catch blocks and return descriptive messages, like shown in Listing 13-16 below. Think about what the AI model needs to be helpful.

Listing 13-16. Graceful error handling in database tools

```
public static async Task<string> SafeQuery(
    AppDbContext db,
    ILogger<AppDbContext> logger,
    string searchTerm)
{
    try
    {
        var results = await db.Customers
            .Where(c => c.Name.Contains(searchTerm))
            .ToListAsync();

        return results.Count > 0
            ? string.Join("\n", results.Select(c => c.Name)) : "No results
            found.";
    }
    catch (Exception ex)
    {
        logger.LogError(ex, "Database query failed");

        return "The database is temporarily unavailable."
            + " Please try again in a few moments.";
    }
}
```

One more thing that often gets overlooked: input validation. AI models can and will pass unexpected values to your tools. An empty search term might return your entire customer table. A negative customer ID makes no sense. A string with 50,000 characters is a waste of a database round-trip. Add basic guards at the top of your tool methods: null checks, length limits, and range validation. Also, do not forget to call `app.UseHttpsRedirection()` in your pipeline. An enterprise MCP server should enforce HTTPS, especially when API keys and bearer tokens travel in headers. And for testing all these patterns, the integration testing techniques from Chapter 11 transfer directly. Swap in an in-memory database provider and exercise your tools end-to-end.

Monitoring and Observability

Your MCP server is running in production. Everything seems fine. Then at 3 AM, your phone buzzes with an alert. Which tools are being called the most? How long are database queries taking? Are there error spikes? Without observability, you are flying blind. Luckily, .NET has excellent built-in support for this through structured logging and OpenTelemetry.

You have already seen `ILogger` used throughout our tools. Structured logging is the foundation because it produces log entries that can be queried and analyzed programmatically. Instead of a flat string like "Looking up customer Alice," you write a structured log with named parameters that tools like Seq or Application Insights can index and search. A sample logging call with useful information can be found in Listing 13-17 below.

Caution Be careful what you log. Search terms, customer names, and email addresses are personally identifiable information (PII). Logging them verbatim can violate GDPR, CCPA, and similar regulations. In production, consider hashing or truncating sensitive values, or use a log scrubbing middleware that strips PII before it reaches your log sink.

Listing 13-17. Structured logging in MCP tools

```
logger.LogInformation(
    "Customer lookup: "
    + "SearchTerm={SearchTerm}, "
    + "ResultCount={Count}, "
    + "Duration={Duration}ms",
    searchTerm, customers.Count, stopwatch.ElapsedMilliseconds);
```

For deeper observability, you can integrate OpenTelemetry. This gives you distributed tracing, which is invaluable when your MCP tools call external APIs. You can see the entire chain from the AI request through your tool to the database and back. You can simple wire this up while initializing your MCP server as shown in Listing 13-18.

Listing 13-18. OpenTelemetry Configuration

```
using OpenTelemetry.Trace;

builder.Services
    .AddOpenTelemetry()
    .WithTracing(tracing =>
    {
        tracing
            .AddAspNetCoreInstrumentation()
            .AddHttpClientInstrumentation()
            .AddConsoleExporter();
    });
```

Tip The `AddConsoleExporter` call is great for development, but in production, you want to export traces to a real backend. Replace it with `AddOtlpExporter()` to send data to Jaeger, Grafana Cloud, Honeycomb, or any OpenTelemetry Protocol (OTLP) compatible service. For Azure, use `AddAzureMonitorTraceExporter()` from the Azure Monitor OpenTelemetry package.

And do not forget health checks. ASP.NET Core has built-in health check support, and it takes about three lines to hook it up. In containerized deployments, orchestrators like Kubernetes use these endpoints to know whether your server is ready to accept traffic. Configuring this is easy as shown in Listing 13-19.

Listing 13-19. Health check configuration

```
builder.Services.AddHealthChecks()
    .AddDbContextCheck<AppDbContext>("database");

// In the pipeline:
app.MapHealthChecks("/health");
```

With structured logging, distributed tracing, and health checks in place, you have a complete view of what your server is doing. When something goes sideways at 3 AM, you will be glad you set this up. Trust me on that one.

Rate Limiting and Quotas

Here is something that catches people off guard: AI models can generate a lot of traffic. An enthusiastic user might ask a question that triggers the AI to call your tools dozens of times in rapid succession. If those tools are hitting a database or an external API, you could easily overwhelm your backend. Rate limiting is not optional; it is your safety valve. Without it, a single runaway conversation can bring down your entire service, so make sure to get this right!

ASP.NET Core includes built-in rate limiting middleware that works perfectly here. Take a look at the configuration in Listing 13-20 that limits each API key to 100 requests per minute.

Listing 13-20. Rate Limiting Configuration

```
using System.Threading.RateLimiting;

builder.Services.AddRateLimiter(
    options =>
    {
        options.GlobalLimiter = PartitionedRateLimiter
            .Create<HttpContext, string>(context =>
            RateLimitPartition.GetFixedWindowLimiter(
            partitionKey: context.User?.FindFirst("sub")?.Value
                ?? context.Request.Headers["X-API-Key"].ToString()
                ?? "anonymous",
            factory: _ =>
            new FixedWindowRateLimiterOptions
            {
                PermitLimit = 100,
                Window = TimeSpan.FromMinutes(1)
            }));

        options.RejectionStatusCode = 429;
    });

// In the pipeline, before MCP mapping:
app.UseRateLimiter();
```

The partition key uses a fallback strategy: first it tries the OAuth subject claim for JWT-authenticated users, then falls back to the API key header, and finally to "anonymous" as a catch-all. This way, the rate limiter works correctly regardless of whether you are using OAuth, API keys, or a mix of both. You can adjust the `PermitLimit` and `Window` values based on your backend's capacity. You might also want tool-level rate limiting for especially expensive operations, like a tool that generates complex reports.

Summary

Look at what you just built. We started this chapter with a pizza server and ended with something that could genuinely run in a production environment. That is a pretty big leap, and you should feel good about it. Here is a quick recap of the key patterns we covered:

- Database integration with EF Core, including `DbContext` registration through DI, seed data for rapid testing, and tools that query and modify data naturally
- REST API wrapping with `HttpClient` and `IHttpClientFactory`, giving AI models access to your existing API infrastructure without rewriting anything
- Authentication and authorization using API key middleware, JWT Bearer with McpAuthenticationDefaults, Protected Resource Metadata via AddMcp(), and scope enforcement in middleware to keep your enterprise resources locked down
- Multi-tool orchestration patterns that let tools work together in sequence, plus convenience tools for common workflows and transaction support
- Error handling and resilience with `Polly` for retry policies and circuit breakers, plus graceful error messages that keep the AI informed
- Monitoring and observability through structured logging, OpenTelemetry tracing, and health checks
- Rate limiting to protect backend services from AI-driven traffic bursts

Here is the thing I want you to take away: none of these patterns are unique to MCP. They are standard .NET patterns applied to a new context. Your existing knowledge of ASP.NET Core, EF Core, and the broader .NET ecosystem transfers directly. If you have built production web APIs before, you already know most of this. MCP just gives your code a new audience: AI models instead of browsers.

We are almost at the finish line. In the next chapter, we will take the production-ready server you have built and actually deploy it. Chapter 14 covers containerization with Docker, cloud deployment options, and making your server discoverable to AI clients. It is the final step in going from code on your laptop to a service that others can use. I would love to see what you build, so let us keep going.

CHAPTER 14

Deploying and Publishing

I was recently putting the finishing touches on an MCP server I had been building for a side project. Everything worked beautifully on my machine. The tools responded, the resources loaded, the prompts rendered perfectly. Then a colleague asked me, "Hey, can I try that?" And just like that, I was staring at the age-old problem every developer knows too well: it works on my machine, but how do I get it to work on yours?

That is exactly what this chapter is about. This is the moment your MCP server goes from "it works on my machine" to "it works everywhere." We will cover containerization with Docker, publishing as a .NET global tool, deploying to Azure, hardening for production, setting up CI/CD pipelines, and finally, we will take a look at what is next for MCP. By the end, you will have everything you need to get your server out into the real world.

Deployment Options Overview

Before we jump into specific strategies, it helps to step back and think about what kind of MCP server you are deploying, because that drives every decision that follows.

For stdio-based servers, the server runs as a local process on the same machine as the client. Distribution is the main concern here, not hosting. You want to make it dead simple for someone to install and run your server. Publishing as a .NET global tool or distributing a self-contained executable are your best bets.

For HTTP-based servers using SSE or the Streamable HTTP transport, you are dealing with a more traditional web service deployment. These servers need to live somewhere accessible over the network, handle concurrent connections, maintain uptime, and scale as demand grows. Cloud platforms like Azure shine here.

G. Versluis, *Building MCP Servers with C#*, https://doi.org/10.1007/979-8-8688-3010-5_14

Here are the main deployment strategies we will explore:

- Docker containers for portable, reproducible deployments
- .NET global tools for easy distribution of stdio-based servers
- Azure App Service and Azure Container Apps for cloud hosting
- CI/CD pipelines for automated building, testing, and deployment

Let us start with Docker, which has become the de facto standard for packaging server applications.

Docker Containerization

Docker is a natural fit for MCP servers. It gives you a consistent, isolated environment that works the same way whether you are running locally, in CI, or on a production server. If you have never used Docker before, the core idea is simple: you define a recipe called a Dockerfile that describes how to build and run your application. Docker then packages everything into an image that can run anywhere Docker is installed.

Creating a Dockerfile

The key to an efficient Docker image is using a multistage build. In the first stage, you use the full .NET SDK to restore, compile, and publish. In the second stage, you copy the published output into a much smaller runtime image. This keeps your final image lean and, as a bonus, reduces the attack surface in production.

This section assumes a little bit of preexisting knowledge about Docker. Using Docker can be a whole book on its own. If you're not familiar with Docker, don't worry too much about it, you'll get the gist. If you do want to learn more, Microsoft has great documentation on getting started with Docker and .NET: `https://learn.microsoft.com/dotnet/core/docker/introduction`.

Listing 14-1 shows a Dockerfile for our weather MCP server.

Listing 14-1. Dockerfile for an MCP server using a multistage build

```
FROM mcr.microsoft.com/dotnet/sdk:10.0 AS build
WORKDIR /src
COPY *.csproj ./
RUN dotnet restore
COPY . ./
RUN dotnet publish -c Release -o /app/publish

FROM mcr.microsoft.com/dotnet/aspnet:10.0 AS runtime
WORKDIR /app
USER app
COPY --from=build /app/publish .
ENTRYPOINT ["dotnet", "DockerDeployment.dll"]
```

A few things worth calling out here. I copy the project file first and run `dotnet restore` separately from the rest of the source code. This is a Docker best practice because it lets Docker cache the restored packages layer. As long as your project file does not change, Docker reuses the cached packages on subsequent builds. When you are iterating quickly, this saves a ton of time.

The second stage starts from the much smaller ASP.NET runtime image. Notice the USER app command. The .NET 10 container images already include a built-in non-root user called app, so you do not need to create one yourself. Running containers as root is a security risk you just do not want to take, and this single line significantly improves your container's security posture. Better safe than sorry!

Building and Running

With the Dockerfile in place, here is how to actually build and run your containerized MCP server. No magic, just a couple of commands as shown below in Listing 14-2.

Listing 14-2. Building and running the Docker container

```
# Build the Docker image
docker build -t mcp-weather-server .

# Run interactively for stdio transport
docker run -i mcp-weather-server

# Run with environment variables
docker run -i \
-e ASPNETCORE_ENVIRONMENT=Production \
mcp-weather-server

# Run an HTTP-based server on port 8080
docker run -d -p 8080:8080 \
mcp-weather-server
```

Notice the `-i` flag when running a stdio-based server. This keeps `stdin` open so the MCP client can communicate through standard input and output. For HTTP-based servers, you use `-d` to run in detached mode and `-p` to map the container port to a host port.

I also recommend creating a `.dockerignore` file to exclude the bin and obj directories, Git metadata, and documentation from the build context. This speeds up builds and keeps your image size down.

Connecting to Your Containerized Server

Great, you have a running container. But how do you actually connect to it? This threw me off a little until it hit me: MCP configurations just need to know how to run a command-line tool or the URL to reach!

So it depends on which transport your server uses. For a stdio-based server like ours, AI clients need to run the container with docker run and communicate through stdin and stdout. For an HTTP-based server, clients connect to the mapped port over the network.

In VS Code with the GitHub Copilot extension, you configure your MCP server in `.vscode/mcp.json` or the user settings. For a Docker-based stdio server, you tell it to run docker as the command instead of dotnet as we've seen throughout the rest of this book. The full command and configuration can be seen in Listing 14-3 below.

Listing 14-3. VS Code MCP configuration for a Docker container

```
{
    "servers": {
        "weather-docker": {
            "type": "stdio",
            "command": "docker",
            "args": [
                "run",
                "-i",
                "--rm",
                "mcp-weather-server"
            ]
        }
    }
}
```

The key here is that the MCP client runs docker run `-i` as the command, passing `--rm` to automatically clean up the container when the session ends. The `-i` flag keeps stdin open for the JSON-RPC communication. From the client's perspective, it does not matter that the server is running inside a container. It is still just stdin and stdout.

For HTTP-based servers, the story is even simpler. Run the container with `-d -p 8080:8080` as shown in Listing 14-2, and then configure your client to connect to `http://localhost:8080`. In VS Code, that would look like setting the url property instead of command and args.

Publishing As a .NET Tool

This is one of my favorite ways to distribute MCP servers, and I will tell you why. Once published to NuGet, anyone with the .NET SDK installed can install your server with a single command. No cloning repos, no building from source, no fiddling with Docker. Just `dotnet tool install` and you are done. For stdio-based servers, it does not get much simpler than that.

Configuring Your Project

Besides running building your command-line tool from source or distribute it as an executable by zipping it up and sending it over, you can also pack it as a .NET tool.

To make your project packable as a .NET tool, add a few properties to your project file as shown in Listing 14-4 underneath. The important ones are `PackAsTool`, which tells the build system to create a tool package, and `ToolCommandName`, which defines the command users will type to run your server.

Listing 14-4. Project file properties for .NET tool packaging

```
<PropertyGroup>
    <PackAsTool>true</PackAsTool>
    <ToolCommandName>mcp-weather</ToolCommandName>
    <PackageId>McpWeatherServer</PackageId>
    <Version>1.0.0</Version>
    <Authors>Gerald Versluis</Authors>
    <Description>A sample MCP server for weather data.</Description>
</PropertyGroup>
```

Packing and Publishing

Once your project file is configured, creating and publishing the tool package is a two-step process. Have a look at the terminal commands in Listing 14-5.

Listing 14-5. Packing and publishing a .NET tool to NuGet

```
# Create the NuGet package
dotnet pack -c Release

# Push to NuGet.org
dotnet nuget push \
    ./nupkg/McpWeatherServer.1.0.0.nupkg \
    --api-key YOUR_NUGET_API_KEY \
    --source https://api.nuget.org/v3/index.json
```

After that, anyone can install and run your server as shown in Listing 14-6.

Listing 14-6. Installing and running the .NET tool

```
# Install the tool globally
dotnet tool install --global McpWeatherServer

# Run it
mcp-weather
```

Users can then reference `mcp-weather` directly in their MCP client configuration as the command to launch the server. That's it! Your server is now a single command away for anyone in the .NET ecosystem.

Tip You can also publish .NET tools to private NuGet feeds if you want to distribute your MCP server within an organization without making it publicly available.

But what about testing your tool locally before publishing it to NuGet? You have two great options. The first is to create a local NuGet feed from a folder. After running `dotnet pack`, point the install command at the output directory.

```
# Pack the tool
dotnet pack -c Release

# Install from the local folder
dotnet tool install --global \
    --add-source ./nupkg McpWeatherServer
```

The second option is even cooler. .NET 10 introduced `dnx`, which works like `npx` from the Node.js world. It lets you run a .NET tool directly from a NuGet package without installing it first. Once your package is on NuGet (or a local feed), you can run it in one shot.

```
# Run a .NET tool without installing it
dnx McpWeatherServer

# Or with the longer form
dotnet tool exec McpWeatherServer
```

The `dnx` command downloads the package if needed, runs it, and does not leave anything installed on your system. This is perfect for trying out MCP servers that others have published, or for CI/CD pipelines where you do not want to persist global tools between runs. Think of it as "just run this thing" without any ceremony.

If you want to learn more about dnx, refer to the documentation here: `https://learn.microsoft.com/dotnet/core/tools/dotnet-tool-exec`.

Azure Deployment

For HTTP-based MCP servers that need to be accessible over the network, Azure provides several excellent hosting options. We will focus on the two most practical ones: Azure App Service and Azure Container Apps.

Azure App Service

Azure App Service is the simplest way to get an MCP server into the cloud. It supports .NET natively, handles TLS for you, and provides built-in scaling. You can deploy directly from your machine using the Azure CLI. Here is how.

Same as with Docker, going over all of Azure and the Azure CLI is a bit out of scope, so this assumes a bit of preexisting knowledge. If you want to learn more about Azure CLI, you can go to: `https://learn.microsoft.com/cli/azure/get-started-with-azure-cli`, and Azure App Service: `https://learn.microsoft.com/azure/app-service/quickstart-dotnetcore`. Whenever you're ready, you can find the commands for creating a resource group, creating the right Azure App Service Plan and web app and deploying your MCP server project below in Listing 14-7.

Listing 14-7. Deploying to Azure App Service with the Azure CLI

```
# Create a resource group
az group create \
--name rg-mcp-server \
--location westus2

# Create an App Service plan
az appservice plan create \
--name plan-mcp-server \
--resource-group rg-mcp-server \
--sku B1 --is-linux

# Create the web app
```

```
az webapp create \
--name mcp-weather-server \
--resource-group rg-mcp-server \
--plan plan-mcp-server \
--runtime 'DOTNETCORE:10.0'

# Deploy your published output
dotnet publish -c Release -o ./publish
cd publish && zip -r ../deploy.zip .
az webapp deploy \
--name mcp-weather-server \
--resource-group rg-mcp-server \
--src-path ../deploy.zip \
--type zip
```

One thing to keep in mind: if your server uses the SSE transport, you need to enable WebSockets in the App Service configuration. The Streamable HTTP transport works out of the box since it uses standard HTTP requests.

For secrets like API keys or connection strings, integrate with Azure Key Vault rather than storing them in app settings directly. I strongly recommend this for any production deployment.

Azure Container Apps

If you are already using Docker, Azure Container Apps is a great choice. Think of it as a simpler alternative to Kubernetes that still gives you the benefits of container-based deployment, with built-in scaling and scale-to-zero to keep costs down.

For more information about Azure Container Apps, look at: `https://learn.microsoft.com/azure/container-apps/quickstart-code-to-cloud`. To give you an idea of how easy it is to deploy through the Azure CLI, have a look at Listing 14-8 for this specific example.

Listing 14-8. Deploying to Azure Container Apps

```
# Create Container Apps environment
az containerapp env create \
--name mcp-env \
--resource-group rg-mcp-server \
```

```
--location westus2

# Deploy directly from source
az containerapp up \
--name mcp-weather-server \
--resource-group rg-mcp-server \
--environment mcp-env \
--source . \
--ingress external \
--target-port 8080
```

The `az containerapp up` command is pretty cool. It handles building your Docker image, pushing it to a registry, and creating the Container App all in one step. For MCP servers that experience variable load, the scale-to-zero capability can significantly reduce your hosting costs during quiet periods.

Production Considerations

Running an MCP server in production is a different beast than running one on your local machine. Here is what you need to think about before your server handles real traffic.

Health Checks

Health checks let your hosting platform know whether your server is alive and ready to handle requests. For HTTP-based MCP servers, implement at least a basic health endpoint that returns a 200 status code. Container orchestrators and load balancers use these to route traffic and restart unhealthy instances.

In .NET, you can add health checks with just a few lines using the `Microsoft.Extensions.Diagnostics.HealthChecks` package. You can even create custom health checks that verify connectivity to your server's dependencies, like databases or external APIs.

Graceful Shutdown

When your server receives a shutdown signal, it should finish processing any in-flight requests before terminating. The .NET Generic Host handles this automatically through the `IHostApplicationLifetime` interface. It responds to SIGTERM and gives your application a configurable window to complete pending work.

This matters especially in containerized environments where containers can be stopped and restarted at any time. If your MCP server is in the middle of a long-running tool execution when shutdown is requested, graceful shutdown ensures the client gets a proper response rather than a dropped connection.

Environment-Based Configuration

Your MCP server should behave differently in development, staging, and production. The .NET configuration system makes this easy with environment-specific `appsettings` files. Use `appsettings.Development.json` for verbose logging and dev-friendly defaults, and `appsettings.Production.json` for optimized settings.

In containerized deployments, environment variables are the preferred way to pass configuration. They can be set in your Docker Compose file, your Kubernetes manifests, or your cloud platform's settings. Avoid hardcoding any configuration values in your source code.

Secrets Management

Never store secrets like API keys, connection strings, or certificates in your source code. In development, use the .NET Secret Manager tool. In production, use a dedicated secrets management service like Azure Key Vault, AWS Secrets Manager, or HashiCorp Vault. These services provide encryption at rest, access auditing, and automatic rotation that are essential for production security.

Crash Reporting and Observability

And seriously, use a crash reporting tool. I cannot stress this enough. When your MCP server is running in production and something goes wrong at 2 AM, you do not want to be guessing what happened. Tools like Sentry, Application Insights, or Seq give you stack traces, breadcrumbs, and context that turn a mystery crash into a fixable bug.

Combine crash reporting with structured logging using `ILogger`, and you will have full visibility into what your server is doing. Trust me, your future self will thank you for setting this up before you need it.

Security Hardening

Security is not optional for production MCP servers. Your server processes requests that could contain anything, and the tools you expose might interact with sensitive systems. Here are the key areas to focus on.

Input Validation

Every input your MCP server receives should be validated before processing. This includes tool arguments, resource URIs, and prompt parameters. Never trust that the input is well-formed or within expected bounds. Validate string lengths, check numeric ranges, and sanitize any input used in database queries or shell commands. The MCP SDK handles protocol-level validation, but application-level validation is your responsibility.

Sandboxing and Least Privilege

Your MCP server should run with the minimum permissions it needs. If it only reads files from a specific directory, do not give it write access to the entire filesystem. If it connects to a database, use a database user with only the required permissions. In containers, run as a non-root user, as we did in our Dockerfile, and consider read-only filesystem mounts where possible.

For tools that execute potentially dangerous operations, implement additional guardrails. Restrict which directories can be accessed, which commands can be executed, and which network endpoints can be reached. Think of it as defense in depth: even if one layer fails, the others still protect your system.

Data Filtering

Be mindful of what data your MCP server exposes. When building resources or tool responses, filter out sensitive information like passwords, internal identifiers, or personal data that the AI model does not need. Remember that everything your server returns could end up in logs, conversation histories, or model training data. Apply the principle of least information: only return what is strictly necessary.

Performance Optimization

A slow MCP server creates a poor user experience. When an AI assistant calls your tool, the user is waiting. Nobody likes waiting. Here are the key techniques to keep your server responsive.

Caching

If your tools call external APIs or query databases, caching can dramatically reduce response times. The `Microsoft.Extensions.Caching.Memory` package provides an in-memory cache that works great for single-instance servers. For distributed deployments, consider Redis through the `IDistributedCache` interface.

Be thoughtful about what you cache and for how long. Weather data might be fine to cache for five minutes, but stock prices need to be fresh. Set appropriate expiration times and consider cache invalidation for data that changes unpredictably.

Connection Pooling

If your MCP server connects to databases or external HTTP services, make sure you are reusing connections. For HTTP clients, use `IHttpClientFactory`, which manages pooling automatically. For database connections, most .NET providers handle pooling by default, but verify your connection strings are configured correctly.

Async All the Way

Throughout this book, we have used async and await for our tool implementations. This is not just a convenience; it is critical for performance. Asynchronous code lets your server handle multiple concurrent requests without blocking threads. Make sure you are not accidentally blocking by calling `.Result` or `.Wait()` on tasks. The rule is simple: if a method is async, every caller up the chain should be too.

Benchmarking

Before optimizing, measure. Use tools like BenchmarkDotNet to profile your tool implementations and identify actual bottlenecks. You might be surprised where the real performance issues are. I was genuinely surprised the first time I profiled one of my servers and found that the bottleneck was not where I expected at all. Measure first, optimize second, and measure again to verify your optimization actually helped.

CI/CD Pipeline

A proper CI/CD pipeline automates building, testing, and deploying your MCP server. This ensures every change goes through the same quality gates and that deployments are consistent and repeatable. GitHub Actions is a popular choice that integrates naturally with GitHub repositories, but ultimately it doesn't matter. Azure DevOps or any other provider will work just as well.

Listing 14-9 shows a GitHub Actions workflow that builds and tests on every push and pull request and publishes a Docker image when changes are merged to the main branch.

Listing 14-9. GitHub Actions workflow for building, testing, and deploying

```
name: Build, Test, and Deploy MCP Server
on:
  push:
    branches: [ main ]
  pull_request:
    branches: [ main ]
env:
  DOTNET_VERSION: '10.0.x'
  REGISTRY: ghcr.io
  IMAGE_NAME: ${{ github.repository }}
jobs:
  build-and-test:
    runs-on: ubuntu-latest
    steps:
      - uses: actions/checkout@v4
```

```
      - name: Setup .NET
        uses: actions/setup-dotnet@v4
        with:
          dotnet-version:
            ${{ env.DOTNET_VERSION }}
      - name: Restore dependencies
        run: dotnet restore
      - name: Build
        run: >-
          dotnet build
          --no-restore -c Release
      - name: Test
        run: >-
          dotnet test
          --no-build -c Release
  docker-publish:
    needs: build-and-test
    runs-on: ubuntu-latest
    if: >-
      github.ref == 'refs/heads/main'
    permissions:
      contents: read
      packages: write
    steps:
      - uses: actions/checkout@v4
      - name: Log in to Registry
        uses: docker/login-action@v3
        with:
          registry:
            ${{ env.REGISTRY }}
          username:
            ${{ github.actor }}
          password:
            ${{ secrets.GITHUB_TOKEN }}
      - name: Build and push image
```

```
        uses: docker/build-push-action@v5
        with:
          context: .
          push: true
          tags: >-
            ${{ env.REGISTRY }}/${{
            env.IMAGE_NAME }}:latest
```

This workflow has two jobs. The `build-and-test` job runs on every push and pull request: it sets up .NET, restores packages, builds the solution, and runs tests. If any step fails, the workflow stops. The docker-publish job only runs when changes hit main. It builds the Docker image and pushes it to the GitHub Container Registry.

Automated NuGet Publishing

If you are distributing your MCP server as a .NET tool on NuGet, you can automate the publishing process with GitHub Actions. The recommended approach is NuGet Trusted Publishing, which uses OpenID Connect (OIDC) to generate short-lived credentials during your workflow run. No long-lived API keys to manage, rotate, or accidentally leak. You set up a trusted publishing policy on nuget.org that links your GitHub repository and workflow file, and from that point on, your pipeline can publish without any stored secrets. An example GitHub Actions workflow file is seen in Listing 14-10 underneath.

Listing 14-10. GitHub Actions workflow for NuGet publishing

```
nuget-publish:
  needs: build-and-test
  runs-on: ubuntu-latest
  if: >-
    github.ref == 'refs/heads/main'
  permissions:
    id-token: write
  steps:
    - uses: actions/checkout@v4
    - name: Setup .NET
      uses: actions/setup-dotnet@v4
      with:
```

```
        dotnet-version:
          ${{ env.DOTNET_VERSION }}
    - name: Pack
      run: dotnet pack -c Release
    - name: NuGet Login
      uses: nuget/login@v1
      id: nuget-login
      with:
        user: YOUR_NUGET_USERNAME
    - name: Publish to NuGet
      run: >-
        dotnet nuget push
        **/*.nupkg
        --source https://api.nuget.org/v3/index.json
        --api-key
        ${{ steps.nuget-login
            .outputs.NUGET_API_KEY }}
        --skip-duplicate
```

To set this up, go to nuget.org, navigate to your account's Trusted Publishing settings, and create a policy that links your GitHub repository and workflow file. The NuGet/login action uses OIDC to request a short-lived token at publish time, so there are no secrets to store or rotate. This is the most secure way to publish NuGet packages from CI/CD and I strongly recommend using it over API keys. For a full walkthrough, see `https://learn.microsoft.com/nuget/nuget-org/trusted-publishing`.

What Is Next?

The Model Context Protocol is still young and evolving rapidly. I don't know about you, but I find this incredibly exciting. We are at the ground floor of something that could fundamentally change how AI systems interact with the world around them.

The MCP specification continues to evolve with new capabilities. Task primitives and workflow support are being discussed in the community, which would allow MCP servers to coordinate multistep operations more effectively. Imagine a server that reports progress on a long-running task or orchestrates a sequence of tool calls on behalf of the client. These features would open up entirely new categories of MCP servers.

Agent frameworks are another area where things are moving fast. Frameworks like Semantic Kernel, AutoGen, and LangChain are adding MCP support, making it easier to build sophisticated AI agents that use MCP servers as their capabilities layer. The combination of agent orchestration with MCP's standardized tool interface creates a powerful foundation for complex AI-powered applications.

The community around MCP is growing fast too. Open-source MCP servers are being published for everything from database access to cloud infrastructure management, from code analysis to creative writing assistance. I encourage you to explore what is out there, contribute to existing projects, and share your own creations. The best way to learn is by building, and the best way to grow the ecosystem is by sharing.

Note The C# MCP SDK is actively maintained and regularly updated. Always check `https://csharp.sdk.modelcontextprotocol.io` for the latest documentation, API changes, and best practices. The ecosystem moves fast, and staying current will help you take advantage of new features as they become available.

Summary

You now know how to take your MCP server from a development project to a production deployment. We covered Docker containerization with multistage builds, publishing as a .NET global tool for easy distribution, deploying to Azure using App Service and Container Apps, setting up CI/CD pipelines with GitHub Actions and NuGet Trusted Publishing, and the critical production considerations of security, performance, crash reporting, and configuration management.

But more importantly, this chapter marks the end of our journey together through this book. When I started writing it, I wanted to create the resource I wished I had when I first started working with MCP. I hope it has been that for you.

We started in Chapter 1, "The Model Context Protocol," by understanding what MCP is and why it matters. You learned how it provides a standardized way for AI models to interact with external tools and data sources. Chapter 2, "MCP Architecture Under the Hood," explored how the protocol actually works.

In Chapter 3, "Setting Up Your Development Environment," you got your machine ready for MCP development. Then in Chapter 4, "Your First MCP Server," you built your very first server. I still remember the fun of seeing that first tool response come back from a server I built myself.

From there, we explored the three core primitives: "Creating Tools" in Chapter 5, "Working with Resources" in Chapter 6, and "Exposing Prompts" in Chapter 7. These three chapters form the heart of what MCP servers can do.

Chapter 8, "Transport Layers," taught you how MCP servers communicate with clients across different transport mechanisms. Chapter 9, "Dependency Injection and Service Integration," introduced the architecture patterns that make MCP servers maintainable and testable in the real world.

In Chapter 10, "Building an MCP Client," you explored the other side of the protocol by building your own client. Chapter 11, "Testing Your MCP Servers," gave you the strategies to make sure your servers are reliable. Skills that will save you countless hours when things go wrong.

Chapters 12 and 13 brought everything together. "Building the Cosmic Pizza Server" showed a fun, real-world application of the concepts you learned, and "Enterprise Integration Patterns" covered what it takes to build MCP servers that hold up in a professional setting. And in this final chapter, you learned how to deploy and share your work with the world.

I hope this book has given you both the knowledge and the confidence to build MCP servers that solve real problems. The Model Context Protocol represents a fundamental shift in how we connect AI models to the real world, and you are now equipped to be part of that transformation. The tools, techniques, and patterns you have learned are not just theoretical; they are practical skills you can apply today.

I genuinely enjoyed writing this book, and I hope you enjoyed reading it. Now go build something fun, share it with the community, and I would love to see what you create. Reach out to me on social media, open an issue on the book's GitHub repository, or just share your MCP server with the world. I may be biased, but I think C# developers are going to build some of the most impressive MCP servers out there.

All the source code from this book is available in the accompanying GitHub repository. Use it as a starting point, experiment with the examples, and adapt them to your needs. Happy coding!

Just before this book went to press, a release candidate for the next MCP specification revision (2026-07-28) was announced: the largest update since the protocol launched. The good news: everything you have learned in this book still works. The C# SDK implements progressive transport fallback, meaning servers built against the current 2025-11-25 spec will continue to function with newer clients without code changes. That said, the upcoming revision brings some exciting capabilities worth keeping an eye on. A fully stateless protocol layer eliminates the need for sticky sessions, making it trivial to scale MCP servers behind standard load balancers. Streamable HTTP transport replaces the current SSE-based approach with something that works natively with cloud infrastructure. Server-rendered UI (called MCP Apps) allows servers to expose rich, interactive interfaces directly to clients—think embedded cards or forms instead of plain text responses. The Tasks extension graduates from experimental to a full specification primitive, giving you standardized patterns for long-running asynchronous operations. And improved OAuth and OpenID Connect alignment makes enterprise authentication even more seamless. Keep an eye on the official C# SDK repository at `https://github.com/modelcontextprotocol/csharp-sdk` and the specification site at `https://modelcontextprotocol.io` for updates. Perhaps these new features will be covered in a future revised edition of this book!

Index

G. Versluis, *Building MCP Servers with C#*, https://doi.org/10.1007/979-8-8688-3010-5

D

J, K

L

M

N

O

P, Q

R

GPSR Compliance
The European Union's (EU) General Product Safety Regulation (GPSR) is a set of rules that requires consumer products to be safe and our obligations to ensure this.

If you have any concerns about our products, you can contact us on

ProductSafety@springernature.com

In case Publisher is established outside the EU, the EU authorized representative is:

Springer Nature Customer Service Center GmbH
Europaplatz 3
69115 Heidelberg, Germany

www.ingramcontent.com/pod-product-compliance
Lightning Source LLC
LaVergne TN
LVHW080023210926
848481LV00011B/3097
* 9 7 9 8 8 6 8 8 3 0 0 9 9 *